INTERPRETING SPANISH COLONIALISM

INTERPRETING SPANISH COLONIALISM

Empires, Nations, and Legends

Edited by *Christopher Schmidt-Nowara*
and *John M. Nieto-Phillips*

UNIVERSITY OF NEW MEXICO PRESS

ALBUQUERQUE

09 08 07 06 05   1 2   3   4   5

LIBRARY OF CONGRESS CATALOGING-IN-PUBLICATION DATA

Interpreting Spanish colonialism : empires, nations, and legends /
edited by Christopher Schmidt-Nowara and John M. Nieto-Phillips.
p. cm.
Includes bibliographical references and index.
ISBN 0-8263-3673-6 (pbk. : alk. paper)
1. Spain—Colonies—America—Historiography.
2. America—Colonization—Historiography.
3. Nationalism—America—Historiography.
4. Imperialism—America—Historiography.
I. Schmidt-Nowara, Christopher, 1966–
II. Nieto-Phillips, John M., 1964–
DP85.3.I68 2005
970'.0971246'071—dc22
2005016793

DESIGN AND COMPOSITION: *Mina Yamashita*

To the progeny of conquest:
Los mestizos, los genízaros,
los coyotes, and all those
of "Some Other Race"

Contents

Acknowledgments

From Christopher Schmidt-Nowara: My thanks to the Graduate School of Arts and Sciences at Fordham University for generously supporting the original conference, entitled "Paradigms and *Paradigmas*," held at the university's Lincoln Center campus on 29 September 2001. Deans Robert Himmelberg and Nancy Busch were encouraging throughout. Thanks also to Maureen Hanratty for making the meeting work. Also invaluable was the assistance of the Latin American and Latino Studies Institute and my friend Elizabeth Wilson, who offered timely advice and expertise on producing the manuscript.

I would also like to thank each of the participants for adhering to the original plan in the immediate aftermath of the attacks of 11 September 2001, when traveling to New York was by no means easy. The events of 9-11, and now those of 3-11 (the 11 March 2004 Madrid train bombings), perhaps affected not so much the crafting of these essays as they will the reading of them. Empire and nation building have resurfaced in public debate, worldwide, with a vengeance, as have memories of colonialism and decolonization. The connections between the histories recounted here and our own era are complicated but relevant.

From John Nieto-Phillips: I would like to thank Jorge Chapa and John Bodnar for their warm welcome to Indiana University in 2003, and for allowing time off from teaching and the wherewithal to see this and other projects through to their completion. I would also like to thank Norris Hundley and Valerie Matsumoto for their comments on an early draft of my article, and Clara Rodríguez and Jorge Chapa for their input on the afterword. Editor-in-Chief David Holtby and the outside reader for the University of New Mexico Press have been especially supportive of this endeavor from the outset. Their feedback has helped bring the manuscript into sharper focus. I especially want to thank Chris Schmidt-Nowara for his critical insights on my work, and for conceiving and organizing the Fordham University conference upon which these articles were based. This collection is a testament to his vision, collegiality, and untiring creative energy.

INTRODUCTION

Interpreting Spanish Colonialism

Christopher Schmidt-Nowara

At the end of his study of the Valley of Mexico, Charles Gibson reminds historians of Spain and Latin America to reflect upon the paradigms that prefigure their approach to sources and the construction of their narratives.

> The Black Legend provides a gross but essentially accurate interpretation of relations between Spaniards and Indians. The Legend builds upon the record of deliberate sadism. It flourishes in an atmosphere of indignation, which removes the issue from the category of objective understanding. It is insufficient in its awareness of the institutions of colonial history. But the substantive content of the Black Legend asserts that Indians were exploited by Spaniards, and in empirical fact they were.[1]

The Black Legend, the story of Spanish cruelty in Europe and in the Americas, has shaped centuries of scholarship, while its counterpart, the White Legend of Spanish benevolence, has been equally significant to representations of Spanish conquest and colonization in the Americas and elsewhere. A chief aim of the essays in this collection is to trace the origins, uses, and legacies of these and other models that have directed historians in their approach to the Spanish colonial past.

The authors of these essays gathered at Fordham University in September 2001 to discuss the motives and methods for writing histories of Spanish colonialism. Our conversations in New York turned on three related topics that have since become major themes in this volume. First, several of the authors

In writing this essay I have benefited from the timely comments of Fred Cooper, Astrid Cubano-Iguina, Antonio Feros, Javier Morillo-Alicea, and an anonymous reader for the University of New Mexico Press. The advice and encouragement of Miranda Spieler were indispensable. John Nieto-Phillips has been a close collaborator from beginning to end. My thanks to all of them. I would also like to thank David Holtby for his interest and engagement throughout, and Sonia Dickey, Maya Allen-Gallegos, Sarah Pilcher Ritthaler, and Ginny Hoffman for their help in completing this book.

question the link between historiography and nation-building by emphasizing the ways that empire continues to shape the historical imagination in Spain and in some of its former colonies.[2] Second, virtually all of the contributors consider the comparability of Spanish colonialism to other colonial regimes. Third, all of the authors address the supposed backwardness of Spain and Latin America and reflect on the idea of backwardness as it has animated concepts of modernity in Europe and in the United States.[3]

NATIONS AND EMPIRES

Theorizing and analyzing the connection between historical writing and nation building has been fruitful for historians in recent years.[4] However, a focus on the nation can run the risk of overlooking the myriad interests at play in any historical project, as these articles make clear. The nation was simply not broad enough for some intellectuals to comprehend the array of cultural and economic relations that comprised a people's society and history, something that becomes clear reading Sam Truett's study of Herbert Eugene Bolton, the twentieth-century U.S. historian of the "Spanish Borderlands," and Dale Tomich's study of Francisco Arango y Parreño, a planter and principle theorist of Cuban plantation agriculture during the Atlantic world's "age of revolution."[5] Arango y Parreño scoured the Atlantic basin in theorizing the necessary conditions for Cuban sugar and slavery's expansion. The Colombian historian José Manuel Restrepo and his Argentine counterpart Bartolomé Mitre, the subjects of Jeremy Adelman's essay on postindependence Latin American historiography, also thought in terms of the Atlantic world by trying to understand their national revolutions in relationship to the American and French revolutions. Restrepo questioned the nation's very existence, an agonizing view shared by Puerto Rican patriots who always pondered their national destiny in the framework of empire, whether Spanish or North American.

Empire also shaped, and continues to shape, the historical imagination in Spain. Antonio Feros and José del Valle address the persistent question of *hispanismo*, Spain's effort to reinvent its colonialism in the Americas and to consolidate a metropolitan national identity after the end of formal colonialism. Though the "disaster" of 1898, Spain's military defeat by the United States, made this project all the more urgent from the Spanish perspective given the loss of Cuba, Puerto Rico, and the Philippines, the effort to redefine the impact and virtues of Spanish conquest and colonization had deep nineteenth-century roots and extended back into the old regime, as a recent work has shown.[6]

The representation of a benevolent Spanish colonizer defended by hispanismo has found a warm reception in the United States over the years, as Sam Truett and John Nieto-Phillips demonstrate. Here, too, the nation was not enough in the crafting of a historiographic tradition. Similar to their Spanish counterparts, U.S. historians like Charles Lummis, a Yankee transplant in the Southwest in the late nineteenth century, portrayed Spanish colonialism as essentially benevolent, if also backward. So successful was Spain's colonial enterprise that the decolonized Americas, such as New Mexico, were still essentially Spanish in their culture.[7]

What for some Spanish and North American historians was (or is) a virtue of Spanish "colonial legacies"—the persistence of language, religion, social structures, and cultural practices—was a curse to others, especially in independent Latin America. Lummis admired the medievalism of New Mexico, while many Puerto Rican patriots preferred the Spanish Ariel to the North American Caliban. In the view of Restrepo and Mitre, however, complete extirpation of the Spanish colonial past was the only way for Colombia and Argentina to move into the future. In Jeremy Adelman's words, "getting rid of Spain was not exactly the same thing as getting rid of colonialism." For these historians, the wars of independence were a rejection of Spain and of the nation's origins in the colony. Argentina, according to Mitre, had opened this rupture already during the colonial period because of Spain's relative neglect of the River Plate region. Thus, in opposition to Spanish tyranny and backwardness, Argentines had the opportunity to craft a primitive democracy and a successful commercial economy. Restrepo, though, was far more gloomy than his *porteño* colleague. Spain had exercised effective control over Nueva Granada and the results were disastrous for the successor nation-states, especially his own Colombia. Not only did the new nation need to resort to ruthless violence to defeat Spain; it also needed to invent national political institutions and a national culture so that it could effectively exercise its freedom and sovereignty. The end of the Spanish American revolutions inaugurated the real war for national independence.[8]

Recent Puerto Rican historiography has been a rich field for discussing the strengths and weaknesses of national histories as Astrid Cubano-Iguina's article makes abundantly clear. One of the characteristics of the 1898 centennial (marking the expulsion of Spain from Cuba, Puerto Rico, Guam, and the Philippines and the advent of U.S. domination) was a close scrutiny of national narratives, especially in the Antilles and Spain. While in Spain 1998 saw a cautious optimism about national triumphs in the twentieth century (more on this below), in

Puerto Rico, the persistence of colonial rule produced an acute questioning of the relationship between nation building and the nation-state, which in turn led to a reassessment of the teleology of national historical narratives. Puerto Rican historians and cultural critics began rewriting nineteenth- and twentieth-century history as they sought to explain an apparently contradictory situation: While Puerto Rico was clearly a "nation" with a distinct sense of identity and history, it had never been a nation-state nor did independence appear likely in the foreseeable future. This disjuncture between the nation and the state, or perhaps the symbiosis between nationalism and colonialism, has produced intense theorizing. Provocative concepts that have characterized Puerto Rico as a *sociedad cimarrona*, a society of runaways, marked by slavery and colonialism and resistance to both through flight, emphasize a profound popular distrust of the state, be it colonial or national.[9] While these works explicitly try to explain the trajectory of Puerto Rican history, they also implicitly address issues in Cuban historiography as Cuba was for many years the positive model against which Puerto Rico's supposed national failings were measured.[10] Cuban patriots directly challenged Spanish rule through force of arms three times in the late nineteenth century (1868–1878, 1879–1880, and 1895–1898); why did Puerto Rican patriots apparently compromise with the colonizer? Now, however, Puerto Rican scholars are more likely to argue that the lack of sustained armed resistance to colonial rule is not proof of a lack of national feeling and identity; resistance and national affirmations took more indirect forms. In Angel Quintero Rivera's judgment, these acts of subversion were more expressive of "an attitude of withdrawal from the State. . . . [D]efiance took the form of flight, not attack."[11]

To Compare or Not to Compare

Why Spanish colonialism as the entry into this interrogation of nation building? As Javier Morillo-Alicea suggests, it allows the historian to encompass metropolis and colonies in a single analytic field. Moreover, it admits that Spanish colonialism is more than colonial Latin America, including the Philippines and, potentially, Spain's other Asian and African colonies. It also reintroduces Spanish domination into discussions of empire and postcolonialism in Latin America and the Philippines, a notable omission in recent studies of the topic that have focused primarily on the United States in the Americas and the Pacific.[12] One consequence of this move is that Spanish colonialism and Latin America become less hermetic fields and open to more explicit comparisons—or, better said, connections—with other European colonialisms and postcolonial nations.

An important reference point for thinking about such connections is Frederick Cooper and Ann Stoler's seminal *Tensions of Empire*, a collection of studies of British, French, and Dutch colonial rule and culture in the nineteenth and twentieth centuries. One of the authors' major hypotheses, which Morillo-Alicea elaborates carefully, is that colonial knowledge crossed the conventional physical and temporal boundaries created by empire and nation builders. While several essays here are in the spirit of Cooper and Stoler's volume, one should note the complete absence of Iberia and Iberian colonialism from their collection, an omission whose historical origins we hope to address, at least implicitly.

Some scholars believe such an omission to be justified and necessary. For example, in one of the most influential collections of essays on postcolonial historiography, Jorge Klor de Alva argues that Spanish rule in the Americas was not comparable to other European colonialisms because it was based on *mestizaje*, the cultural and biological assimilation of the conquered peoples of the Americas. Moreover, the creole elite that led the charge for independence in the early nineteenth century shared metropolitan ideas about political rights and racial privilege; the wars of independence were not revolutions but civil wars between essentially homogenous European and American elites. The characteristics of Spanish rule in the Americas were thus quite different from British and French colonialism in Africa and Asia where a clearly European conquering and governing class ruled over unassimilated, subjugated, and racially distinct indigenous masses.[13]

Most Spanish and Latin American history written in the United States from the nineteenth to the mid-twentieth century shared some of these assumptions about the peculiarities of their subject. For U.S. scholars such as Washington Irving and William Hickling Prescott in the nineteenth century or the founders of the *Hispanic American Historical Review* in the early twentieth, the history of Latin American was the history of "Spain in America," of Spanish ways and institutions implanted in the New World that permanently shaped the historical trajectory of Latin America even after independence. A perusal of the early issues of the *HAHR*, still the field's flagship journal, shows an overwhelming preponderance of studies of the colonial period, many based on research in Spanish archives, principally the Archivo de Indias in Seville. The reader almost senses that the rulers of the new empire are learning from the makers of the old.[14]

But Latin American and Iberian history in the United States cannot be reduced, though it can be related, to the reasons of imperial interest. Historians had other motives as well. As John Nieto-Phillips and Sam Truett note in their studies of the making of Borderlands and Southwestern history, historians, both professional and amateur, in the late nineteenth and early twentieth centuries saw Spain and the postcolonial Americas as a romantic, medieval other to their own modern, materialist culture. Their work shared much with the master historians of the nineteenth century like Prescott, especially in their sense of historical time in the Iberian orbit; like their predecessors they emphasized continuity and even stagnation.[15] But unlike Prescott, they represented Spain's medieval and colonial institutions and beliefs as admirable alternatives to Anglo-American modernity. Rolena Adorno has made pertinent observations on this characteristic of early Latin American studies and Hispanism in the United States. In her introduction to a new edition of Irving Leonard's *Books of the Brave*, she noted the different perspectives of Leonard's generation and her own in the United States that led to a quite different reading of Leonard's foundational work: "[T]oday's readers (including myself) question, in fact reject, that the conquests could be interpreted as acts of enviable valor, or that the invasion of America by Spain could be excused because all western Europe participated."[16] Adorno's observations are telling. As she remarks, North American Hispanists and Latin Americanists in the early to mid-twentieth century had downplayed their precursors' emphasis on Spanish cruelty and chosen instead to focus on the heroic and assimilative aspects of Spanish empire-building in the Americas. The conquistadors and friars of Leonard, Charles Lummis, Herbert Eugene Bolton, Lewis Hanke, and Paul Horgan, among others, were romantic figures who implanted an essentially medieval European culture in the Americas. Though this culture had caused Spain and Latin America to lag behind the Anglo-American world in the modern period, it also preserved noble virtues absent in the more materialist United States. Spain and postcolonial Latin America (and parts of the United States like New Mexico) thus became living museums where the idealism of great figures like Bartolomé de las Casas persisted.[17]

Klor de Alva's strong and provocative thesis and the tradition of North American hispanism, however, obscure two major trends in Latin American historiography that suggest the possibility of comparisons and connections with other colonial and postcolonial societies. First, social historical scholarship over several decades, beginning perhaps with Gibson's *The Aztecs under Spanish Rule*, has sought to reconstruct the attempts of the conquered native peoples to defend their lifeways in the face of multiple colonial assaults such as *encomienda*, *reducciones*, or the Church's efforts to extirpate "idolatry." Nancy Farriss's study of the Maya in Yucatán or James Lockhart's of the Nahua of

Central Mexico indicate lasting divisions between Native Americans and Spaniards, colonized and colonizer, that complicate the visions of a hispanicized America postulated by Klor de Alva.[18]

Second, some scholars of the conquest who tend to emphasize mestizaje and the success of the conquerors in eradicating aspects of indigenous culture nonetheless point out that mestizaje is a multivalent process; it is not simply the imposition of the conqueror's institutions, language, religion, and values upon the conquered. Serge Gruzinski and Nathan Wachtel, for instance, argue that in the case of Mexico and the Andes, the "Occidentalization" of the indigenous peoples paralleled the impact of indigenous cultures on the Spanish creoles, though this was a contest fought under grossly uneven conditions of power. In another work, Gruzinski characterizes Amerindians and Spanish conquerors in sixteenth-century Mexico as bound together "like prisoners in a maze" as they struggled to build new societies after the cultural and physical displacements caused by the "shock of conquest."[19]

Regarding the national period, Florencia Mallon argues that mestizaje was not only a hegemonic ideology but also a tool of resistance and counterhegemony. On the one hand, "*mestizaje* . . . emerges as an official discourse of nation formation, a new claim to authenticity that denies colonial forms of racial/ethnic hierarchy and oppression," while on the other, "we have mestizaje as a liberating force that breaks open colonial and neocolonial categories of ethnicity and race. This is a resistant mestizaje, one that questions authenticity and rejects the need to belong as defined by those in power."[20] To Mallon's typology we must add the nostalgic longings of Spain's postcolonial elites of the nineteenth and twentieth centuries who deployed mestizaje in their own process of nation building, as Antonio Feros persuasively shows in his essay, an effort that not only downplayed the peculiarities of nation formation in Latin America and the Philippines but also the diversity of national identities within Spain itself, as José del Valle observes.

Fernando Ortiz's influential theory of transculturation, which seeks to encompass the multiplicity of influences that shape American cultures, also helps us to think of mestizaje in more complex ways:

> I am of the opinion that the word *transculturation* better expresses the different phases of the process of transition from one culture to another because this does not consist merely in acquiring another culture, which is what the English word *acculturation* really implies, but the process also necessarily involves the loss or uprooting of a previous

culture, which would be defined as deculturation. In addition it car-
ries the idea of the consequent creation of new cultural phenomena,
which could be called neoculturation. In the end . . . the result of every
union of cultures is similar to that of the reproductive process
between individuals: the offspring always has something of both parents but is always different from each of them.[21]

If we understand mestizaje in the more robust sense used by Gruzinski,
Wachtel, and Mallon and inflected by Ortiz's paradigm of transculturation,
Spanish colonialism, and the historiography of Spanish colonialism, perhaps
become less resistant to comparison. For instance, concepts like hybridity that
pervade contemporary studies of colonialism and postcolonialism in the British,
French, and Dutch orbits seek to comprehend social and cultural phenomena
not dissimilar from those understood under the heading of mestizaje. Indeed,
the leading edge of colonial and postcolonial studies has been the interrogation
of essential categories like colonizer and colonized by showing how power, identity, and resistance follow unpredictable routes that escape any easy dichotomies,
calling into question the neat distinction between Iberian and Northern
European colonialisms posited by Klor de Alva. As Stuart Hall trenchantly
argues, postcolonial theory obliges scholars to scrutinize "the over-determining
effects of the colonial moment, the 'work' which its binaries were constantly
required to do to *re-present* the proliferation of cultural difference and forms of
life, which were always there, within the sutured and over-determined 'unity' of
the simplifying, over-arching binary, 'the West and the Rest.'"[22]

As we see in Cooper and Stoler's *Tensions of Empire*, this assault on colonial
categories has produced works that call attention to the interconnectedness of
colonial and metropolitan politics and cultures and to the struggles in colonial
societies over miscegenation and the boundaries of Europeanness. It has also led
to rich rereadings of canonical European texts in search of what Peter Hulme,
borrowing from Althusser, calls the "inner darkness of exclusion," the silenced
colonial encounter that is always already present in European culture.[23] The
point is not to collapse mestizaje into contemporary theorizations or celebrations of hybridity. Rather, it is to suggest that mestizaje, while peculiar and specific, is not necessarily incomparable to hegemonic and counterhegemonic
discourses and lived processes in other colonial and postcolonial societies; thus,
one might emphasize the strategic uses of mestizaje as a form of identity and as
an ideological paradigm to make claims about peculiarity, abnormality, and
incomparability, an approach adopted by several of the authors here.

BETWEEN BACKWARDNESS AND MODERNITY:
USE AND ABUSE OF PECULIARITIES

If emphasizing Spanish and Latin American difference and peculiarity is one tendency in colonial and postcolonial history, celebrating Spain's normality is another, though of more recent vintage. Among historians of Spain, the effort to link Spanish history to broader European trends has often ended with the increasingly lame conclusion that Spain was just like the rest of western Europe. This claim seeks to right the more modern inflection of the Black Legend, what Richard Kagan has called "Prescott's Paradigm," that emphasizes not Spanish cruelty, but backwardness, not only in a European but also in an American and Atlantic context.[24] Assimilating Spain into western European history reached a climax in the recent centennial of 1898 (the Spanish-Cuban-American War). While members of Spain's Generation of '98 such as Miguel de Unamuno and Pío Baroja lamented Spanish backwardness and decay in the aftermath of rapid defeat by the United States and the loss of the still extremely valuable Caribbean and Pacific colonies, Spanish historians a century later emphasized Spain's fit within the mainstream of western European history.[25] Though clearly thinking of Spain's transition to democracy and vibrant place in the European Union, they curiously also folded the so-called disaster of 1898 into this discourse on normality. An essay by Juan Pablo Fusi captured this mood by contrasting 1998 to 1898:

> The contrast between both fines de siglo was, of course, much greater. The Spain of 1998 did not live, like that of 1898, locked into pessimism; the former, for instance, did not internalize its history . . . as the history of a long and inevitable decadence, as did the men of 1898. Indeed, one would say that Spain faced the end of the twentieth century with an optimistic perspective and . . . as a dynamic, democratic, and European country; a country that over time and despite suffering grave setbacks (the civil war, the Franco regime) had reencountered modernity.[26]

While one can agree or disagree with Fusi's conclusions, and he was by no means alone in his optimism about both present and past, one may question his leap from historical revisionism to his affirmation of Spanish modernity (and normality). What such a move fails to do is to question the very paradigms of modernity that the image of Spanish and Latin American backwardness animate and legitimize. In other words, if Spain is surprisingly modern, then what does that say about the meaning of modernity?[27]

This question leads back to the Black and White Legends. If dominant models of capitalist modernity—liberal and Marxist—emphasize constant social change and economic innovation, then they must omit the Spanish empire, for scholars and theorists have widely characterized it as remarkably resistant to change. In the minds of historians such as Prescott, the Spanish empire ossified at the exact moment of its greatest glory. From the Reconquista onward, Spain and its colonies were governed, indeed, terrorized, by the Inquisition and its medieval ecclesiastical mindset. Tradition, hierarchy, and obedience defined both metropolitan and colonial society. By contrast, among the more dynamic North European powers, especially England and the Netherlands, individual rights, secular values, and economic modernization, rooted deep in Reformation and Enlightenment ideals, flourished in the metropolis and, especially, the colonies.

Scholars of the Spanish colonial and postcolonial world have long rejected this tidy dichotomy, however. For instance, studies of Latin American slave societies suggest greater similarities to their English, Dutch, and French counterparts, especially in highly developed plantation societies like Cuba. Dale Tomich makes this case. The eighteenth-century planter and colonial official Francisco Arango y Parreño engaged the ideas of Adam Smith, the Physiocrats, and Spanish political economists like Gaspar Melchor de Jovellanos to construct a sophisticated plan for the modernization of the Cuban plantation belt. From his generation onward, creole and peninsular planters invested heavily in slave labor, railways, and advanced processing technology to build the world's most dynamic and efficient sugar economy, completely revolutionizing Cuban society. In Spain, similar processes transformed Catalan industry and the Valencian *huerta* during the early to mid-nineteenth century. Nearly everywhere scholars of Spain and its colonies have looked, they have found examples of economic innovation and social transformation. Surely, the Marxist and liberal models of change and renewal are useful in comprehending these phenomena. Why, then, do these parts of the colonial and postcolonial world remain marginal to dominant views of capitalist modernity in its varied manifestations?[28]

Thus, the critique of nation building and the issue of comparability led the authors to discuss the relationship of the phenomena Spain, Spanish colonialism, and Latin America to dominant paradigms of modernity. This topic has a long pedigree and has attracted significant attention. Richard Kagan's article "Prescott's Paradigm" is a recent intervention. Surveying the trajectory of Spanish historiography in the United States in the nineteenth and twentieth centuries, Kagan has argued that U.S. historians represented Spain as an archaic, backward, Catholic other to the modern, progressive, Protestant United States, an opposition that persists to the present. In Latin American history, the debate has been even more robust. Think of Ernesto Laclau's critique of Andre Gunder Frank and Immanuel Wallerstein. Laclau rejected the characterization of Latin America as feudal and argued that its apparent economic backwardness was the condition of European economic modernization. In other words, Latin America was the crucible, not the dustbin, of capitalist modernity.[29]

Most of the writers here tend to share Laclau's perspective about Latin America and the legacies of Spanish colonialism. However, rather than try to redefine modernity, they have sought to understand the intellectual history of Spanish and Latin American backwardness that girds both the Black and the White Legends by moving between comparability and peculiarity and critiquing the interests at play in the construction of both difference and normality. These moves do not imply the venerable methods of comparative history that generally treat the objects of comparison as spatially and temporally discrete, compartmentalized phenomena. Rather, the authors tend to think in terms of connections and borrowings especially regarding forms of knowledge such as political economy, colonial exhibitions, and historical narratives.[30] For the most part, the writers they write about argued vigorously for the peculiarly archaic qualities of Spanish colonialism. Indeed, perusing the essays on hispanismo, patriotic Latin American histories, and North American boosterism, the reader senses that she or he is witnessing Spanish and Latin American backwardness in the making, though made for varied motives and ends. But backwardness was not the only story. While writers like Restrepo, Mitre, Lummis, and the founders of the *Revista de Indias* firmly defended this reading, though in diverse ways, Arango y Parreño and Spain's late-nineteenth-century colonial minister, the Catalan man of letters Víctor Balaguer (discussed in Morillo-Alicea's essay), were optimistic modernizers, sanguine about the metropolis and colony's potential to replicate the successes of other states and economies.

Moreover, the flow of colonial knowledge was not one-way: Spain and its former colonies were exporters, not just importers, of colonial innovations.[31] Historians of Spanish colonialism are beginning to conceptualize the relationship between Spain and other colonial powers in ironic and critical fashion. Like Cooper and Stoler, they see the universal discourses to emerge from the Enlightenment forming a hinge moment in the definition of Spanish and European colonialisms and their legacies. In Cooper and Stoler's words: "Conquest, exploitation, and subjugation are old themes in world history. What was new in the Europe of the Enlightenment, of the development of liberalism, of the French Revolution, and of the classical economists was that such processes were set off against increasingly powerful claims in late eighteenth-century discourse to universal principles as the basis for organizing a polity."[32] In the view of prominent Enlightenment thinkers like Adam Smith, the Abbé Raynal, Cornelius De Pauw, and Voltaire, Spain and its empire failed to measure up to universal standards of economic efficiency, scientific rationality, and political justice because of their enslavement to traditional notions of privilege and intellectual authority, judgments that would carry over into the nineteenth century in the works of historians like Prescott, though eighteenth-century Spaniards and Creoles themselves contested these verdicts with great intellectual vigor and imagination, as Jorge Cañizares-Esguerra has recently shown.[33]

Smith in particular condemned the Spanish colonial enterprise because of the Crown's massive expenditures on behalf of the Church and the mining sector and its efforts to build an exclusive commercial system that favored the metropolis over the colonies. While he also criticized British colonialism as "mercantilism," he nonetheless saw it as superior because the English monarchy paid relatively little attention to the colonists (this characterization is similar to Mitre's view of Spain and the River Plate, as Adelman shows). This neglect unintentionally gave colonial subjects substantial political and economic liberty, a liberty that produced tremendous wealth not only for the colonists but also for the metropolis itself. In Smith's ironic judgment, the more neglectful and haphazard the colonial enterprise, the more successful it ultimately became because a weak state unintentionally encouraged economic growth.[34]

However, in the eyes of some scholars of Spanish colonialism, it was precisely this *laissez-faire* model of colonial rule trumpeted and theorized by Smith that England and other European powers began to abandon with the turn toward Asia and Africa beginning in the latter part of the eighteenth century. Instead, they built interventionist colonial regimes that not only regulated the economy more carefully but also sought to control and "civilize" the subject population, a mission whose contours resembled the supposedly archaic ambitions and strategies of the Spanish empire. In the words of Josep M. Fradera, a leading historian of Spanish colonialism in the eighteenth and nineteenth centuries:

> In reading about the efforts of the East India Company to control peasant tribute, or about the debates in Calcutta and Batavia over just government (for example, during the impeachment of Hastings), or about the function of native intermediaries, the Spanish historian cannot help but smile because these are echoes, two centuries later, of

similar debates held by Spanish functionaries or by the theologians of Salamanca. The Spanish colonial enterprise is less a historical anomaly than the origin of a historically dense process that must be explained from the start.[35]

It is precisely that sort of connection, not only temporal but also intellectual, cultural, and political, that most (but not all) of these essays suggest and pursue. In conceptualizing knowledge of Spanish colonialism and postcolonialism in relationship to a broader history of colonialism and decolonization, this volume does not intend to stand the hierarchy of colonial and postcolonial studies on its head by simplistically claiming that Spain created the template for subsequent conquests and colonial societies. Nor is it joining in the perceived assault against area studies, a source of some anxiety and speculation of late.[36] Rather, it argues that the islands, continents, peninsula, and archipelago discussed in the essays that follow, while unique and exceptional, were not and are not a world apart, though for the most part, they have formed distinct historiographic traditions. The causes for that apparent isolation lay not only in neglect by scholars of U.S. and northern European colonialisms but especially in the active construction of difference, in a variety of ways and for many motives, by scholars of Spain and its former colonies.

NOTES

1. Charles Gibson, *The Aztecs under Spanish Rule: A History of the Indians of the Valley of Mexico, 1519–1810* (Stanford: Stanford University Press, 1964), 403.

2. On the persistence of empire in shaping political discourse, this time in the case of French West Africa, see also Frederick Cooper, *Colonialism in Question: Theory, Knowledge, History* (Berkeley: University of California Press, 2005).

3. The idea for this meeting arose from a forum in the *American Historical Review* in which the authors explored historical paradigms, such as Frederick Jackson Turner's idea of the Frontier, used to comprehend the making of colonial and national borders in North American history. See Jeremy Adelman and Stephen Aron, "From Borderlands to Borders: Empires, Nation-States, and the Peoples in Between in North American History," *American Historical Review* 104 (June 1999): 814–41. The responses are Evan Haefeli, "A Note on the Use of North American Borderlands"; Christopher Ebert Schmidt-Nowara, "Borders and Borderlands of Interpretation"; John R. Wunder and Pekka Hämäläinen, "Of Lethal Places and Lethal Essays"; and Adelman and Aron, "Of Lively Exchanges and Larger Perspectives," *American Historical Review* 104 (October 1999): 1222–39.

4. Important studies of the link between historical writing and nation building that are particularly relevant to this introduction include Richard Kagan, "Prescott's Paradigm: American Historical Scholarship and the Decline of Spain," *American*

Historical Review 101 (April 1996): 423–46; idem, ed., *Spain in America: The Origins of Hispanism in the United States* (Urbana: University of Illinois Press, 2002); Carolyn Boyd, *Historia Patria: Politics, History, and National Identity in Spain, 1875–1975* (Princeton: Princeton University Press, 1997); Louis A. Pérez Jr., *The War of 1898: The United States and Cuba in History and Historiography* (Chapel Hill: University of North Carolina Press, 1998); Gabriel Haslip-Viera, ed., *Taíno Revival* (New York: Centro de Estudios Puertorriqueños, 1999); Carlos Serrano, *El nacimiento de Carmen: Mitos, símbolos y nación* (Madrid: Taurus, 1999); José Alvarez Junco, *Mater dolorosa: La idea de España en el siglo XIX* (Madrid: Taurus, 2001); Jorge Cañizares-Esguerra, *How to Write the History of the New World: Histories, Epistemologies, and Identities in the Eighteenth-Century Atlantic World* (Stanford: Stanford University Press, 2001); Jorge Duany, *The Puerto Rican Nation on the Move: Identities on the Island and in the United States* (Chapel Hill: University of North Carolina Press, 2002); and Stephen Jacobson, "'The Head and Heart of Spain': New Perspectives on Nationalism and Nationhood," *Social History* 29 (2004): 393–407.

5. Bolton's most famous work is *The Spanish Borderlands: A Chronicle of Old Florida and the Southwest* (New Haven: Yale University Press, 1921). In this volume, Sam Truett concentrates on another of his paradigm-building efforts: Herbert E. Bolton, "The Epic of Greater America," *American Historical Review* 38 (April 1933): 448–74. Arango y Parreño is one of the protagonists of Manuel Moreno Fraginal's seminal study of the Cuban sugar complex in the late eighteenth and early nineteenth centuries, *El Ingenio*, 3 vols. (Havana: Editorial de Ciencias Sociales, 1978).

6. Cañizares-Esguerra, *How to Write*. On the modern period, see Frederick Pike, *Hispanismo, 1898–1936* (Notre Dame: University of Notre Dame Press, 1971).

7. See Charles Lummis, *The Land of Poco Tiempo* (New York: C. Scribner's Sons, 1893).

8. Stuart Schwartz notes similarly dystopian constructions of the colonial past in Brazilian historiography. See his "The Colonial Past: Conceptualizing Post-*Dependista* Brazil," in *Colonial Legacies: The Problem of Persistence in Latin American History*, ed. Jeremy Adelman (New York: Routledge, 1999), 175–92.

9. Angel Quintero Rivera, "The Camouflaged Drum: Melodization of Rhythms and Maroonaged Ethnicity in Caribbean Peasant Music," *Caribbean Quarterly* 40 (1994): 27–37; idem, "Vueltita, con mantilla," in *Hispanofilia: Arquitectura y vida en Puerto Rico, 1900–1950*, ed. Enrique Vivoni Farage and Silvia Alvarez Curbelo (San Juan: Editorial de la Universidad de Puerto Rico, 1998), 249–74; Arcadio Díaz Quiñones, "1898," *Hispanic American Historical Review* 78 (1998): 577–81; idem, *El arte de bregar: Ensayos* (San Juan: Ediciones Callejón, 2000); and Duany, *The Puerto Rican Nation on the Move*.

10. Noel Luna, "Cuba y Puerto Rico no son: Conversación con Arcadio Díaz Quiñones," *Encuentro de la Cultura Cubana* 26/27 (2002–2003): 209–22.

11. Quintero Rivera, "Vueltita, con mantilla," 263.

12. See Amy Kaplan and Donald Pease, eds., *Cultures of United States Imperialism* (Durham, N.C.: Duke University Press, 1993); and Gilbert Joseph, Catherine LeGrand, and Ricardo Salvatore, eds., *Close Encounters of Empire: Writing the Cultural History of U.S.–Latin American Relations* (Durham, N.C.: Duke University Press, 1998). See also

James D. Fernández, "'Longfellow's Law': The Place of Latin America and Spain in U.S. Hispanism circa 1915," in Kagan, *Spain in America*, 122–41.

13. Ann Laura Stoler and Frederick Cooper, "Between Metropole and Colony: Rethinking a Research Agenda," in *Tensions of Empire: Colonial Cultures in a Bourgeois World*, ed. Frederick Cooper and Ann Laura Stoler (Berkeley: University of California Press, 1997), 1–56; Jorge Klor de Alva, "The Postcolonization of the (Latin) American Experience: A Reconsideration of 'Colonialism,' 'Postcolonialism,' and 'Mestizaje,'" in *After Colonialism*, ed. Gyan Prakash (Princeton: Princeton University Press, 1995), 241–75. See also Jaime Rodríguez O., ed., *The Origins of Mexican National Politics* (Wilmington, Del.: Scholarly Resources, 1997); and idem, *The Independence of Spanish America* (Cambridge: Cambridge University Press, 1998). Rodríguez O. also questions whether Spanish America was indeed a colonial society but bases his argument on the political ideologies and institutions of creole and metropolitan patriotic liberalism. Finally, see Mark Thurner's recent critique of Klor de Alva in "After Spanish Rule: Writing Another After," in *After Spanish Rule: Postcolonial Predicaments of the Americas*, ed. Mark Thurner and Andrés Guerrero (Durham, N.C.: Duke University Press, 2003), 20–25.

14. "The Founding of the Review," *Hispanic American Historical Review* 1 (1918): 8–23. In the introduction to the inaugural issue, the founders note that the idea originated at the Panama-Pacific Exhibition and the various congresses held for the event in the San Francisco Bay area in 1916. In effect, surveying the spectacle of the United States' new imperial possessions provided the impetus for creating a forum to study the ideas and institutions built by the U.S.'s Spanish predecessors.

15. For a careful discussion of this approach to Latin American history, see Jeremy Adelman, "Introduction: The Problem of Persistence in Latin American History," in Adelman, *Colonial Legacies*, 1–13.

16. Rolena Adorno, "Introduction," in Irving Leonard, *Books of the Brave* (Berkeley: University of California Press, 1992), x. Also insightful are James Dunkerley's discussion of U.S. Latin Americanists, such as Richard Morse, in his *Americana* (London: Verso, 2000), 101–242. Dunkerley finds a similar effort to construct colonial and postcolonial Latin America as almost utopian alternatives to the dystopian features of modernity in the United States.

17. The debate between Lewis Hanke and Benjamin Keen is an important touchstone in assessing these changes. See Benjamin Keen, "The Black Legend Revisited: Assumptions and Realities," *Hispanic American Historical Review* 49 (1969): 703–19; Lewis Hanke, "A Modest Proposal for a Moratorium on Grand Generalizations: Some Thoughts on the Black Legend," *Hispanic American Historical Review* 51 (1971): 112–27; and Benjamin Keen, "The White Legend Revisited: A Reply to Professor Hanke's 'Modest Proposal,'" *Hispanic American Historical Review* 51 (1971): 336–55. Keen's survey of approaches to the work and life of Las Casas also gives a good sense of the changing nature and perspectives of U.S. Latin American studies. See Benjamin Keen, "Introduction: Approaches to Las Casas, 1535–1970," in *Bartolome de las Casas in History: Toward an Understanding of the Man and His Work*, ed. Benjamin Keen and Juan Friede (DeKalb: Northern Illinois University Press, 1974), 3–63.

18. Gibson, *The Aztecs under Spanish Rule;* Nancy Farriss, *The Maya under Spanish Rule: The Collective Enterprise of Survival* (Princeton: Princeton University Press, 1984); Steve Stern, *Peru's Indian Peoples and the Challenge of Spanish Conquest: Huamanga to 1640* (Madison: University of Wisconsin Press, 1982); James Lockhart, *The Nahuas after the Conquest: A Social and Cultural History of the Indians of Central Mexico, Sixteenth through Eighteenth Centuries* (Stanford: Stanford University Press, 1992).

19. Serge Gruzinski and Nathan Wachtel, "Cultural Inbreedings: Constituting the Majority as a Minority," *Comparative Studies of Society and History* 39 (1997): 231–50; and Gruzinksi, *The Mestizo Mind: The Intellectual Dynamics of Colonization and Globalization*, trans. Deke Dusinberre (London: Routledge, 2002), 50.

20. Florencia Mallon, "Constructing *Mestizaje* in Latin America: Authenticity, Marginality, and Gender in the Claiming of Ethnic Identities," *Journal of Latin American Anthropology* 2 (1996): 171.

21. Fernando Ortiz, *Cuban Counterpoint: Tobacco and Sugar*, trans. Harriet de Onís (Durham, N.C.: Duke University Press, 1995), 102–3. Emphasis in the original. For a brilliant gloss of Ortiz, see Gustavo Pérez-Firmat, *The Cuban Condition* (Cambridge: Cambridge University Press, 1989).

22. Stuart Hall, "When was the 'postcolonial'? Thinking at the Limit," in *The Post-Colonial Question*, ed. Iain Chambers and Lidia Curti (London: Routledge, 1996), 249. Emphasis in the original. See also Ann Laura Stoler, *Race and the Education of Desire: Foucault's History of Sexuality and the Colonial Order of Things* (Durham, N.C.: Duke University Press, 1995).

23. Peter Hulme, "Subversive Archipelagos: Colonial Discourse and the Break-up of Continental Theory," *Dispositio* XIV (1989): 8–9. See also Hulme's *Colonial Encounters: Europe and the Native Caribbean, 1492–1797* (New York: Methuen, 1986).

24. Kagan, "Prescott's Paradigm." For an overview of recent modern Spanish historiography, see "Spain: A Special Issue," *Social History* 29 (2004).

25. On the Generation of '98 and the fascination with Spanish decadence see the recent essays, Carlos Serrano, "Conciencia de la crisis, crisis de la conciencia," 335–403, and José Alvarez Junco, "La nación en duda," 405–75 in *Más se perdió en Cuba: España, 1898 y el fin de siglo*, ed. Juan Pan-Montojo (Madrid: Alianza, 1998).

26. Juan Pablo Fusi, "España: El fin del siglo XX," *Claves de razón prática* 87 (Noviembre 1998): 9. Stephen J. Summerhill and John Alexander Williams discuss the emphasis on Spain's successful integration into Europe during the multiple celebrations of 1992. See Summerhill and Williams, *Sinking Columbus: Contested History, Cultural Politics, and Mythmaking during the Quincentenary* (Gainesville: University Press of Florida, 2000), ch. 5.

One might note that the other '98 anniversary, that of Philip II's death in 1598, produced similar efforts not only to emphasize Spain's Europeanness but also to revise the image of "el Rey prudente," the historical figure most associated with Spanish cruelty in the Black Legend. Important examples include the lavish and quite sophisticated collections published by the Sociedad Estatal de la Conmemoración del Centenario de Carlos V y Felipe II, including *El siglo de Carlos V y Felipe II: La construcción de los mitos en el siglo XIX*, 2 vols., ed. Jesús Martínez Millán and Carlos Reyero (Madrid: Sociedad Estatal de la

Conmemoración del Centenario de Carlos V y Felipe II, 2000). The same was true among some English-language scholars. See especially Henry Kamen, *Philip of Spain* (New Haven: Yale University Press, 1997); and Kamen, *The Spanish Inquisition: A Historical Revision* (New Haven: Yale University Press, 1998). A skeptical view can be found in Richard Kagan's review of the latter in *New York Times Book Review*, 14 April 1998.

27. For an influential discussion of the relationship between theories of modernization and national historiographies, see David Blackbourn and Geoff Eley, *The Peculiarities of German History: Bourgeois Society and Politics in Nineteenth-Century Germany* (New York: Oxford University Press, 1984). See also Alberto Medina Domínguez's mordant observations on the Spanish discourse of modernity in the context of European postmodernity, "Simulación y simulacro," *Quimera* 188/189 (2000): 27–31

28. Manuel Moreno Fraginals, *El Ingenio*; Juan Pan-Montojo, "El atraso económico y la regeneración," in *Más se perdió*, 261–334; Rebecca J. Scott, *Slave Emancipation in Cuba* (Princeton: Princeton University Press, 1985); Josep M. Fradera, *Indústria i mercat: Les bases comercials de la indústria catalana moderna (1814–1845)* (Barcelona: Crítica, 1987); Laird Bergad, *Cuban Rural Society in the Nineteenth Century: The Social and Economic History of Monoculture in Matanzas* (Princeton: Princeton University Press, 1990); Jesús Millán García-Varela, *El poder de la tierra: La sociedad agraria del bajo Segura en la época del liberalismo: 1830–1890* (Alicante: Diputación Provincial de Alicante, 1999). For a general discussion of these issues in contemporary Spanish historiography, see Mónica Burguera and Christopher Schmidt-Nowara, "Backwardness and Its Discontents," *Social History* 29 (2004): 279–83.

29. Kagan, "Prescott's Paradigm"; Ernesto Laclau, "Feudalism and Capitalism in Latin America," *New Left Review* 67 (1971): 19–38. Like Laclau, Enrique Dussel seeks to invert the terms of Latin American backwardness by pinpointing the beginning of "modernity" at 1492. See Dussel, "Eurocentrism and Modernity (Introduction to the Frankfurt Lectures)," *boundary2* 20 (1993): 65–76.

30. See Frederick Cooper, "Race, Ideology, and the Perils of Comparative History," *American Historical Review* 101 (1996): 1122–38. See also Stoler and Cooper, "Between Metropole and Colony"; and Adelman and Aron, "From Borderlands to Borders."

31. For a fascinating example, see Eddy Stols's recounting of Crown Prince Leopold's visit to the Archivo de Indias in Seville in the mid-nineteenth century: "Los imperios ultramarinos de Carlos V y Felipe II en la historiografía e imaginativa expansionistas belgas (1830–1914)," in *El siglo de Carlos V y Felipe II*, vol. 2: 383–405.

32. Stoler and Cooper, "Between Metropole and Colony," 1.

33. Cañizares-Esguerra, *How to Write*, esp. chs. 3–5. See also Anthony Pagden, *Lords of All the World: Ideologies of Empire in Spain, Britain, and France c. 1500–c. 1800* (New Haven: Yale University Press, 1995).

34. See Adam Smith, *An Inquiry into the Nature and Causes of the Wealth of Nations*, ed. R. H. Campbell, A. S. Skinner, and W. B. Todd (Oxford: Clarendon Press, 1976), vol. 2: 567–72. See also the comparison of "monopoly" in the English and Iberian empires in vol 2: 609–10.

35. This quotation is from an interview I conducted with Fradera on the subject. See Christopher Schmidt-Nowara, "After 'Spain': A Dialogue with Josep M. Fradera on

Spanish Colonial Historiography," in *After the Imperial Turn: Thinking through and with the Nation* (Durham, N.C.: Duke University Press, 2003), 164. For overviews of recent Spanish work, see Schmidt-Nowara, "Imperio y crisis colonial," in Pan-Montojo, *Más se perdió*; Consuelo Naranjo, Miguel A. Puig-Samper, and Luis Miguel García Mora, eds., *La nación soñada: Cuba, Puerto Rico y Filipinas ante el 98* (Madrid: Doce Calles, 1996), 31–89; Fradera, *Gobernar colonias* (Barcelona: Península, 1999); and Javier Morillo-Alicea, "'Aquel laberinto de oficinas': Ways of Knowing Empire in Late-Nineteenth-Century Spain," in Thurner and Guerrero, *After Spanish Rule*, 111–40.

Other works that theorize the connections between the colonial and postcolonial Americas and other empires and independent nation-states include Thurner and Guerrero, *After Spanish Rule*; Frederick Cooper, Florencia Mallon, Steve Stern, Allen Isaacman, and William Roseberry, *Confronting Historical Paradigms: Peasants, Labor, and the Capitalist World System in Africa and Latin America* (Madison: University of Wisconsin Press, 1993); Peter Hulme, "Including America," *Ariel* 26 (1995): 117–23; Patricia Seed, *Ceremonies of Possession in Europe's Conquest of the New World, 1492–1640* (Cambridge: Cambridge University Press, 1995); Joseba Galindo, ed., "The Hispanic Atlantic," special section of *Arizona Journal of Hispanic Cultural Studies* 5 (2001): 91–193; and Irene Silverblatt, *Modern Inquisitions: Peru and the Origins of the Civilized World* (Durham, N.C.: Duke University Press, 2004).

36. Arjun Appadurai, *Modernity at Large: Cultural Dimensions of Globalization* (Minneapolis: University of Minnesota Press, 1996); Benedict Anderson, *The Spectre of Comparisons: Nationalism, Southeast Asia, and the World* (London: Verso, 1998).

PART ONE

Modernity among the Ruins

Fig. 1. View of Havana in the mid-nineteenth century.
La Habana al medio del siglo XIX, engraving by J. Bachman,
New York, 1851. From Levi Marrero,
Cuba: Economía y sociedad vol. 9
(Madrid: Editorial Playor, 1983).

INTRODUCTION

Christopher Schmidt-Nowara and John Nieto-Phillips

*T*he division of these essays into "colonial" and "postcolonial" categories is hardly definitive, since continuities and connections across different epochs are immediately evident. Moreover, "colonial" and "postcolonial" do not divide neatly into discrete temporal units: Puerto Rican patriots pondered the fate of their nation under colonial rule at the same time that Colombian and Argentine historians crafted their national narratives in the decades following the Spanish American revolutions. However, it has seemed useful to us to explore the "tensions of empire" in the context of a persistent, if ever-changing, colonial rule, as opposed to the histories and memories of empire composed in the context of political independence and imperial collapse.

From the following essays emerges a curious and perhaps surprising tension: While many intellectuals found questions of peculiarity and backwardness to be paramount, others were confident about partaking of broader currents of colonial knowledge and the efforts to modernize the metropolis and the colonies.

In the essays by Astrid Cubano-Iguina and Antonio Feros, we find both Spaniards and Puerto Ricans seeking to define the peculiar characteristics of Spanish colonialism in opposition to "Anglo-Saxon" powers—Great Britain and the United States. In making this juxtaposition, *criollos* and *peninsulares* alike were well aware of imperial conflicts in the Caribbean, a site of great power rivalry since the sixteenth century but with particular nineteenth-century inflections. For example, it was only after the British government applied persistent pressure on the Spanish government that Spain, in 1870, finally abolished the slave trade to Cuba. Moreover, Cuba's hawkish northern neighbor, as Louis A. Pérez has shown, made well known its pretensions as the ultimate arbiter of Cuba's fate.[1] As a rhetorical defense against Yankee and British imperialism, then, the glorified Spanish past, what we might call the White Legend, arose in part from the tension *between* empires. But hispanismo was equally rooted in tensions *within* the empire: between creoles and Spaniards, separatists and autonomists, Spanish nationalists and their metropolitan critics. Indeed, both authors emphasize how the discussion of empire in both Spain and Puerto

Rico provided a means for cultural and political elites to silence dissent in domestic politics, such as regional nationalisms in Spain or popular political demands in Puerto Rico, a function of imperial rhetoric unique neither to the Spanish empire nor only to the empires of the past.

While Cubano-Iguina and Feros call attention to the sense of threat and vulnerability that shaped Spanish and Puerto Rican histories, Dale Tomich and Javier Morillo-Alicea present us with confident modernizers perched, as we know through historical hindsight, on the verge of monumental changes. Tomich shows that the Cuban planter Francisco Arango y Parreño, much like the Argentine Bartolomé Mitre or the Puerto Rican José Julián Acosta y Calbo, searched restlessly for paradigms and predecessors to help him theorize the conditions necessary for Cuba's plantation belt to take off. In doing so, Arango collapsed many of the binary oppositions that girded classical liberal theory. To create the most productive plantation complex in Caribbean history, Arango emphasized the centrality of a supposedly archaic labor system, chattel slavery; empire was not antithetical to the market, but its practical shell. Moreover, Arango confidently foresaw the success of his vision of an export-driven econ-omy under the protection of a colonial metropolis, Spain, which was pilloried by Adam Smith and others for its archaic fascination with bullion and inatten-tion to commerce.

Morillo-Alicea wrestles with the question of Spain's apparent marginality to Europe's Age of Empire. Indeed, we lead off with his essay because it ele-gantly reflects on various kinds of boundaries. Like Tomich, Morillo-Alicea finds important borrowings from other colonial regimes—for instance, in Víctor Balaguer's enthusiastic patronage of the Exposición Filipina held in Madrid in 1887 while Balaguer was the government's Ministerio de Ultramar (Minister of Overseas Provinces). Morillo also inflects Cooper and Stoler's argument about cross-colonial forms of knowledge and rule by examining how the colonial state utilized ruling strategies from the Caribbean to undertake initiatives in its Pacific colonies.[2] For Balaguer and the Ministerio's functionar-ies, Spain's peculiarities were fully compatible with the innovations of nine-teenth-century European colonialism. Moreover, the metropolis's governing institutions and forms of knowledge were not simply premodern artifacts, pet-rified since the days of the Hapsburgs; they were also tools used by nineteenth-century Spanish liberals to undertake vast changes in the "imperial archipelago."

NOTES

1. Louis A. Pérez Jr., *The War of 1898: Cuba and the United States in History and Historiography* (Chapel Hill: University of North Carolina Press, 1998).

2. Ann Laura Stoler and Frederick Cooper, "Between Metropole and Colony: Rethinking a Research Agenda," in *Tensions of Empire: Colonial Cultures in a Bourgeois World*, ed. Frederick Cooper and Ann Laura Stoler (Berkeley: University of California Press, 1997), 1–56.

CHAPTER ONE

UNCHARTED LANDSCAPES
OF "LATIN AMERICA"

The Philippines in the Spanish Imperial Archipelago

Javier Morillo-Alicea

José Rizal, the Filipino nationalist hero, and his contemporary José Martí, the Cuban revolutionary with whom he had so much in common, never met. Rizal certainly knew of the revolutionary upheavals in the Caribbean sister colony from 1868 forward, and we know from his correspondence that he was well aware of the work of the *antillano* abolitionists and reformers who had agitated in Madrid for years, at times contemporaneously with his own residence there. Rizal did come close to seeing Martí's homeland firsthand when in 1896 he received permission to travel there from the Philippine island of Dapitan, where he had lived in forced exile for four years. After hearing of the outbreak of the second insurrection in Cuba, Rizal wrote to Ramón Blanco y Erenas, Captain-General of the Philippines, requesting that he be allowed to serve in Cuba as a physician for Spanish forces in the Caribbean island. The request was delayed for so long that when the Captain-General finally did give his approval a year later, Rizal had, he wrote to friends, forgotten about the petition.

From this approval one might surmise that Blanco did not seriously consider the prospect that Rizal might, once in Cuba, do anything other than serve on the side of the Spanish military. Officials may have seen the move as an opportune one; Rizal's novels and political mobilization had made him dangerously popular in the Philippine archipelago. Blanco may have considered

I wish to thank Christopher Schmidt-Nowara for inviting me to participate in the "Paradigms/Paradigmas" conference, as well as the participants for their very helpful comments on an earlier draft of this essay. I also wish to thank John T. Stiles, whose careful readings of the many drafts greatly improved the final product. All mistakes, of course, remain mine. All translations, unless otherwise noted, are mine.

the benefits of Rizal's voluntary exile more than the possibility that once in Cuba, he might side with—or, at the very least, learn from—people who, like him, were strong critics of and threats to the empire. In any case, it was not Spanish concerns with their Cuban problem that interrupted Rizal's travel but rather a very local Philippine situation: the outbreak of the Katipunan rebellion. Apparently determined to display a strong hand against reformers and rebels alike (and, in the process, to eliminate the distinction between the two), officials returned Rizal, who was already en route to Cuba, to Manila to face trial for treason. Found guilty, he was executed in 1896.

What Rizal was thinking on his way to Cuba, we cannot know, although interpretations of his intentions have played an important role in Filipino historiography. To historian Renato Constantino, for example, the physician's attempt to enlist in the service of the metropole's armed forces proved him a Spanish loyalist, bound by his class interests to be a reformer, not a revolutionary.[1] Rizal knew that had he reached Cuba, he would have encountered the regime of Gen. Valeriano Weyler, a man he knew well from the latter's time as Captain-General of the Philippines. Although the Rizal family's unhappy history with Weyler, to which I will return later, should cast doubt on any easy reading of his intentions in traveling to Cuba, my aim here is not to counter Constantino's certainty with another. Instead, I evoke the image of Rizal on a boat, almost but not reaching Cuba, because it suggests an interesting question about Spain's nineteenth-century empire: Why was there never a meaningful alliance formed between colonial reformers and separatists in the Caribbean with their counterparts in the Philippines? While Puerto Rican poet Lola Rodríguez de Tió once famously declared that Cuba and Puerto Rico were "de un pájaro las dos alas" (two wings of the same bird), no one ever suggested that the wings of her conceptual avis might span as far as the "Pearl of the Orient." The distance of geography cannot explain it all. Oceans may have separated the poor men in Cuba and the Philippines who made up the majority of both uprisings, but many elites had the privilege of travel that could bridge worlds. The Filipino *ilustrado* consciousness that Rizal is representative of, after all, developed not in the Pacific but in the metropolitan capital, the same Madrid that was home to so many *antillano* intellectuals and politicians.

I begin with this counterfactual question, this "historical negative"[2] as a starting point for a reflection on Spain's nineteenth-century empire and on the nature of colonial state power in the Age of Empire. My aim is not to anachronistically castigate nineteenth-century actors for not forging alliances; this essay, in fact, does not seek to explore the histories of reform and revolution in the colonies led by people like Tió, Rizal, and Martí. The absence of an anticolonial imaginary that placed struggles in the various colonies on the same plane is interesting to me because it stands in stark contrast to the state that colonial critics struggled against. My object here is to understand the nature of that state's power. While seeing commonalities between the colonies was not unthinkable to nationalists and reformers, for the state it was a necessity and a source of strength. The colonial bureaucracy had clear understandings of the connections between its possessions; a wide-angle view of empire was central to its power and its ability to fight rebellion. This power rested in its ability to do what colonial critics from the islands could not do as easily: use lessons learned in one colony to address situations in another.

This essay analyzes the state's wide-angle view of empire by taking the colonies of Cuba, the Philippines, and Puerto Rico as a single entity, what I call the Spanish Imperial Archipelago. Focusing as well on the particulars of the Philippines' place in that imperial archipelago, this essay reflects an attempt by a "Latin Americanist" to engage with the history and historiography of that former Spanish colony. Although part of the Spanish empire from the sixteenth century until 1898, the Philippines has been largely ignored by Latin American studies, with some notable exceptions.[3] This essay represents a small contribution to plotting a different conceptual map than that offered by area-studies boundaries, a cartography that helps us better understand the nineteenth-century empire. In order to chart the map of the imperial archipelago, I draw on the work of historians of Spain and its empire that have seriously revised the commonly held notion of the nineteenth-century empire as a relic, a mere teetering giant on its way to being slain by the United States.[4] Challenging the idea of a Spain forever caught in the dark ages—what historian of Spain Richard Kagan has described in anglophone scholarship as "Prescott's Paradigm"—recent work has painted a picture of the nineteenth-century empire as vibrant, vast, and, yes, modern.[5] By giving serious attention to both the Antilles and the Philippines in his research on the "imperio insular," Josep Fradera's work has forged a more complex understanding of the economic and political ties that linked metropole and colonies.[6] Although not literally a translation of Fradera's "imperio insular," my conceptualization of the Imperial Archipelago owes much to his.[7]

Placing side-by-side colonial histories that may on the surface seem incommensurable, this essay is also a meditation on historical comparisons and connections that learns from and expands on the insights of work by scholars in colonial studies. Frederick Cooper has suggested that traditional models of comparative history, by defining the objects of inquiry as two discrete entities to be judged against each other, obscures the ways that seemingly different, isolated phenomena might actually be *connected* by histories that intersect. This does not entail that historical comparison be abandoned, for as Cooper writes, "a global, interactive approach to history needs comparison, and comparison needs interactive and global analysis."[8] This is particularly important if we take seriously Ann Stoler's recent suggestion that theorizing comparison in the history of empire requires attention not only to scholarly practices of historical inquiry, but just as importantly "to practices of colonial comparison by governments themselves."[9] This is important because empires learned from one another; colonialism itself was a comparative project.

While learning from Stoler's project of comparing empires to each other, here I suggest another, equally important space from which to analyze colonialism as a comparative project. While colonies often served as Europe's "laboratories of modernity," it is also true that a single empire's colonies could serve as laboratories for each other.[10] Colonial-studies scholars such as Bernard Cohn and the contributors to Cooper and Stoler's collaborative project *Tensions of Empire* have all shed important light on the workings of colonial knowledge through a dialectical understanding of the colony-metropole relationship. Their insights inform my discussion, below, of the Philippines and its relationship to Spain. The colony-metropole focus, however, has understood the workings of colonial knowledge in a largely vertical manner, i.e., through attention to the relationship of a metropole and one of its colonies. I expand on this work by first drawing attention to the significance of the horizontal connections that existed between the colonies of a single empire. Through a discussion of the bureaucratic and military apparatuses that made disparate islands into an empire, I suggest that the political strength of the nineteenth-century Spanish empire at times derived from its ability to view its various colony-metropole relationships on the same plane.

The two sections of this essay that follow analyze the nineteenth-century Spanish empire through an attention to connections and comparisons, respectively. The first section takes an empire-wide focus through a discussion of the Ministerio de Ultramar, or Overseas Ministry, which starting with its creation in 1863 centralized the empire's multiple paper trails into a single Madrid office.[11] The second section moves us from empire to colony, to the Philippine islands Josep Fradera has described as Spain's "most peculiar colony."[12] While for Fradera the peculiarities stem from the organization of the state's finances there, here I draw another aspect of Philippine history that distinguishes it from the

Antillean possessions. This section revisits an event that Philippine historiography has seen as an important marker in the development of ilustrado national consciousness: an 1887 Philippine Exposition in Madrid featuring live exhibits of indigenous peoples that projected, Rizal and others argued, an image of the colony as primitive and uncivilized. This particular racialization, I argue, made the colony the object of a "civilizing mission" similar to that of other European powers in Asia. It is also a crucial factor in explaining why the "fraternity" with which metropolitan politicians could sometimes embrace the Antillean islands was rarely extended to the Southeast Asian colony. The connections between colonies that I suggest in the first section and the particularities that set them apart from each other that I explore in the second do not contradict each other. The state's ability to see commonalities across colonies with different histories was precisely its source of strength.

The Nineteenth-Century Imperial Archipelago: Movements of People and Paper

There were two central and related components to the state's wide-angle view of empire: its ability to move people and paper. The story with which I began, of Rizal's interrupted voyage across the Imperial Archipelago, is a useful starting point for grasping the importance of the first. As mentioned, had the Filipino colonial critic made it to Cuba, he might have come face-to-face with Valeriano Weyler, a man he knew well and who, in turn, knew him as well. Weyler, famous in Cuban and United States historiography as the Spanish villain in the Hearst newspaper reports of the insurrection, had previously made his reputation as a hard-liner against colonial reform as Governor-General of the Philippines. Weyler assumed that position in 1888, replacing a more liberal predecessor. By the time of Weyler's elevation to the post, Rizal had already attracted the attention of the Church and state with the European publication of his landmark novel, *Noli me tangere*, in which he presented a devastating picture of the colony as corrupted by the religious orders and their ability to suppress all Liberal reform. His family, meanwhile, was in the midst of a legal battle over land with one of those religious orders when Weyler took office. Siding with the Dominican order, the Governor-General played a direct role in the Rizals' eviction, along with sixty other families, from the Dominicans' Calamba estate.[13]

Weyler's connection to both islands suggests the manner in which the state used knowledge, practices, and personnel from one colony to inform policies in another. It was in the Philippines that he implemented harsh policies of relocation that he would later rework in Cuba as the infamous *reconcentraciones*.

General Blanco, Weyler's successor, was loudly criticized by the Madrid press for appearing weak when faced with the Katipunan rebellion that broke out in 1896 and for initially granting Rizal's request to travel to Cuba. By December of that year Blanco was replaced by General García de Polavieja, who sought permission from the central government to implement Weyler's reconcentraciones to assist in suppressing the growing revolt in the Philippines. Aware by this time that the Cuban campaign had provoked international criticism, Polavieja was careful to note that in the Asian colony he would ensure that the reconcentraciones did not result in the starvation and cruelty that made Weyler infamous in the Antilles.[14] The symbiotic relationship of military policy in the Philippines and Cuba came full circle when in October 1897, the new Liberal government in Madrid, under pressure from the United States, moved Weyler out of Cuba, replacing him with Ramón Blanco, the "weak" Governor-General of the Philippines.

The movement of people included not just agents of the state like Weyler and Blanco but also the involuntary travel forced upon many of its colonial subjects. The empire had a long history of exiling politically dangerous persons from one corner of the empire to another, a history Blanco perhaps drew on when granting Rizal leave to Cuba. Government changes in the metropole at times meant the deportation of peninsular Liberals to the Philippines, something one historian of the Philippines suggests contributed to the spread of Liberal ideas in the colony.[15] The African island-colony of Fernando Po was at one time considered a possible destination for the deportation of freed Cuban blacks—a "problem" created, of course, by the most significant case of involuntary movement of people, the Atlantic slave trade. The island would later serve as a destination for many insurgents deported from Cuba during its insurrections.[16] And Puerto Rican prisons often housed wards from other colonies, including the 1880 imprisonment of Cuban insurgent José Maceo, brother of Antonio, the famous revolutionary leader.

While the above examples revolve around military matters, imperial circuits were not limited to the strategic decisions of a state fighting rebellion on two fronts, nor were these circuits restricted to the transfer of political prisoners. In 1877, a Chinese man who appears in the archive of the Consejo de Estado in Madrid as "José María Segundo, Asiático," requested a pardon from the Crown from his prison cell in San Juan, Puerto Rico. José María had not committed any crimes in Puerto Rico; he was serving time there after having been convicted of homicide in Cuba, where he had been a contract laborer.[17] Having labored in Cuba and served prison time in Puerto Rico, a full understanding of José María's situation also takes us to the colony in Southeast Asia. As the institution of slavery and, especially, the slave trade were increasingly challenged through the nineteenth century, Cuban sugar planters began to seek other forms of labor. It was through Spanish presence in the Philippines and the trade with China it facilitated that Cubans were first able to gain access to Chinese indentured labor.[18] José María is one of at least six Chinese laborers who requested pardons from the crown from the *presidio* in Puerto Rico.

The voluntary and involuntary relocations of individuals across the Imperial Archipelago were facilitated by a bureaucracy that managed the state's paper trails and sought to control the flow of information. The 1863 creation of the Overseas Ministry centralized management of the empire in a single office in Madrid.[19] The ministry marked the culmination of a long history of discussion that began with the Napoleonic invasion that sparked the Spanish American wars of independence. One side of the discussion, which revolved around whether the overseas territories were to be seen as equal partners in the nation, was represented by the 1810 call of the Cortes de Cádiz for representatives from all of the colonies (although not in proportion to the overseas populations). The subsequent 1812 Constitution claimed to reject "the old system of conquests and colonies" in favor of a relationship based on "reciprocal love and of the union of interests with those of the Peninsula." This love would be reflected concretely in the form of parliamentary representation for the "overseas provinces." If the remaining colonies were to be treated as provinces, as the wording of the constitution suggests, then it would follow that they would be administered in the same manner as the Iberian provinces—that is, through existing ministries. As Josep Fradera has pointed out, however, the century is best characterized not by the fraternal embrace of 1812 but by the year 1837, a date that marks the expulsion of overseas delegates from the Cortes and the promise, unfulfilled for the whole of the century, that the overseas territories would be governed by "special laws."[20] These two actions framed the ongoing nineteenth-century debate over how best to administer the reconfigured empire, a debate that was only resolved by the establishment of the Overseas Ministry. The ministry's creation marked a victory for Liberals, for whom centralization of colonial administration was key to bringing it in line with the administrative logic of other European empires, particularly the British.

The office handled all affairs of the colonies under a wide bureaucratic umbrella that managed justice, budgets, and government. While in the peninsula, for example, all criminal matters were handled through the Ministry of Justice, criminal matters of the colonies were handled in the Office of Justice within the Overseas Ministry. This meant that, in the metropole, the same public servants who received reports of land disputes in the Philippines also received and dealt with news from Puerto Rico and Cuba. This centralizing logic permeated colonial administration from 1863 onward. The ministry's archive was the embodiment of the state's wide-angle view, a perspective that could be put to use by using experiences in one colony to inform the administration of another.

In practice, this broad perspective allowed the state to play the colonies off one another. Perhaps the most striking example of this is in the Antilles, where Puerto Rico's lack of rebelliousness vis-à-vis Cuba could make the former island a test case for colonial policy. While 1868 had seen three revolutions in the empire—in Madrid, Cuba, and Puerto Rico—the latter's Grito de Lares was quickly suppressed. Much to the chagrin of leaders like Ramón Emeterio Betances, the island population was never roused to action in a manner parallel to Cuba, where the Grito de Yara set off the Ten Years War and, in retrospect, could be read as the beginning of a thirty-year revolution against the Spanish metropole.[21] The absence of armed struggle, however, meant that Puerto Rico could serve as what Agustín Sánchez Andrés has described as an "experimental field" for the development of new colonial policies.[22] Right up until the 1897 granting of the Carta Autonómica, the island was the scene of a series of concessions that, while not made available to the Cubans in arms, were in part aimed at demonstrating to them that the state could be trusted to institute reforms.

This is not meant to suggest that handling various colonies could not also present problems for the state. Overseas Minister Víctor Balaguer, a man with a particular interest in the Philippines, once lamented the attention that the rebellious island of Cuba took away from the Southeast Asian colony, writing: "But then there is Cuba, Cuba, which since 1870 has monopolized all of the hours of the minister, taking control of him body and soul."[23] Nor is my discussion of the visibility of the Imperial Archipelago to the state meant to suggest that the bureaucratic webs that the ministry spun, linking the Philippines, Cuba, and Puerto Rico to Madrid, made the state all-powerful or omniscient. Using the image of the imperial archive as a metaphor for British rule, Thomas Richards has rightly argued that colonial power depended on an illusion of total knowledge—a "fantasy of empire"—that real bureaucratic practice could not actualize.[24] The Royal Decree that created the ministry, as well as the various regulations that governed its workings, taken at face value suggests the state paid meticulous attention to efficiency, accuracy, and, above all, probity in administration.

On the ground, the reality was that the bureaucratic apparatus was a lightning rod for colonial critics in every corner of the empire. Rafael María de Labra, the noted Liberal crusader for colonial reform, saw the colonial problem as centered in the Overseas Ministry, a place where "most employees only know of overseas matters from what they read in the records" they shuffled.[25] Labra saw the colonial state's ability to control information about its possessions as paramount to understanding its power.

> [I]t is well known that one of the most powerful resources available to reactionaries and monopolists in the colonies of all countries is the ability to mislead public opinion and wear down the observer, whether through the chaos and confusion of administrative measures taken in the colonies, or by making it difficult for anyone to receive direct or immediate knowledge of actions taken Overseas that, in many cases, contradict those administrative measures.[26]

It was thus not a fear of absolute state power that motivated Labra's criticism; rather, it was the fact of the slowness of state action and the mistakes made by bureaucrats not knowledgeable of colonial affairs that was the source of his consternation. The tension Labra describes between a state that was both bumbling and powerful is also what gives the 1887 novel by Cuban Ramón Meza, *Mi tío el empleado*, its biting, satirical brilliance. Meza presents the colonial administration of Cuba as a comical world where bureaucrats move paper back and forth without ever having a clear idea of the contents of the records; it is also clear, however, that people like the uncle in the title gained much power from its corruption.[27] The reality of colonial practice Ramón Meza describes fictionally in Cuba resonates strongly with José Rizal's contemporaneous concerns for morality in administration in the Philippines. Writing about the ills of Spanish colonialism to his friend, the Austrian Orientalist Ferdinand Blumentritt, Rizal was sure to include "better government employees" in what he considered was a modest list of reforms necessary in the colony.[28]

The common criticisms of bureaucratic practice across the empire, and the fact that these rarely translated into collective action, brings us again to the "historical negative" with which we began. I should stress once again, that the aim is not to judge reformers in different colonies as short-sighted but merely to point out the disadvantages they faced against a centralizing state. The moments of possibility we do find in the historical record suggest that colonial critics were aware of the importance of the state's wide-angle view, even if they could not easily mobilize an equally broad counternarrative. Labra's description, quoted above, of the power of colonial states as centered in their control of information suggests such an understanding. Given this, it is perhaps not surprising, then, that Labra was also one who saw cross-colonial alliances as a possibility to be pursued. Although born in Cuba, Labra was raised in the peninsula and considered himself a metropolitan Spaniard. Strongly committed to a vision of Liberalism that would afford the overseas territories political autonomy within the state, this metropolitan was a vocal critic of colonial policies and a consistent advocate of reform. In an 1873 pamphlet addressed to Puerto Rican electors, Labra called on island liberals to look beyond their local situation to the empire as a whole. Convinced of the need to learn from each other's struggles, Labra wrote, "on several occasions I lobbied for the creation of a Colonial-Reformist Center in Madrid . . . and the founding of a newspaper, with the aim of making known the aspirations of our Colonies."[29]

Labra was at the center of another attempt to bring together *antillanos* and *filipinos*. The Filipino ilustrado group had once even entertained the possibility of an alliance for colonial reform, but not much ever came of these rumblings. When Evaristo Aguirre, a member of the group, wrote to Rizal—by then having left Madrid for Germany—about talk of such a coalition, he was decidedly less than enthusiastic. Of the antillanos, he wrote: "I have yet to become friendly with any of them, as I find in every one of them large doses of exaggerated vanity and egotism." Although he had kind words to say about Labra, who was to be the coalition's leader, he reminded Rizal that as a Republican in the middle of the monarchy Labra had a limited voice. Comparing the situation of their colony with the Antillean islands, Aguirre wrote pessimistically: "Could the Philippines, represented by a small group of young men in Madrid, present itself as a viable candidate for autonomy (as Labra suggests), when this has been flatly denied to Cuba and Puerto Rico, claiming that this is a path toward independence?"[30]

Aguirre's comparative impulse here is interesting, and his silence about the reasons for his pessimism compelling. Without elaborating any further than the lines quoted above, Aguirre presents the differences between the Antillean colonies and the Philippines as self-evident. Nor does he expand on the egotism and vanity he sees in the attitude of antillanos. He does not dwell on—perhaps he does not need to—something that would have been obvious to Rizal and others: differences of race in the Philippines and the Antilles. While in the Antilles Spanish Liberals had a significant class of white *criollos* lobbying for reform, in the Philippine colony most, though not all, were classified in race and class terms as *mestizos*.[31] There is ample evidence to suggest that Aguirre, a creole from the Philippines who would have been considered "white," was highly attuned to the racial politics of colonial control and anticolonial mobilization.

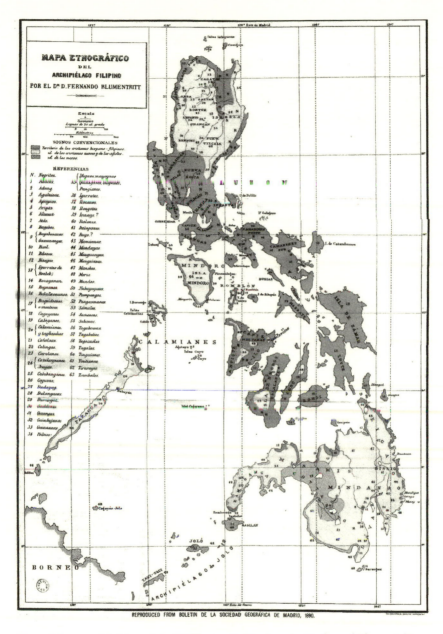

Fig. 2. Ethnographic Map of the Philippine Archipelago, by Ferdinand Blumentritt. From http://www.univie.ac.at/Voelkerkunde/apsis/aufi/blumen/blumap.htm (28 May 2002).

His letters to Rizal detail an emerging rift among criollos and mestizos in the student community. As a creole it is not surprising that Aguirre would have argued against a race-based definition of Filipinoness that would have excluded white men like himself.[32] Although I will return to this rift in the group in the next section, for now what is important is that it suggests a way to read Aguirre's silence regarding the difference between antillanos and filipinos, between the Caribbean islands and the Philippines. I conjecture that the reasons he left unstated for his pessimism about making common cause with anti-colonial antillanos, their supposed character flaws notwithstanding, is directly related to the racial privilege of which they would have been, and most certainly were, the beneficiaries. The racially heterogeneous societies of the Caribbean colonies had a sizeable population of white people, peninsular and Creole—people whom metropolitans, regardless of their colonial politics, could view racially as persons with whom they could dialogue. This, I suggest, is what was so self-evident to Aguirre that he did not need to expand upon it in his correspondence to Rizal.

In this section, I have mapped some of the historical connections that bind together, materially and conceptually, the nineteenth-century colonies of Latin American and the Philippines into an "imperial archipelago." I have argued in particular that the notion of imperial archipelago is not just a theoretical imposition on geographically dispersed and disparate places, but that the archipelago was in fact actualized and instantiated by the wide-angle view of empire that was available to the colonial state. Though the state's powers of control, exercised through the movement of people and papers, was sensed by some reformers, they were largely unable to counter them. Having made the case for understanding the imperial archipelago through the connections between colonies, I now turn to one aspect of the Philippines that distinguished it from Spain's other colonies, namely the peculiar ways in which it was differentially racialized within the imperial archipelago.

CHARTING RACE IN IMPERIAL ARCHIPELAGO: THE PHILIPPINES

In an effort to chart the place of the Philippines in our imagined cartography of the Imperial Archipelago, let us first turn to another map, one published in 1890 by José Rizal's friend and correspondent, Ferdinand Blumentritt.[33] Having heard of Blumentritt's study of Philippine language and ethnology, Rizal initiated correspondence with him in 1886, beginning a friendship that would last until his death ten years later. I draw on this map to discuss one of the factors that set the colony of the Philippines apart from the Antillean colonies: the particular racialization of the Philippine colony as an object of anthropological curiosity. Never having visited the Philippines himself, Blumentritt's late-nineteenth-century research and writing are representative of the era's "armchair anthropology," a term most often used to describe the work of Victorian British anthropologists whose ethnographic accounts of "primitive" life relied on the travel, missionary, and scientific writings of others.[34] The landscape of this "Ethnographic Map of the Philippine Archipelago" offers viewers a lesson not only in geography but in "primitive" ethnology, overlaying Filipino place names with ethnic designations of the archipelago's inhabitants and indigenous groups.

A similar ethnological map of Spain's Caribbean possessions would not have existed. This is not to say that the racial composition of Puerto Rico and Cuba, both racially heterogeneous islands with slave economies for most of the century, were not of interest to the colonial state or to anthropology.[35] The interest in them was very different, however, from the practices of racialization in the Philippines, where the state's interest in race coincided with contemporary anthropology's concern with the "primitive." The Antilles, where indigenous populations were but a historical memory, were of little interest to the nascent discipline that inherited what Michel-Rolph Trouillot has called the West's "savage slot."[36] I turn now to the production of racialized knowledge about the colony and, in particular, how that knowledge was transported for metropolitan consumption through an event common in contemporary Europe: the colonial exposition.

Víctor Balaguer expressed his lamentation about the inattention given to the Philippines in one of the two *Memorias* he wrote about his years spent as Overseas Minister.[37] In *Islas Filipinas*, Balaguer continued the effort he began as minister to put the Philippine archipelago at the center of metropolitan attention. Balaguer was not alone in bemoaning the "profound ignorance that reigns with regards to all aspects of our Archipelago." Spanish geographers had for some time been lamenting the dearth of knowledge about the Philippines and had begun the task of correcting that lacuna.[38] While successive Madrid governments after 1868 were understandably concerned with the Cuban problem, Balaguer wrote floridly about the need to expand Spanish knowledge of the Asian possessions so that these islands might "awaken the fondness of some, incite the interests of others, and earn the love of all." The former minister declared his special affection for the Philippines, which, "by virtue of their distance from the metropole, command more attention and require more care."[39] To this end, Balaguer's memoria served a dual function. First, it told the story of Balaguer's interest in the Philippines and what he felt to be one of his greatest achievements as Overseas Minister, organizing Madrid's first-ever Philippine Exposition, in 1887. Second, through the description of the 1887 fair Balaguer was also arguing forcefully for continuing that project through an entire series of similar exhibitions about the islands. While Cuba was a problem, the Philippines represented potential, a potential for which Balaguer expressed hope: "The Philippines is meant to be . . . and it shall be."[40]

Madrid experienced that potential firsthand at the Philippine Exposition, inaugurated by the Queen Regent María Cristina in June 1887. Officially, the purpose of the exposition was to showcase the economic, particularly agricultural, potential of the distant territories. As Filipino critics of the exposition were quick to point out, however, the event had an equally important mission: to bring the exotic home. Alongside the export products, there were scientific presentations of native flora and fauna, while the principal attraction of the site was the "native villages" that would be recreated and populated by actual "natives" themselves, transported from Manila for the event. Through this event Balaguer was bringing home not just the Philippines but the very practice of colonial expositions, events that in a letter to Balaguer Archbishop Pedro Payo of Manila described as "one of the most recent practices of modern life."[41] This was Balaguer's pet project; while in 1895 he would write about it as a crowning achievement, at the time it was suggested that he only agreed to helm the Overseas Ministry if he could organize the exposition.[42]

I turn to this 1887 Exposition in order to complicate Balaguer's celebratory description of it in *Islas Filipinas*. My aim is twofold. First, a look at his correspondence with Archbishop Pedro Payo, the man charged in Manila with organizing the exposition and collecting exhibition items and peoples, will provide a window into the obstacles the state encountered in trying to bring the Philippines to Madrid. Rather than present the exhibition as *the* Spanish view of the Philippines, Balaguer and Payo's correspondence will point to some of the contestations and disagreements—the "tensions of empire"—that occurred *within* the colonial state.[43] The second goal is to analyze a tension from without, through a look into a different, parallel world of correspondence and political activity: the *colonia* of Filipino students centered in Madrid, some of whom fiercely opposed the ministry's plans to display live exhibits of "primitives" from the islands. Historian of the Philippines John Schumacher has looked at the exposition as a pivotal moment in the creation of a Filipino national identity, arguing that the ilustrados' defense of the exhibited Filipino natives caused them to view as brethren those with whom they would have had very little contact at home.[44] In revisiting the exposition here, I pay specific attention to the ways in which ilustrado depictions of "primitives" at times coincided with that of the colonial state, a fact that, I suggest, is indicative of the state's power to set the terms of debate.

In preparing for the exposition, Balaguer corresponded extensively with Archbishop Payo, whose appointment as head of the commission organizing the exposition is indicative of the special role the Church played in the Philippines. In his first letter to the Minister, Payo detailed the obstacles he faced in trying to prepare for this event. He complained of the lack of time he had to work and of the character of the island's inhabitants, who were not inclined to participate in "modern" practices such as the exposition. He wrote:

> The inhabitant of these islands, as a general rule, is of an excellent condition, submissive to authority, with great abilities in the arts, and prone to following good examples where he sees them; but whether it is due to the climate, or as a trait of his race, the truth is that he lacks initiative and is inactive, not easily stimulated into action, except only when he can see immediate results coming from little effort.[45]

Payo returns repeatedly in his correspondence to the deficiencies of native character. In a second letter written before Balaguer had answered the first, Payo described himself at a loss to know how to inspire poor people to take the project as a personal goal without "exercis[ing] pressure and violence," which, he says, would probably have no effect anyway.[46]

Lack of initiative alone, however, did not explain the enormous obstacles Payo faced. The dearth of scientific knowledge about the islands inhibited his efforts. Because "the day when we have complete statistics for all of its branches is still far away," it would be impossible for him to gather materials for exhibit in the time frame given him. The economic situation of the archipelago was a hindrance as well. The archbishop found it impossible to excite locals about the exposition when the colony suffered from a "general malaise" due to drought and poverty. Payo underscored his frustration by comparing the exposition to a similar one held in a neighboring empire. "You are aware, Sir," he wrote to Balaguer, "of the amount of time that went into preparations for the colonial exposition celebrated in England, and it cannot be logically expected that in the Philippines, with less time and fewer resources, we accomplish as much or more than British empire."[47]

Balaguer's replies to the archbishop did little to address the worries of his correspondent, much less assuage them. He wrote that while he did not wish to contradict the archbishop's opinions, recognizing that "perhaps nobody has more knowledge than you of the country," he also had to insist that everything proceed as planned. He stressed that the Queen Regent saw the exposition as a tribute to the memory of her deceased husband, the late King, and that the ministry had to make good on its commitment, "for to the contrary we would play an extremely sad role before the world." Payo was assured that the commission's financial shortfall would be remedied and that he had the full support of the administration. "In a word," Payo was warned, "we must do the impossible before retreating."[48]

As the letters of archbishop and minister crossed oceans by boat, others concerned with the Philippines were also thinking, talking, and writing about the coming exposition. On 24 October 1886, around the time that Balaguer might have been receiving Payo's first letter, Evaristo Aguirre, member of the colonia born in the Philippines to Spanish parents, wrote to Rizal, who was by then studying in Germany. There was some discussion among the colonia in Madrid about whether it was best to participate in the preparation of the event and help shape it or whether that would just prove an exercise in futility. Aguirre, whom we met earlier, expressing skepticism about a Filipino-Antillean alliance, fell quite distinctively in the latter camp. Responding to Rizal's questions about the exposition, Aguirre wrote at length, in a letter dripping in irony and sarcasm: "Well! And now you hear of the project of the Filipino-Savagery exposition that come Spring is to open to satisfy the curiosity of all the uncouth south of the Pyrennes? . . . And so you hoped [our] dirty laundry would be aired at home? That is a habit of the clean, my dear man."[49] Aguirre dismisses out of hand official claims that the purpose of the event was to promote the colony's commerce. "What, then, is the purpose of the exposition? For that, to expose the country as God brought it to the world: let whoever wishes come and see it."[50] The exposition, in Aguirre's formulation, leaves the Pacific archipelago literally exposed, naked to the world. The source of this nudity is the plan to exhibit "naturales" of the Philippines as objects for peninsular curiosity, which inspired Aguirre's suggestion of the exposition's only real goal: presenting the archipelago as backward and thereby justifying the metropole's "civilizing mission."[51]

Rizal relayed these characterizations to Ferdinand Blumentritt, dismissing the event as "not . . . a Philippine Exposition but an Exposition of Igorots, who will play their musical instruments, cook, sing, and dance."[52] His words are indicative of the general thrust of Filipino criticism of the event, focusing as it did on the matter of the live exhibits. At issue was who could accurately represent the Philippines. It is in this problem of representation, played out in the debates about the display of "Igorots" and others, that we see something of a convergence between the communications between Filipinos on the one hand and letters of the two agents of the state on the other. As noted above, first on Payo's list of obstacles were the perceived deficiencies of Filipino character. While Payo did not distinguish between different groups of islanders, for the ilustrados drawing those distinctions was crucial. By describing the event as a display of "Filipino-Savagery" and accusing the government of "airing the dirty laundry" of the colony, men like Aguirre accepted the state's representation of "native" difference. Each side used this image of difference differently, of course: the state to justify its colonial project and the ilustrados to argue that native Filipinos were inappropriate representatives of the islands.[53]

As Payo's subsequent communications reveal, however, the notion of "native character" could be deployed to take different, sometimes contradictory, positions. These same *naturales* figure differently in a subsequent letter of the archbishop to the minister, where native "docility" serves the purpose of explaining the failures not of the colonized but of their colonizers:

> The docility of the inhabitants of these islands, and their respect for the counsel and decisions of their authorities, leads me to believe that if the Exposition is not as successful as is expected, we must not lay blame on the producers but rather on the lack of zeal on the part of those who have the moral obligation of leading them.[54]

Whereas native indifference to the project of the exposition had previously led Payo to find fault with them, in this letter he expiates their sin. While this might seem to mark a shift on the archbishop's part, it seems more indicative of the very malleability of categories like "docility" and "native." It also points to larger debates over the "morality" of colonial administration, especially in the Philippines. Complaints about the quality of civil servants sent to the Philippines were heard not just from colonial critics but from successive governors-general as well.[55] A moral administrator, in Payo's formulation here, was one who led his charges to follow corrects paths if only they were provided with good examples. The fact that the administration was not moral in this respect turns Payo colonial critic, harshly condemning civil servants' "lack of experience and knowledge about the country."[56] Shifting the blame for the colony's problems from the colonized to the colonizers, Payo here makes claims that might well have resonated with Rizal and his fellow reformers.

If the local agents of the state were the problem then they, too, had to be properly disciplined if this—and, by implication, any other—project was to be completed successfully. Payo forwarded with his letter a published announcement sent to provincial administrators, "in which I have tried every means, from persuasion to threat, and attempt to dissipate all objections or protestations that could be made in favor of not participating on the part of exhibitors."[57] While previously, with regard to producers, Payo had mentioned the futility of force or coercion, with regard to officials he threatened it freely. While the naturales' imagined docility could be blamed for their faults, administrators had no such excuse.

Payo's criticism of the state is not the only way in which his analysis might have resonated with that of some in the colonia filipina. Just as Payo saw the naturales here as passive recipients of the state's largesse (or its ineptitude), they are similarly inscrutable to Evaristo Aguirre. In a second letter to Rizal, he expresses frustration with those who would allow themselves to appear as live exhibits and suffer humiliation. He wrote emotionally to his friend about the pain he felt at seeing the Philippines "lend itself so easily, without even a passive resistance, nor a protest, to come here to play the fool and play a sad role in this exposition. Why do these people come so easily . . . led like sheep to slaughter? Could it be that among people over there who think like us there is no one with clear vision to take initiative?"[58] Another Filipino, Eduardo Lete, while disagreeing with Aguirre's boycott of the event, presented a similarly docile image of the people being exhibited. In a letter to Rizal, Lete challenged those who thought him a traitor for taking a job with the exposition, claiming he did so out of love for the patria. "I think I have been able to do more for the benefit of our *patria* being inside [the exposition]," he wrote, recounting how he taught the "Igorots and other peoples" not to humble themselves before Spaniards. Giving proof of their gratitude for his vigilance, he wrote, "let it suffice to say that the Igorots followed me wherever I went."[59]

The absence in contemporary press accounts and correspondence of a sense of Igorot agency is most salient when one considers the harsh reality encountered by some of those transported to and spoken for in Madrid. Upon receiving shipments of goods and people from Manila, Balaguer wrote to Payo to advise him of the condition of their arrival. In one letter the minister complains that a shipment of plants had not arrived in good condition but reports happily that "the two *moros* from Mindanao are superior to the ones from Joló, and they are drawing much attention." Cold weather had killed all of the snakes and many of the birds, he informed Payo, adding: "Among the personnel, we have not had to suffer more losses than of the poor *mora* Basalia. . . . I would regret deep in my soul if we suffered a second misfortune."[60] By the time he wrote this, Balaguer was no doubt aware that Basalia's death had been well reported in the press and that members of the colonia were publicly expressing their outrage.[61] By the end, there were more such misfortunes. The public criticism may have had some impact on Balaguer's decision to grant a government pension to the family of Dolores Neissern, a woman from the Carolina Islands who died after the exposition opened. This, he said, should be done "with the aim of demonstrating the interest of the *Patria* in all of its children. I believe it is something that should be done if we are to preserve our good name and increase our prestige."[62]

Expressions of outrage not only goaded the state into action but also had a profound effect on the internal politics of the community of Filipino students itself. The community's newspaper, *España en Filipinas*, which had begun as a rather moderate voice for reform, became during the time of the exposition a key venue for discussions of reformist and radical politics. Schumacher notes that "[a] racial element appears to have figured in all their dissidences," adding that "there was a tendency to attribute antipathies due to personal motives or other differences of opinion to racial antipathies."[63] As previously mentioned, Evaristo Aguirre had rejected the notion, espoused by some, that his Creoleness made him less than authentically Filipino. Although the criollos involved with the newspaper had generally fallen on the side of tempering the publication's voice, it is interesting that it is the publication of an ode Aguirre wrote to memorialize Basalia that caused the paper's demise. His description of Basalia as a "Daughter of people which in rude combat / Unconquered resists the foreign yoke," drew the attention of Spaniards who saw Aguirre and *España en Filipinas* as decidedly separatist. Schumacher credits this controversy as sealing the fate of the newspaper, as the more moderate members withdrew their financial support.[64]

Aguirre's ode to Basalia points to some difficulties in interpreting the controversy over the exposition as a whole. His seeming identification with Basalia, on the one hand, would seem to qualify Renato Constantino's interpretation of ilustrados as being ideologically constrained by an elite class status that prohibited any true identification with the masses.[65] On the other hand, it is nonetheless important not to dismiss accounts that credit the exposition with fostering a shared Filipino identification across social status. Schumacher's description of this newfound spirit is telling: "Now a new feeling of solidarity with the Igorots and Moros at the exposition was displayed by the educated, middle, or upper-class Filipinos in Madrid, some of them partly or completely of Spanish blood."[66] Yet the one-sidedness of this picture of a sense of kinship is symptomatic, for even if we accept the sincerity of ilustrado identification with the Filipinos on display, we do not know if the objects of Eduardo Lete's protection, the "Igorots and other people," returned the compliment.

By calling attention to the elite group's racial composition as wholly or partly white, Schumacher points to the cultural and racial logics that made those displayed so seemingly inscrutable to Aguirre, Lete, and Archbisop Payo. The initial reactions to the ministry's plans for the exhibition, well before any of the live exhibits had stepped foot in Spain, clearly reveal the discomfort felt by some of the students with being inappropriately represented. Rizal and others would have been aware of anthropological and popular notions that viewed primitives through evolutionary frameworks even before the incorporation of Darwinian theory. Primitive society was studied as a key to the past of all humanity, ideas that suggested, in effect, that "they are today as we were long ago." These images of primitives as existing in the same space but a different time as Europeans—what Johannes Fabian has called the denial of coevalness[67]—can be seen in the ethnographic accounts of someone like Guillermo Galvey. Galvey was a lieutenant colonel and amateur anthropologist who led violent military campaigns fighting contraband tobacco production in the Cordillera. He wrote an 1842 ethnographic treatise that unflatteringly described the Igorots as diseased and "repulsive." Explaining the relevance of this description, Galvey added, "They are exactly the same race as our Christian Filipinos, and as they have no mixture of European blood, can serve as their primeval type."[68] Judging by some denigrating press accounts, the exposition confirmed that all Filipinos were uncivilized. Skeptical ilustrados were correct to assume that a welcoming audience in the metropole would find explanatory power in intellectually accessible ideas like Galvey's. Their discomfort is indicative of a keen awareness, however incompletely articulated, that the cultural understandings of race that undergirded the displays of the primitive did not leave them—or their politics—untouched or unaffected.

Given the common depictions of the exhibited peoples as docile, in need of the leadership of either responsible state officials or magnanimous ilustrados, we should pause for further reflection on these so-called *igorrotes* about whom so much was being written. Although various ethnic groups were exhibited, including Muslims from the southern islands and members of the ethnic group known as "Negritos," it was the Igorots who became emblematic of the exposition. In the colony the term *igorrote* generally referred to peoples from the Gran Cordillera Central of Luzón, although the term encompasses six different ethnolinguistic groups. Historian W. H. Scott writes that the one thing these different groups had in common was that they "resisted assimilation into the Spanish Empire for three centuries."[69] In fact, by the time of the exposition's 1887 opening, only five years had passed since the abolition of the state's tobacco monopoly in the Philippines—a restriction on private tobacco production that the Cordillera peoples were well known for violating. While the monopoly had proven a highly successful venture for the state, the centralization of wealth in the hands of Spaniards had a negative impact on most inhabitants. "Ironically," writes Scott, "the only Filipinos to share in the enjoyment of this profit were Igorots."[70] Igorots, many of whom had been tobacco farmers prior to the imposition of the monopoly, quickly adapted to the demand for tax-free contraband tobacco during that period, something that put them at sometimes violent odds with the military. It is ironic, as well, that the "primitives" on display had played such a pivotal role in resisting an enterprise so central to the transformation of the Philippines into a modern, revenue-producing colony—and did so well before the corruption the monopoly engendered became a rallying point for colonial critics.[71] Thus, from centuries of missionary and military contact the Igorots had been far from isolated, and their resistance to the state was far more calculating than the above images of docility would imply.

Scott's important outline of the long history of Igorot-Spanish relations also gives the lie to a commonly held assumption about the primitive that was central to nineteenth-century anthropology. That nascent field of inquiry depended on a "savage slot," on a notion of the primitive as untouched by civilization, with little or no connection to the European societies that produced observers such as anthropologists and visitors to colonial expositions.[72] The power of the "savage slot" allowed for both Rizal's dismissal of the event as "Exposition of Igorots," as well as for the particular draw Madrid journalists seemed to feel toward them, one of whom described an Igorot man as "one who, in times past, had been a cannibal. Today he seems the most inoffensive man in the world."[73] That the Igorots—whom early Spanish missionaries accused of being warrior headhunters, a charge unsubstantiated in the historical record—could be represented both as savage and as capable of progress seems to confirm Aguirre's suspicion that the exposition was meant to serve as justification for a civilizing mission. Scott's history of the Igorots as actors that were a thorn in the side of the colonial state, which historiographically restores to them an agency absent in the representations of both Payo and the ilustrados, suggests as well just how much those two narratives of docility coincided. As we have seen in the exposition, anthropological notions of the primitive served the state's interest in a particular way in the Philippines, even if the uses of docility—sometimes to blame natives, sometimes to indict colonial officials—were slippery and logically inconsistent. The fact that the most vocal critics of the state project—to whom these inconsistencies were invisible—accepted some of these notions of the primitive even as they disagreed with its effects, suggests the power of that state to define the terms of discussion.

Despite ilustrado protests, and the "misfortune" of native deaths, the exposition was regarded by both the mainstream press and Balaguer himself, in his later memoirs, as an enormous success.

Conclusion: "El Demonio de las Comparaciones"

I close with another moment of possibility. A year after Rizal's execution, Ramón Emeterio Betances, the Puerto Rican abolitionist and activist on behalf of Cuban and Puerto Rican independence, wrote in a letter to the Cuban Gonzalo de Quesada about his communications with the Hong Kong Committee of Filipino insurgents. Betances praises the efforts of the Filipinos, describing how news of a battle between them and Spanish forces had led him to think, "now begins the war." This image of a single war, a united combat against a common enemy, has led one of Betances's biographers, somewhat hyperbolically, to credit him with "initiat[ing] the process of uniting the revolutionary movement in the Philippines and the Cuban insurrection."[74] Whether this alliance would have occurred had the United States not intervened in the war, we of course cannot know. I call on this moment of possibility here as a reminder that while an alliance between anticolonial forces that replicated the state's wide-angle view of empire may have been thinkable, it was not fully realizable at this particular moment in the history of modern empire.

This moment of possibility suggests the two goals I have set out to accomplish in this essay. Betances's joy at hearing of rebellion in the Philippines suggests his awareness that the state's power stemmed from its controlling the whole of its empire. In the first section of this essay, I argued for rethinking the Spanish empire of the nineteenth century as a unit I have called the "imperial archipelago." The links provided by the state's bureaucratic and military apparatus allowed it to apply lessons learned in one colony to situations in another. The above story of a possibility also points to my second goal, to reflect on the differences within the imperial archipelago that made some alliances more thinkable and practical than others. Betances is known for his activism on behalf of the Cuban rebellion, having served as the insurgency's diplomatic representative in Paris. Despite contemporaneous years of activism in Madrid, antillanos and filipinos never forged common alliances and, as Evaristo Aguirre's words remind us, certain concessions that might be made for the Caribbean islands seemed inconceivable for the Philippines. The second section of this essay, focusing on one corner of the empire, the Philippines, looked at one important factor that distinguished that colony from the Antilles. The Philippine Exposition in Madrid showed the way that the "Pearl of the Orient" was the object of scientific and colonial gaze that classified it as a site of primitiveness, one in need of a "civilizing mission" before it could be considered a candidate for Liberal reforms.

Colonial cartographers drew up maps to lay claim to lands, to define them as owned. That is not my aim here, in suggesting a recharting of the landscapes of "Latin America"—to claim, as one trained in the history of Latin America, to stake a claim to the Philippines for my region of study. Rather, I have tried to suggest, that in the process of rethinking historiographies of "Borders and Borderlands" of nations and empires, we also reevaluate the conceptual maps that may keep us from seeing the connections between seemingly incommensurable worlds.[75] In a move away from borders and borderlands of Latin American studies, I have sought to explore the connections that tied together the histories of Cuba, Puerto Rico, and the Philippines, that linked them in an imperial archipelago. I have also tried to remain mindful of comparisons— those of contemporaries as well as my own—that tell us something about the particular place of the Philippine islands in that archipelago.

While standard regional demarcations might make the Philippines an uneasy fit in Latin American studies, Benedict Anderson suggests that placing that archipelago into the history of Southeast Asia is not without its problems. The Philippines serves Anderson as a starting point for *The Spectre of Comparison*, a collection of essays on Southeast Asian history that also serves as an extended reflection on historical comparison. Anderson writes, "Rizal and his comrades of the 1880s and 1890s were so extraordinarily unlike anyone I could think of in other parts of Southeast Asia, and indeed their 'time' was so out of sync with Southeast Asian time, that it was necessary to consider them outside a standard Southeast Asian framing."[76] Considering instead the history of the Philippines as a crucial component of the imperial archipelago suggests some of the ways in which, viewed up against the faraway islands of Cuba and Puerto Rico, its "time" may not seem so "out of sync."

Anderson takes the title of his book from Rizal's novel *Noli me tangere*, from a passage with which, giving Rizal the last word, I would like to close. As Rizal's protagonist, Crisóstomo Ibarra, travels through Manila in a carriage, he stops to ponder the city's gardens. Having recently returned from his studies in Europe, Ibarra's memories of his travels interrupt his appreciation for Manila. Rizal writes, "that devil comparison put before him the botanical gardens of Europe, in countries where much effort and gold are needed to make a leaf bloom or a bud open." Ibarra's urge to compare seems beyond his control, caused by a trickster demon or devil (which Anderson translates as "spectre"), one he cannot tame upon returning home. Like the real-life ilustrados the character represents, Ibarra returned to the colony after having lived in a European climate of Liberal intellectual ferment. The comparison Ibarra almost reflexively draws seems almost painful for him to contemplate—it could only have lain bare the irony that men like him could have been much more vocal in their criticisms of the state in the metropole than they could have been once back in the colony. Ibarra, following the demon's urging, looks across the ocean—but not toward the Caribbean: rather, toward the relationship he knows better.

"On the other side is Europe," thought the young man, "Europe with her beautiful nations in constant agitation, searching for happiness, dreaming at dawn and full of disappointment with the advent of night . . . happy in the midst of its castastrophes."[77]

NOTES

1. *Neocolonial Identity and Counter-consciousness* (New York: M. E. Sharp, 1978), 269. More recently, Floro C. Quibuyen has cited a 1917 memoir from a contemporary and friend of Rizal's who claimed to have heard from him that his intention was to "study the war in a practical way [and] go through the Cuban soldiery if he thought he would find there solutions which would remedy the bad situation in the Philippines." See *A Nation Aborted: Rizal, American Hegemony, and Philippine Nationalism* (Quezon City: Ateneo de Manila University Press, 1999), 51–53. For an interpretation of Rizal's life and death and the relationship of those attempts to understand him outside of nationalist binaries, see Reynaldo Ileto, "Rizal and the Underside of Philippine History," in his collection of essays, *Filipinos and Their Revolution: Event, Discourse, and Historiography* (Quezon City: Ateneo de Manila University Press, 1998).

2. Ann Laura Stoler, "Developing Historical Negatives: Modernist Visions of the Colonial State," in *From the Margins: Historical Anthropology and Its Futures*, ed. Brian Axel (Durham: Duke University Press, 2002), 156–85. With her concept of the "historical negative," Stoler suggests mining imagined, but not realized, state projects for what they tell us about the conditions of possibility present in the past. Here, I turn to an imagined *anti*-colonial historical negative but for the same purpose.

3. For a well-known example of one Latin American historian's engagement with the history of the Philippines, see John Leddy Phelan, *The Hispanization of the Philippines: Spanish Aims and Filipino Responses, 1565–1700* (Madison: University of Wisconsin Press, 1967); Phelan's interesting examination of religious history has been revised considerably by Vicente Rafael, *Contracting Colonialism: Translation and Christian Conversion in Tagalog Society under Spanish Rule* (Durham: Duke University Press, 1993); see as well Reynaldo Ileto's *Pasyon and Revolution: Popular Movements in the Philippines, 1840–1910* (Quezon City: Ateneo de Manila University Press, [1979] 1997). Although it covers a much

later period, Ileto's now classic study is a fascinating interpretation of the role of popular appropriation of the Catholic passion in popular rebellions.

4. See Angel Bahamonde and José Cayuela, *Hacer las Américas: Las élites coloniales españolas en el siglo XIX* (Madrid: Alianza Editorial, 1992); Josep Fradera, "Quiebra imperial y reorganización política," *Op.Cit.* 9 (1997): 289–317, and "Why were Spain's special overseas laws never enacted?" in *Spain, Europe and the Atlantic World*, ed. Richard Kagan and Geoffrey Parker (Cambridge: Cambridge University Press, 1995), 334–49; and also by Fradera, *Gobernar Colonias* (Barcelona: Ediciones Península, 1999); Juan Pan-Montojo, ed., *Más se perdió en Cuba: España, 1898 y la crisis de fin de siglo* (Madrid: Alianza, 1998); Christopher Schmidt-Nowara, *Empire and Antislavery: Spain, Cuba, and Puerto Rico, 1833–1874* (Pittsburgh: University of Pittsburgh Press, 1999).

5. Richard Kagan, "Prescott's Paradigm: American Historical Scholarship and the Decline of Spain," *American Historical Review* (April 1996): 423–46.

6. See the following works by Josep M. Fradera, "Quiebra imperial"; "Why were Spain's special overseas laws never enacted?"; and *Gobernar Colonias*.

7. Lanny Thompson-Womacks uses the term "imperial archipelago" to describe U.S. imaginary of the post-1898 possessions described in the genre of "Our New Possessions" Literature. While Thompson-Womacks conceives of this more as a colonial imaginary, as representation, Fradera's "imperio insular" looks at the historical ties—political and economic—that made the possessions an empire. See Lanny Thompson-Womacks, "'Estudiarlos, juzgarlos, y gobernarlos': Conocimiento y poder en el archipiélago imperial estadounidense," in *La nación soñada: Cuba, Puerto Rico y Filipinas ante el 98*, ed. Consuelo Naranjo, Miguel A. Puig-Samper, and Luis Miguel García Mora (Madrid: Doce Calles, 1996), 685–94.

8. Frederick Cooper, "Race, Ideology, and the Perils of Comparative History," *American Historical Review* (October 1996): 1135.

9. Ann Laura Stoler, "Tense and Tender Ties: The Politics of Comparison in North American History and (Post) Colonial Studies," *The Journal of American History* (December 2001), http://www.historycooperative.org/journals/jah/88.3/stoler.html (5 June 2002).

10. Bernard Cohn, *Colonialism and Its Forms of Knowledge: The British in India* (Princeton: Princeton University Press, 1996); Frederick Cooper and Ann Laura Stoler, eds., *Tensions of Empire: Colonial Cultures in a Bourgeois World* (Berkeley: University of California Press, 1997).

11. This essay is part of a larger dissertation research project entitled, "Imperial Paper Trails: Bureaucratic Knowledges of Spanish Colonialism, 1863–1900."

12. Josep Fradera's *Filipinas, la colonia más peculiar: Las finanzas públicas en la determinación de la política colonial, 1762–1868* (Madrid: C.S.I.C., 1999).

13. On the Calamba estate dispute, see Floro Quibuyen, *A Nation Aborted*, 23–30. As Quibuyen suggests, Rizal's first-hand experience with Weyler should, at the very least, question any automatic assumption that his request to serve in Cuba betrayed a belief in the validity of the metropole's military effort there.

14. On the Madrid press's denunciations of Blanco and on Polavieja's subsequent reversals of policy, see Alicia Castellanos Escudier, *Filipinas: De la insurrección a la intervención*

de EE.UU., 1896–1898 (Madrid: Sílex, 1998), 143–88.

15. John N. Schumacher, *The Propaganda Movement, 1880–1895: The Creators of a Filipino Consciousness, the Makers of Revolution* (Manila: Solidaridad Publishing House, 1973), 4.

16. On failed plans to send Cuban blacks to Fernando Po, see Ibrahim K. Sundiata, *From Slaving to Neoslavery: The Bight of Biafra and Fernando Po in the Era of Abolition, 1827–1930* (Madison: University of Wisconsin Press, 1996), 50–54. On the strategic use of political exile during the Cuban insurrection, see María del Carmen Barcia, "Los deportados de la guerra de Cuba, 1895–1898," in *La nación soñada*, 635–46.

17. "José María 2.0, asiático, confinado en presidio solicita se alce de su condena la cláusula de retención," Archivo del Consejo de Estado, Sección de Ultramar, U-052-086.

18. See Denise Helly, "Introduction," *The Cuba Commission Report: A Hidden History of the Chinese in Cuba* (Baltimore: Johns Hopkins University Press, 1993), 11.

19. For an overview of the administrative history leading to the founding of the ministry, see Agustín Sánchez Andrés, "El Ministerio de Ultramar en España: Estructura administrative y política colonial (1863–1899)," *Historia y Sociedad* vol. 8: 51–66. This article stems from the exhaustive administrative history Sánchez Andrés detailed in "La política colonial española (1810–1898): Administración central y estatuto jurídico-político antillano" (Ph.D. thesis, Departamento de Historia Contemporánea, Universidad Complutense, Madrid, 1996).

20. Fradera, "Why were Spain's special overseas laws never enacted?" 334–49. The 1812 Constitution is quoted by him on p. 337.

21. Ada Ferrer calls the period a "thirty-year revolution" in *Insurgent Cuba: Race, Nation, and Revolution, 1868–1898* (Chapel Hill: University of North Carolina Press, 1999).

22. Sánchez Andrés, "El Ministerio de Ultramar en España."

23. "Pero ahí está Cuba, Cuba, que desde 1870 viene monopolizando todas las horas del ministro, apoderándose de él en cuerpo y alma." Víctor Balaguer, *Islas Filipinas* (Madrid: R. Angles, 1895), 4.

24. Thomas Richards, *The Imperial Archive: Knowledge and the Fantasy of Empire* (London: Verso, 1993).

25. Rafael María de Labra, *La autonomía colonial: Discurso pronunciado por D. Rafael María de Labra en la sesión del Congreso de 14 de junio de 1883* (Madrid: Imprenta de Aurelio J. Alaria, 1883), 9.

26. Rafael María de Labra, *La reforma política en ultramar* (Madrid: Tipografía de Alberto Alonso, 1902), 135.

27. Ramón Meza, *Mi tío el empleado* (Madrid: Ediciones de Cultura Hispánica, Instituto de Coopeación Iberoamericana, 1993).

28. José Rizal to Ferdinand Blumentritt, 26 January 1887, *The Rizal-Blumentritt Correspondence* (Manila: José Rizal Centennial Commission, 1961), vol. 2, pt. 1, 44.

29. Rafael María de Labra, *A los electores de Sábana Grande (Puerto-Rico)* (Madrid: Imprenta de M. G. Hernández, 1873), 56.

30. Evaristo Aguirre to José Rizal, 26 September 1887, *Epistolario Rizalino* (Manila: Bureau of Printing, 1930 [hereafter *ER*]), 198. I will return to this letter later.

31. Unlike Latin America, where the term denotes persons of mixed Spanish and indigenous parentage, in the Philippines the term *mestizo* most often described people with Chinese ancestry.

32. On the rift in the *colonia*, see John Schumacher, *The Propaganda Movement*, 69–71, and Flor C. Quibuyen, *A Nation Aborted*, 89–93.

33. http://www.univie.ac.at/Voelkerkunde/apsis/aufi/blumen/blumap.htm (28 May 2002).

34. George W. Stocking, *Victorian Anthropology* (New York: Free Press, 1987).

35. On anthropology and race in Cuba, see Armando García González, "En torno a la antropología y el racismo en Cuba en el siglo XIX," in *Cuba: La perla de las Antillas*, ed. Consuelo Naranjo Orovio and Tomás Mallo Gutiérrez (Madrid: CSIC, 1994), 45–64. On anthropology's relative neglect of the Caribbean as a field of inquiry, see Michel-Rolph Trouillot, "The Caribbean Region: An Open Frontier in Anthropological Theory," *Annual Review of Anthropology* vol. 21 (1992): 19–42.

36. Michel-Rolph Trouillot, "Anthropology and the Savage Slot: The Poetics and Politics of Otherness," in *Recapturing Anthropology: Working in the Present*, ed. Richard G. Fox (Santa Fe, N.M.: School of American Research Press, 1991), 17–44.

37. Balaguer was appointed to head the Overseas Ministry on three separate occasions, but twice only briefly: In 1871, he served just over a month before the fall of the Malcampo government ended his tenure; in 1874 he was minister from January to May; his longest term as minister occurred from 1886 to 1888. See Balaguer's two-volume *En el ministerio de Ultramar* (Imprenta y Fundición de Manuel Tello, 1888).

38. On Spanish geography in the nineteenth century in the context of the Age of Empire, see Horacio Capel, "The Imperial Dream: Geography and the Spanish Empire in the Nineteenth Century," in *Geography and Empire*, ed. Anne Godlewska and Neil Smith (Oxford: Blackwell, 1994), 58–73.

39. Balaguer, *Islas Filipinas*, 5, 2.

40. Ibid., 54.

41. Letter from Archbishop Pedro Payo to Minister Víctor Balaguer, 27 September 1886, Museo-Biblioteca de Víctor Balaguer (hereafter MBVB), Exposición de Filipinas. Correspondencia (hereafter EFC), doc. 1.

42. Filipino ilustrado Evaristo Aguirre wrote to José Rizal in 1887, "according to what I hear, he accepted the Overseas Ministry on the condition that it be celebrated." See Evaristo Aguirre ("Cahuit") to José Rizal, 31 January 1887, *ER*, 223.

43. Frederick Cooper and Ann Laura Stoler, *Tensions of Empire*. This approach to colonial expositions is suggested by Paul Kramer as a corrective to those who see in these events a single, unified vision of empire on display: "the reality was much less neat and orderly." See "Making Concessions: Race and Empire Revisited at the Philippine Exposition, St. Louis, 1901–1905," *Radical History Review* vol. 73 (1999): 77. The literature on colonial expositions is now quite vast. See, for example, Robert Rydell, *All the World's a Fair: Visions of Empire at American International Expositions, 1876–1916* (Chicago: Chicago Univesity Press, 1984); Zeynep Çelik, *Displaying the Orient: Architecture of Islam at Nineteenth-Century World's Fairs* (Berkeley: University of California Press, 1992); Timothy Mitchell, *Colonising Egypt*, 2nd ed. (Berkeley: University of California Press,

1977), especially the introductory chapter; Mauricio Tenorio Trillo, *Mexico at the World's Fairs: Crafting a Modern Nation* (Berkeley: University of California Press, 1996).

44. Schumacher, *The Propaganda Movement*, 65–69.

45. Payo to Balaguer, 27 September 1886, MBVB, EFC, doc. 1.

46. Payo to Balaguer, 16 October 1886, MBVB, EFC, doc. 2.

47. Payo to Balaguer, 27 September 1886, MBVB, EFC, doc. 1.

48. Balaguer to Payo, 17 November 1886, MBVB, EFC, doc. 4.

49. Evaristo Aguirre to José Rizal, 24 October 1886, *ER*, 204.

50. Ibid.

51. Ibid, 206.

52. José Rizal to Ferdinand Blumentritt, 22 November 1886, in *The Rizal-Blumentritt Correspondence* (Manila: José Rizal Centennial Commission, 1961), vol. 2, pt. 1, 22.

53. I do not mean to suggest that Aguirre and Rizal had no concern for the people themselves. They both, for example, express concern for the health of the participants, a concern that turned out to be prophetic. What I am arguing and will develop further later, is that the ability of the ilustrados to represent—in both senses of the term—the Philippines, was circumscribed both by state power and the realities of social status in the colony that created distinctions between, for example, "mestizos" and "Igorots."

54. Payo to Balaguer, 31 December 1886, MBVB, EFC, doc. 8.

55. Ibid. Forging a "moral administration" was of concern to Balaguer who attempted to undertake administrative reforms during his tenure as minister.

56. Ibid.

57. Ibid.

58. Aguirre to Rizal, 31 January 1887, *ER*, 225.

59. The phrase Lete uses is "igorrotes y demás gentes," underscoring that Igorots as a category tended in ilustrado correspondence over the exposition to be a synecdoche for all naturales. Eduardo Lete to José Rizal, 20 June 1887, *ER*, 281–82.

60. Balaguer to Payo, 15 June 1887, MBVB, EFC, doc. 16.

61. On the public debate about Basalia's death, see John Schumacher, *The Propaganda Movement*, 66–69.

62. Balaguer to Payo, 27 July 1887, MBVB, EFC doc. 18.

63. Schumacher, *The Propaganda Movement*, 70.

64. Ibid., 71.

65. Constantino, *Neocolonial Identity*.

66. Schumacher, *The Propaganda Movement*, 67.

67. Johannes Fabian, *Time and the Other* (New York: Columbia University Press, 1983), esp. 1–35.

68. Quoted in W. H. Scott, *The Discovery of the Igorots: Spanish Contacts with the Pagans of Northern Luzon* (Quezón City: New Day Publishers, 1974), 221.

69. Scott, *The Discovery of the Igorots*, 2. In explaining his title, Scott writes, "the process by which the Spaniards met the Igorots, gradually learned more about them, and then spread that knowledge abroad may be called the Discovery of the Igorots." The role of the Madrid Exposition in this "Discovery" is covered briefly on pp. 275–78.

70. Ibid., 211.

71. On the tobacco monopoly and state finances in the colony, see Fradera, *La colonia más peculiar*; H. de la Costa, *Readings in Philippine History* (Manila: Bookmark, 1965), reprints documents concerning the creation of the monopoly as well as its Liberal critics of the nineteenth century (pp. 115–20 and 169–72, respectively).

72. Trouillot, "Anthropology and the Savage Slot."

73. "En la Exposición de Filipinas," *El Imparcial*, 8 May 1887.

74. See Félix Ojeda Reyes, *La manigua en París: Correspondencia diplomática de Betances* (San Juan: Centro de Estudios Avanzados de Puerto Rico y el Caribe, 1984), 11. The 13 August 1897 letter from Betances to Gonzalo de Quesada is reproduced on pp. 132–33. I am thankful to historian Luis Agraít of the University of Puerto Rico, who, after hearing my paper at the "Paradigms/Paradigmas" conference, suggested that I pursue Betances's communications with the Hong Kong Committee as a further example of the unrealized potential of cross-colonial alliance.

75. Jeremy Adelman and Stephen Aron, "From Borderlands to Borders: Empires, Nation-States, and the Peoples in Between in North American History," *American Historical Review* 104, 3 (June 1999): 814–41. Looking at nineteenth-century Spanish impressions of its empire, I follow Christopher Schmidt-Nowara's suggestion that discussions of "Borderlands" take into account the perspectives of other national historiographies. My empire-wide focus further suggests the need to move beyond the Americas to understand the workings of an empire whose colonies were separated by oceans and not borders on land. Christopher Schmidt-Nowara, *The American Historical Review* 104, 4 (October 1999): 1226–28.

76. Benedict Anderson, *The Spectre of Comparison: Nationalism, Southeast Asia, and the World* (London: Verso, 1998), 24.

77. José Rizal, *Noli me tangere* (Caracas: Biblioteca Ayacucho, 1976), 51; my translation is adapted from Ma. Soledad Lacson-Locsin, *Noli me tangere* (Honolulu: University of Hawaii Press, 1996), 51. I have chosen to translate the phrase as "*that* devil comparison" because I think the original Spanish phrasing suggests that Ibarra's urge to compare is caused by a sort of trickster demon—the character does not seem to *want* to compare; after traveling from Europe he has no choice.

Fig. 3. Portrait of Francisco Arango y Parreño.
From Francisco J. Ponte Domínguez, *Arango y Parreño:
Estadista colonial cubana* (Havana: Molina y Cia, 1937),
frontispiece.

CHAPTER TWO

THE WEALTH OF EMPIRE

Francisco Arango y Parreño, Political Economy, and the Second Slavery in Cuba

Dale Tomich

INTRODUCTION

*P*lanter, statesman, and economic reformer Francisco Arango y Parreño (1765–1837) was the spokesman for Havana's emergent planter elite and was also among the major architects of Cuba's sugar boom during the first half of the nineteenth century. In 1792, in the midst of the slave insurrection in Saint Domingue, Arango, Apoderado General of the Havana *ayuntamiento*, addressed a series of memorials to the Spanish Crown culminating in *Discurso sobre la Agricultura de la Habana y Medios de Fomentarla*.[1] These documents at once articulated the interests of the Havana planter class and formulated Arango's program for the transformation of Cuban economic life. Widely regarded as key texts of Cuban history, they provided the theoretical framework for the development of Cuba into the world's leading sugar producer from the 1820s into the twentieth century. At the same time, they express the creation of new zones of slave production as part of the political and economic restructuring of the world economy that I have elsewhere called the "second slavery."[2] An examination of these works thus calls attention to the continual re-formation of slavery and other forms of compulsory labor as part of the historical development of the capitalist world economy and to the ways that highly specific local actions at once shape and are shaped by global processes.

The *Discurso* draws its effectiveness from Arango's acute awareness of the ways U.S. independence, the French Revolution, and the Haitian slave insurrection were

This article was previously published in *Comparative Studies in Society and History* 45, 1 (January 2003). We would like to thank the editors and Cambridge University Press for permission to republish it.

restructuring the Atlantic economy and his profound understanding both of the possibilities that this political economic conjuncture opened for Cuba and of what was required for Cuba to take advantage of these conditions.[3] Arango's concern was to secure conditions for Cuba's long-term dominance over the trade in tropical goods, above all sugar, beyond the immediate advantage from what he then perceived to be the temporary disruption of order in the neighboring French colony.[4] At this decisive moment, he systematically conceptualized the emerging conditions of the Atlantic economy from the perspective of the Havana planter elite. The keystone of his proposals was his call for the free entry of slaves into Cuba and for the removal of Spanish mercantile restrictions in order to permit free trade in tropical produce for Havana planters. In his conception, free trade went hand in hand with the expansion and renovation of sugar production through the systematic application of slave labor, agricultural and industrial improvement, and better slave management. His project theoretically and practically reconstitutes slave relations and sugar production within new economic, political, and ideological domains and formulates a program for Cuba's economic and social transformation.

Emphasis on the Atlantic dimension of Arango's thought reveals its innovative character. In these works, the revitalization of slave labor and expansion of the sugar frontier in Cuba appear not as the persistence of archaic economic and social forms, but as active and formative aspects of what Giovanni Arrighi refers to as "the British systemic cycle of accumulation,"[5] the restructuring of world economic and political relations that coincided with free trade and the integration of world markets, the industrial revolution in Britain, the crisis of colonial slavery in the British and French West Indies, and anticolonial rebellion elsewhere in Latin America. Arango's project itself is articulated within modern forms of thought. The new discipline of political economy provides Arango with the means to formulate his program for increasing the wealth of Cuba and his justification for slavery. He reconceptualizes slave labor within the framework of free trade, individual self-interest, efficient management, and systematic technological innovation. Indeed, the *Discurso* demonstrates not the incompatibility, nor even the simultaneous coexistence of liberal ideas and proslavery thought, but the ways these positions derive from the shared conceptual field of political economy.

This common grounding is perhaps nowhere more evident than in Arango's theoretical affinity with and appropriation of Adam Smith. Despite the differences between them, the proximity between these two thinkers, stemming from their common theoretical origin in physiocracy and agrarian thought, and

COMPENDIO

DE LA OBRA INGLESA

INTITULADA

RIQUEZA DE LAS NACIONES.

HECHO

POR EL MARQUES DE CONDORCET

Y TRADUCIDO AL CASTELLANO

CON VARIAS ADICIONES DEL ORIGINAL

POR

DON CARLOS MARTINEZ DE IRUJO,
Oficial de la primera Secretaria
de Estado.

DE ORDEN SUPERIOR

MADRID: EN LA IMPRENTA REAL
MDCCXCII.

Fig. 4. First Spanish translation (1792) of Adam Smith's *The Wealth of Nations*. From Levi Marrero, *Cuba: Economía y Sociedad*, vol. 10 (Madrid: Editorial Playor, 1984), 38.

by their conceptions of free trade, labor, and self-interest, give grounds to question the boundaries and supposed antimonies between proslavery thought and liberal political economy. Examination of the *Discurso* and other texts at once discloses the compatibility and interdependence of liberal political economy and proslavery thought in Arango's project and problematizes Smith's liberalism by drawing out the ways it is compatible with slavery.

This interpretation may be contrasted to approaches that regard slavery in the Americas as an anomalous or archaic social and economic relation that is incompatible with modern forms of productive organization, market, and state.[6] From this latter perspective, slavery is destined to be superseded by the emergence of a liberal economic, political, and social order. Such interpretations continually juxtapose a linear conception of (liberal, capitalist) modernity against an equally linear conception of premodern slavery. Here, the social relations of slavery may coexist with the world market and liberalism, but each term is conceived as an independent, internally unified, and mutually exclusive social category.[7] These abstracted attributes are localized in discrete social spaces, each of which is assigned a distinctive temporality. Thus, Cuba remains fixed as the site of slavery and racial ideology, while true capitalism, the real bourgeoisie, and authentic liberalism are taken to occur elsewhere.

From this perspective, the coexistence of slavery, the free market, and Enlightenment thought, both internationally and as part of the world view of the Creole elite itself, is regarded as at once a defining feature and a central paradox of the nineteenth-century Cuban slave regime. Arango, the planter class, Cuban slavery, and racial ideology are excluded from full membership in historical modernity. With "one foot in the bourgeois future and the other in the remote slave past,"[8] they are viewed as hybrid products of the self-contradictory attempt to combine irreconcilable opposites. The history of slavery in nineteenth-century Cuba is understood as a narrative of flawed and unfinished liberalism.[9] Cuban slavery and racial ideology are characterized by their incompleteness and immaturity.[10] Liberal practices and ideas are construed as out of place in the colony: Colonial forms of liberal thought are viewed as deformed versions of their metropolitan analogues. The historical trajectory of Cuban slavery and the planter class is defined by its failure to conform to the progressive development of liberal capitalism.

What is lost here is precisely the self-consciousness of the Cuban planter class and its project of social and economic transformation. Such perspectives are unable to conceive of the Cuban planter elite as an active and reflexive subject, engaged in practical activity and capable of appropriating and transforming fields of knowledge and social ideas in order to grasp their historical condition in their own terms and act practically on it.[11] Instead, they present Cuban planters as caught between two already formed and incompatible bodies of ideas: On the one hand, their thought is imprisoned within ideological forms that directly reflect anterior, determinant, and virtually immobile slave relations of production. On the other hand, they are passive recipients of a fixed and complete liberal ideology, which is imported from the outside and which they are unable fully to assimilate.

Rather than conceiving of the opposition of liberalism and proslavery thought as resulting from the juxtaposition of distinct temporalities (premodern and modern) in one place, I would like to argue that it is more fruitful to think of these two intellectual currents as expressions appropriate to different places in the same time—the time of the world market. The specificity of Arango and Cuban slavery during the nineteenth century is to be found not in the continuous interplay of homogeneous prebourgeois and bourgeois forces, but in a compound, internally complex modernity that is historically formed within heterogeneous and plural relations of slavery and world economy. Enlightenment thought and liberal political economy are not "out of place" in Cuba. Rather, they are constitutive elements of Cuban proslavery thought. Indeed, I would like to suggest that the particular conjuncture of liberal political economy and proslavery ideas that characterize Arango's *Discurso* discloses not an anomaly within the national space of Cuba, but the temporal discontinuity of slavery in the Atlantic world, that is, the remaking of slavery and world inequalities in a new cycle of accumulation.

ARANGO, THE *DISCURSO*, AND THE CONJUNCTURE
OF THE ATLANTIC ECONOMY

Son of a prominent Havana family, Francisco de Arango y Parreño was a leading figure of the nascent Havana sugar elite. This group, including such figures as José Ignacio Echegoyen, Nicolás Calvo, Ignacio Pedro Montalvo y Ambulodi (the Count of Casa-Montalvo), Bonifacio Duarte, and Nicolas Peñalver, reshaped Cuban economy and society in the first part of the nineteenth century and transformed Cuba into the wealthiest plantation colony in the world.[12] Arango was a new kind of intellectual with a new relationship to power.[13] His ideas most often found expression in political memorials. Intellectually precocious and well educated, Arango studied at the Seminario de San Carlos and the University of Havana in Cuba, where he received a bachelor of law degree in 1786. After a period practicing law before the Audiencia in Santo Domingo, he

completed his studies in Spain, where he received his doctor of law degree in
1789. In Madrid, he attracted the attention of high functionaries of the Court
including Prime Minister Floridablanca. At the same time, he was a friend of
Gaspar Melchor de Jovellanos and other figures of the Spanish Enlightenment.
In this milieu, he developed a cosmopolitan outlook. He was familiar with the
works of Raynal, Montesquieu, Quesnay, Smith, and Genovesi among others.
Although he had not yet attained his legal majority by 1788, he was then
appointed Apoderado General of the Havana *ayuntamiento* at the age of 23. In
this capacity, he addressed the *Discurso sobre la agricultura de la Habana y
Medios de Fomentarla* to the Spanish Crown in 1791.[14]

Arango drafted the *Discurso* with great urgency following the arrival in
Madrid of the news of the slave insurrection in the French colony of Saint
Domingue. The situation in the French sugar colonies began to deteriorate
with the outbreak of revolution in France. But it was the slave uprising that created an unprecedented opportunity for Cuba. Arango quickly grasped the significance of the moment: "[S]eeing them [the French] immersed in a calamity
that, if it does not destroy all of the prosperity of that colony will retard it
indefinitely, it is necessary to look at it not only with compassion, but with
political eyes, and, with the faith of a good patriot and a good vassal, announce
to the best of kings the opportunity and the means to give to our agriculture
of the Islands advantage and preponderance over that of the French."[15] He urged
the King that it was necessary for Cuba to take advantage of the disruption of
Haiti in order to raise itself "to a level of power and wealth capable of withstand-
ing competition even when your rival recovers. . . . Take advantage of the
moment to bring to your soil the wealth that the narrow territory of Guarico
[Saint Domingue] gave to the French nation."[16]

Arango was concerned with what would happen to Cuba after the immediate effects of Haiti were over. The windfall profits generated by the revolt in
Saint Domingue were inadequate to guarantee Cuba's long-term development.
Arango feared that the return to order would be ruinous. He argued that for
Cuba to maintain its position in the face of English and French competition,
agricultural and commercial reform was an urgent necessity: "The very advantage that we enjoy today in the sale of sugars can be disastrous for us if we do
not know how to take advantage of it. I have already said, and I repeat, that if
we wish to encourage this branch of industry we must work as though we were
in the times preceding the insurrection of the negroes of Guarico so that when
they [the French] return we do not find ourselves in the sad condition that we
were in before."[17]

The *Discurso* articulates just such a systematic program of reform. In it, Arango brings to bear both the theoretical perspectives of political economy and Enlightenment thought and his profound practical knowledge of Cuba. More than a pastiche of incompatible premodern and modern elements, this remarkable document combines a theoretically informed vision with practical political concerns. The text is organized in a format similar to that used by Jovellanos in his *Informe sobre Industria y Comercio* (1790) and his *Informe sobre la Ley Agraria* (1794).[18] It begins with a summary history of Cuban economic development that contrasts the colony's stagnation under Spanish mercantilist policies with the growth and prosperity that it experienced as a result of the English invasion of 1762, which promoted the importation of slaves and open commercial policies. Arango then compares the colonial policies of Spain, England, France, and Portugal in order to identify Cuba's technical and economic disadvantages in relation to its chief competitors. Through his incisive and uncompromising treatment of these problems, Arango discloses the root causes of these difficulties and forcefully advocates full and immediate exploitation of Cuba's potential for production of tropical export staples. Described by historian Levi Marrero as "the magna carta for the subsequent development of the sugar industry," the *Discurso* not only argues for the particular reforms that triggered Cuba's economic transformation, but gives conceptual coherence to practices and policies that were to guide Cuban development at least until 1868 if not beyond.[19]

POLITICAL ECONOMY, AGRICULTURE, AND *FELICIDAD*

Although the *Discurso* is a policy proposal, not a systematic treatise, it nonetheless demonstrates the Enlightenment sources of Arango's thought. Arango himself describes his program for the economic and social transformation of Cuba as one of "propagating enlightenment" (*propogar las luces*). Indeed, he formulates his project for increasing the productivity (*rendimento*) of colonial agriculture within the intellectual framework of political economy. The appearance of this discipline during the second half of the eighteenth century provided a new vocabulary with which to conceptualize wealth and the perception that agriculture, industry, and commerce were the means to produce and accumulate it.[20] Even if we do not seek to ascertain the genealogy of specific ideas in the *Discurso*, it is clear that Arango was influenced by diverse neomercantilist, physiocratic, agrarian, and liberal theorists including Quesnay, Jovellanos, Campomanes, Genovesi, and Galliani, as well as Adam Smith. In the last decades of the eighteenth century, enlightened liberal agrarians such as

Jovellanos and Campomanes drew on physiocratic arguments about agriculture and free trade. Yet they were neither doctrinaire physiocrats nor even systematic theoretical economists. Rather, they used political economic discourse as an instrument of practical policy and progressive reform. In a manner similar to that of other Latin American thinkers, such as Argentines Manuel Belgrano and Mariano Moreno, Arango relied on these apparently eclectic intellectual sources to diagnose the condition of Cuba and to elaborate the program that would lay the groundwork for subsequent Cuban economic development.[21]

Arango draws on the new discipline of political economy to reassess the nature and sources of wealth in the Americas. He argues:

> No one still denies or doubts that true wealth consists of agriculture, of commerce and the arts, and that if America has been one of the causes of our decadence, it was because of the disdain that we had for the cultivation of its fertile lands, because of the preference and protection that we accord to mining, and because of the miserable method with which we conduct our commerce.[22]

This conception of wealth signals a decisive shift away from mercantilism and from mining as the source of prosperity within the Spanish empire and toward productive agriculture and commerce.[23] Arango identifies the extraction of precious metals, mercantilism, monopoly, and the balance of trade as causes of Spain's poverty and decadence. In opposition to them, he defends the "enlightened view" that "the prosperity (*felicidad*) of the nation . . . consists principally in developing (*fomentar*) colonial agriculture."[24] Viewed in this light, Arango's argument for the redeployment of slave labor in Cuba signals not the persistence of an already existing archaic form of social organization, but the revitalization of the colonial economy through agricultural production and trade. He breaks decisively from static conceptions of wealth based on the domination of fixed territorial spaces that are represented by the colonial mining economy and mercantilism ("the space of places").[25] Instead, he formulates a dynamic conception of well-being or abundance (felicidad) as the result of fertility, productive activity, and the circulation of commodities and wealth ("the space of flows")[26] that characterizes the new conjuncture of world economy.

In accordance with agrarian conceptions, Arango held that Cuba's advantage over other sugar producers resided in the superior fertility of its soil. Its greatest potential source of wealth was agriculture and industry based upon agriculture. For Arango, export crops, especially sugar and coffee, were the appropriate activities for Cuban agriculture, especially since no other Spanish colonies supplied such products. (This preference defined and justified the sugar elite's domination not only of slaves but also of cattle ranchers and tobacco smallholders.) Yet, he argued, commercial restrictions offset the natural advantage of Cuba's soil productivity. Such restrictions increased the cost of labor, equipment, and credit; impeded technical progress and good management; and inhibited the development of markets. For Arango, Spain's mercantile policies were the cause of Cuba's torpor: free trade provided the means to overcome it.[27]

Arango's demand to increase the supply of slave labor to Cuba was an integral part of a comprehensive "development project" that was grounded in principles of political economy. In the *Discurso* Arango reconceptualizes slavery, agriculture, and commerce to redefine Cuba's place in the world economic conjuncture. He links the necessity of free trade and access to foreign markets, especially that of the newly independent United States, to unrestricted access to slave labor and scientific transformation of production processes. Implied here is a reformulation of slavery within the new conditions of science and technology, productivity, and free trade, and, further, the understanding that the market and free trade are the most efficient mechanisms for determining price, quantity, and quality of goods (including slaves). These are the means to promote Cuba's prosperity and possible domination of the world sugar market.

Arango, familiar with the most advanced political economic ideas of his time, does not present slavery as archaic or anomalous. He sees no contradiction between slave labor and free trade. Rather, he constructs slavery within the presuppositions of free trade. In his view, slave labor is the means to achieve Cuba's integration into the world market and secure the colony's prosperity and progress.[28] Conversely, free trade is the condition for the expansion and consolidation of the Cuban slave system.

THE SLAVE TRADE: *LIBERTAD ABSOLUTA*

In Arango's conception, the future of enlightened agriculture and the prosperity (felicidad) of the nation rested upon the slave trade. He maintained that the experience of three centuries and reason proved that the export staples (*frutos de retorno*) of the American colonies—and not their precious metals—contributed in innumerable ways to the well-being of the metropolis. However, the promise of colonial agriculture was undercut by insufficient population. Although enlightened administrations were preoccupied with the development

Fig. 5. A bas-relief of a slave ship from the palace of the king of Abomey. From Isabelle Auget, *La traite des nègres* (Genève: Éditions Minerva, 1971), 52.

of commercial agriculture, the colonies lacked the necessary hands for the lands that they wished to cultivate. Arango looked to the slave trade to resolve this problem. The west coast of Africa, he contended, provided the source of manpower that was most appropriate for this project.[29] African slaves were, in his words, the hands that would "animate agriculture and provide [by their labor] abundant fruits."[30]

In Arango's view, African slaves were the necessary building block for the development of plantation agriculture in Cuba, and free trade was the means to obtain them. He is concerned, above all, with the concrete conditions of slave supply to Cuba, and his case for free trade is presented within the context of tactical imperatives and political conditions obtaining both in Spain and in Cuba. It develops as an argument with monopolists and various vested interests over royal *cédulas* that regulated the slave trade for periods of limited duration. Nonetheless,

Arango sustains the position that not only is free trade the most adequate and efficient means to assure a sufficient supply of slaves, but that the market mechanism would provide optimal conditions of quantity, quality, and price.

In his first document written as Apoderado in 1788, Arango was determined to seek the remedy for what he viewed as the evil caused by the scarcity of negroes in the colony. Absolute liberty to trade with other nations in this branch of commerce, he argued, would be the most useful remedy.[31] In the following year, in his "Primer papel sobre el comercio de negros," Arango elaborated this argument. He criticized Spain's failure to engage directly in the slave trade. He complained that Denmark, Holland, Portugal, France, and, above all, England each supplied more slaves to the Americas than Spain. At the same time, Spain's need for slaves was greater than that of all of the others combined.[32] The only way for Cuba to get out of this predicament, he insisted, was to obtain slaves from rival nations. Arango contended that the utility for colonial agriculture of absolute free trade in slaves was so evident as to require no discussion. In his words, "the advantages that granting absolute liberty to the nations will bring to the American colonist leap out at first glance."[33] The necessary force of market competition, he argued, would produce a commodity in which price, means of payment, and ease of obtaining slaves for the colonial purchaser were maximized.[34] In contrast, monopoly was the least satisfactory solution. A single firm, charged with providing Cuba with negroes, he asserted, could "tyrannize us, bringing insufficient numbers of slaves of whatever quality they desire, and at arbitrary prices."[35]

Arango's "Primer papel sobre el comercio de negros" (1789) appears to have influenced the subsequent legislation of the slave trade. The royal cédula of 28 February 1789 broke the monopoly system. It ran for two years and allowed all Spanish subjects to go abroad to buy slaves and bring them to designated ports (initially Havana and Santiago) where they could enter Cuba duty free. Foreign ships could also import slaves to Havana duty free, but had only 24 hours to unload their ships, and the ships had to be less than 300 tons. The cédula did not attempt to fix prices but did regulate other aspects of the trade.[36]

Arango reasserted his argument for free trade in 1791 when he petitioned the Crown to extend its permission to engage in free trade in slaves.[37] He opposed a simple extension of the cédula of 1789. His argument for a longer extension of free trade in slaves reveals his critique of the monopoly system and his conception of the role of the free market in supplying slaves to Cuba. Arango compared the monopoly held by Philip Allwood (the Havana agent for the Liverpool firm of Baker and Dawson) before 1789 with the preceding two-year period, during which the Crown had opened the slave trade. Negroes were scarce and expensive under

Allwood's contract.[38] In contrast, Arango reported that some 4,000 slaves arrived in Havana in the first nineteen months following the enactment of the cédula of 1789. This was followed by another two thousand arrivals in a subsequent two-month period. Almost half of the first group were imported by Baker and Dawson because of Allwood's strong local contacts. Arango attributed the increase in imports during the more recent period to the effects of the uprising in Saint Domingue. Unable to gain access to their normal market outlet, slave traders brought their cargoes to Cuba. However, Arango warned that under normal circumstances, Cuba was not the most favorable market, and, for that reason, it risked the loss of the slave trade when order was restored in Saint Domingue.[39] He argued that if, under such unstable conditions, the King conceded to the local commercial authorities who wanted to expel Allwood and other foreigners (presumably to the advantage of Cuban/Spanish interests who wanted to control the slave trade themselves), Baker and Dawson would discontinue sending slaves to Cuba, or worse. Cuba would then be reduced to depending on one or another isolated adventurer who would be attracted to the great scarcity, or to the wretched alternative of forcing its own planters to go themselves to find slaves in the other islands. (This argument implies that Arango did not necessarily want to exclude Allwood, who, after all, remained a major slave trader, but rather sought to expose him to the discipline of the market and competition. This position recalls Smith's view that the market competition would, in Smith's words, constrain the "mean rapacity" and "monopolizing spirit" of merchants and manufacturers and promote instead industry and frugality.[40])

Arango argued that Cuba needed to reorganize the terms of its slave trade for the long term and develop a stable and non-speculative market as the surest supply of slaves. In his view, the slave trade could not make firm and constant progress if it were maintained on its current footing.[41] If the Crown were to grant only another two-year extension of "free trade" in slaves, such a short period would merely encourage speculators who wanted to make a quick profit on their first voyage. Businessmen of standing, who were precisely those that Cubans wanted to attract, do not expose themselves in this way. Instead, they invest with the security of recovering on the second or third voyage what they might lose on the first.[42] Serious slaving required investment and profits over the long term.[43] Of course, such merchants would provide Cuba with a more stable supply of slaves (and perhaps of better quality) at better prices. Arango maintained that it was in the King's interest that his American vassals have the negroes that they need at the lowest prices and with just terms of payment. Consequently, he urged that the unrestricted traffic in slaves be extended for six to eight years in order to secure a nonspeculative trade. Thus, even as his position was inscribed within tactical necessities, Arango provided the theoretical justification for the superiority of the market and free trade (*libertad absoluta*) as a mechanism of supplying slaves.

FRUTOS DE RETORNO AND FREE TRADE

While the *Discurso* called for opening up the slave trade to Cuba, it further provided a systematic argument for free trade in tropical products as the means to increase the wealth and prosperity of the island. Not only did Arango argue for the removal of mercantilist restrictions and the expansion of the slave trade, but he also called for free trade for Cuba's exports (especially sugar, coffee, and tobacco) in addition to free importation of the agricultural implements and machinery necessary to improve Cuban production.[44] While the slave trade and the demand for labor were the key elements in Arango's economic reform program, they were tied to free trade for the products of Cuban agriculture.

For Arango, the immediate problem was that Cuba was too poor in its current state to generate an adequate slave trade.[45] In his view, Cuba was at the beginning of a developmental curve with high demand for slaves, but little ability to pay. Havana could not offer foreign slave traders attractive prices, prompt sales, or security of payment. Further, for those merchants who dealt only in slaves (i.e., those who specialized in the direct trade between Cuba and Africa and were interested in a rapid turnaround), Cuba produced nothing that could be exchanged for slaves on the African coast.[46] Consequently, Arango emphasized the need to generate income that could be used to purchase slaves. He argued that only the income from export crops, especially sugar, offered a sufficient return to attract foreign merchants.

In the *Discurso*, then, Arango delineates the interdependence of free trade, agricultural productivity, and Cuba's position in world markets. He demonstrates that in order to develop their potential productive advantage, Cuban planters required a cheap and abundant supply of slaves and agricultural equipment that could only be secured through free trade. At the same time, they needed larger and more profitable outlets for their produce. Cuban export staples had to be traded where they brought the best return. Only through its entry into expanding and increasingly competitive world markets—above all, that of the United States—could the Cuban sugar industry generate the revenue necessary to pay for slaves and other inputs.[47]

However, in order to place their products in open markets or in markets where they were at a disadvantage, Cuban planters had to be competitive with foreign rivals: Market competition required Cuba to increase the productivity of its industry. For Arango, free trade was important not simply because it provided unrestricted access to slaves, but because in itself, it created conditions to revive Cuban agriculture. It was not enough to secure the hands that animated colonial agriculture and provided abundant crops, he insisted. The planter (*labrador*) had to be provided with a reward corresponding to the hardships he had undertaken. In order to realize the value of new slave production, it was necessary to eliminate the obstacles to the profitable sale of his produce.[48] The free entry of slaves and machinery in combination with profitable outlets for agricultural products would stimulate the industry and application of the colonists.[49]

Arango's policy was predicated on Cuba's natural advantages over its competitors. "The natural order," he declared, "demands that the possessors of the most fertile lands should govern this branch of agriculture (sugar): but the exact opposite has occurred."[50] Cuban agricultural development was subordinated to Spanish mercantilist policy and the requirements of the Spanish state and domestic market. Spain did not provide an adequate outlet for Cuban production. Further, it subjected Cuban produce destined for foreign markets to heavy taxation and commercial restrictions. Under these conditions, once they had gained freedom to import slaves, Cubans had no market for their increased output.[51] Their only alternative, in Arango's view, was to find a permanent outlet for their produce in foreign markets. Tariff adjustments and regulation of the consumption of Cuban products in Spain were insufficient. Spanish policy had to promote conditions that would make Cuban industry competitive with its rivals in foreign markets.[52] His goal was to establish a "happy equilibrium" between the supply of slave labor and the production of export crops.[53]

While Arango argued that the market was the most effective means for providing Cuba with necessary inputs of slave labor and agricultural equipment as well as outlets for its produce, he emphasized the role of the state in promoting competitive conditions for productive capital. Instead of subordinating its commercial and colonial policies to metropolitan interests, Spain would have to encourage colonial produce to enter foreign markets and support the development of colonial agriculture so that it could compete in them. Each of the major crops of Cuba—sugar, tobacco, livestock (cattle), and *aguardiente de cana*—were in one way or another subject to heavy duties, taxation, monopoly, and restricted access to markets that limited trade and retarded their development.[54] Arango maintained that no branch of agriculture in Havana had arrived at the degree of perfection of which it was capable, and all of them had powerful rivals with which they had to compete.[55]

Instead of subjecting colonial industries to duties and limiting their access to foreign markets, the state should treat each branch according to its own condition. Like a good parent, the state should treat them as children or adolescents and aid and encourage them until they were able to withstand competition from their powerful rivals in foreign markets.[56] The interests of the treasury should be subordinated to the free circulation of goods, the development of production, and increased abundance. Colonial industries should be supported, not taxed, until they were sufficiently strong to bear the weight of duties and prohibitive laws.[57]

AGRICULTURAL REFORM: REASON VS. THE TYRANNY OF IGNORANCE

From Arango's perspective, free trade in slaves and access to foreign markets would create the conditions for Cuban development and stimulate Cuban producers. However, in order to be competitive with the colonies of other countries in foreign markets, Cuban agriculture required the amelioration not just of trade, but of production itself. Arango argued that, although Cuba was more fertile than its rivals, agricultural and manufacturing techniques, slave management, and scientific knowledge were superior in foreign colonies. The French and British colonies had greater order and economy in their sugar mills. The equipment and the techniques that they employed were superior to those of the Cubans at each stage of the process of sugar production. Consequently, they were able to produce sugar much more cheaply and efficiently than Cuba.[58] The problem in Cuba, according to him, was not the fertility of the soil, but "the industry of man."[59]

Arango argued that the different state of prosperity and vigor in which the French and English held commerce and the arts enabled their colonists to enjoy all the goods and implements that they needed at better prices.[60] He therefore proposed an end to tariffs on the importation of agricultural implements in order to bring Cuba to the level of its foreign competitors. Cuba had progressed by allowing the importation of foreign implements, but the supply was far from what was needed. Duties on these items, Arango contended, were a burden for the agriculturist, were of no advantage to the King, and did not encourage industry in Spain. Machines and primary materials, he insisted, were free of duties in all enlightened nations (*naciones ilustradas*).[61] An open and competitive market for slaves and free importation of agricultural implements and machinery would bring Cuba more or less to the level of its foreign rivals.[62]

However, Arango insisted that isolated innovations were insufficient to resolve Cuba's problems. Instead, he advocated the systematic adoption of scientific agricultural and industrial techniques and the mechanization of Cuban sugar mills. Arango framed his project for agricultural reform within the rhetoric of enlightenment. In his view, the reform of Cuban agriculture pitted interest and reason against custom. The hold of customary practices was strong in Cuba. Arango felt despondent at seeing his compatriots, "destitute of any principle, putting their faith in blind practice and, consequently, being exposed to the most crass errors." Reason was worth little against an old, constant, and uniformly observed custom.[63] Most Cubans remained tied to familiar practices even in the face of favorable results from new ones. Successful innovation encountered skepticism and those who sought to discredit it and make it appear ridiculous. Reform would have to overcome the "tyranny of ignorance." Nonetheless, Arango remained hopeful that self-interest would stir the attention of colonial planters and oblige them to hear the voice of reason.[64]

Arango's purpose was to "propagate the enlightenment." He sought not only to adopt new productive techniques, but to transform the scientific and political economic culture of the Cuban planter class—to remake both the colonial economy and colonial subjects. To this end, he proposed a commission to tour Europe and the neighboring French and British sugar islands to study the methods employed by French and British planters. "What we must do, aside from the diverse economic and political observations that must be noted, is to see the organization, utensils, and machines that the foreigners use to cultivate and process their crops. We must acquire from all of them a profound knowledge in order later to compare the foreign methods with our own in each branch of agriculture and to see if the result gives us advantages or disadvantages."[65]

Arango viewed the commission as part of a broader effort to implant scientific agriculture in Cuba and to create an appropriate institutional framework to support a new critical and self-reflective orientation toward production. He called for the formation of an agricultural society, the Junta Protectora de la Agricultura, to promote improved agricultural and manufacturing techniques and estate management. Arango envisioned this society as an autonomous organization under the control of the Havana planters that could put the resources of Cuba at the service of agricultural development, above all, that of the sugar industry. Its primary concern would be to search for the most refined means to propagate enlightenment practices in agriculture (*buscar los medios más exquisitos de propagar las luces sobre la agricultura*) and to examine each of the advantages that, according to the commissioners' report, foreign agriculture enjoyed over Cuban agriculture. The goal of the society would be "to employ the weapon of reason in conversations and discussions in order to demonstrate to the public its *interest* [my emphasis] and to lead it to abandon its long-established concerns."[66] In addition, Arango stressed the need to make the most recent technical information available to Cuban planters and to bring to Cuba the scientific knowledge of physics, chemistry, botany, and political economy that it so badly needed.[67] Arango called for the combined effort of government, and enlightened planters to develop technical and scientific education to support the sugar industry, improve the technical level of qualified labor, and reform slave management.[68]

FREE TRADE AND EMPIRE

Arango's conception of free trade and productive colonial agriculture dramatically redefines the relations between metropolis and colony. His frame of reference is not the national political space of Cuba, but rather the Spanish American empire. He describes himself not as Cuban, but as "*habanero*" and "*hacendado*," and he writes as a vassal of the King. While he regards Havana as his *patria*,[69] the *Discurso* suggests that he treats the nation as a political entity that encompasses both the peninsula (Spain) and the overseas territories. His conception of "*riqueza nacional*" refers simultaneously to the wealth of both.

In his project, economic life is not subordinated to the social or political order. Instead, economic relations shape the social order. Different socioeconomic sectors and relations are evaluated in terms of profitability and productivity, not substantive political or social relations. Spain and Cuba are to be linked through relations of private property and the market. In contrast to mercantilist conceptions of colonialism, which simply subordinate colonies to metropolitan interests, Arango's formulation of the market, productivity, and property rights establishes a community of interests between colonial property holders and the Spanish state—a terrain more subject to negotiation between interested parties than to metropolitan fiat. The removal of political and economic obstacles will unchain the self-interest of colonial property holders. Consequently, the prosperity of both metropolis and colony will increase through production and trade.

Arango's conception of the market and social relations is more comprehensive and thorough-going than that of his European counterparts. In Europe, the debates between mercantilism, agrarianism, and physiocracy that were formative of political economy evolved within dualistic oppositions between interior and exterior, superfluous and necessary, natural and artificial. In large measure, they turned around the question of whether wheat and other grains, as source of subsistence of national populations and support of armies, were strategic goods that were key to the self-sufficiency and independence of the state, or whether they were the source of profit and destined for foreign commerce.[70] For example, in his celebrated *Informe sobre la ley agraria*, Arango's friend and contemporary Gaspar Melchior de Jovellanos argues for free trade for Spanish produce except for grain. He supports free trade in grain within Spain but contends that grain exports should be prohibited unless there was an excess beyond the needs of internal consumption.[71] For Jovellanos, the principal object of a country's production is its internal consumption. He gives the metropolis priority over the colonies. Colonies, he contends, are useful as an outlet for the surplus (*sobrante*) of metropolitan production. This surplus is "nothing more than what remains after internal consumption." In his view, to deprive the metropolis of the produce of national industry in order to provide it to the colonies would be like aiding poverty outside while allowing hunger to remain in the house.[72]

In contrast, the character of Cuban agriculture compelled Arango to link Cuban prosperity inextricably and immediately to the market. He views the produce of Cuban agriculture as "frutos de retorno," which by their nature were destined for exchange in international markets. In response to an official query that the Junta of Agriculture proposed by Arango should also protect commerce, Arango responded: "To protect agriculture from outside influences, and particularly in a country in which all commerce consists of the export of its crops, is . . . the same as protecting commerce. If I did not speak at length about commerce, it was because I could do not more than to sketch my ideas . . . that for the moment we should not make the mistake of making agriculture dependent on commerce as we appoint the members of the Junta. The hands depend upon the body, and for the same reason the merchants in an agricultural country should not dictate terms, but rather receive them from those who with their sweat nourish and support commerce."[73]

Here, Arango conceptually goes beyond the physiocrats' opposition of natural economy and commerce,[74] while practically he promotes the interests of productive agricultural capital against those of monopolistic merchants. In his view, Cuban agriculture is indissolubly linked to overseas trade. As frutos de retorno, or *produtos de extracción*, all of its crops are intended for export. Agricultural production is necessarily fully integrated into the market. Whereas Jovellanos treats consumption as an a priori deduction from the product and refers to the surplus (sobrante) as the remainder, Arango's use of surplus (sobrante) suggests permanently expanded Cuban production under which the requirements of Spanish consumption are subsumed. Spain, in his view, would lose nothing by encouraging its colonies to sell their produce in foreign markets. It would always have enough for its domestic consumption. The problem Cuba faces is not that of subsistence but that of competition in international markets.[75]

Under the stimulus of the market, Arango conceives of Cuba as an engine of imperial economic development. Free trade and the development of colonial production, he argued, would benefit not only Cuba, but Spain as well. "This in reality is not a favor. It profits the State, which without losing anything or setting anything aside, will find itself at the end of a certain period of time with an income that it did not have previously and with a group of vassals that is capable of helping it."[76] Free trade would perfect the factories, augment the Royal Treasury, and increase the population of the island. With it, Arango proclaimed, Spain would arrive at the fullness of its prosperity.[77] Thus, he urged the King to take advantage of this unique moment which could *"give an incredible stimulus (fomento) to the national wealth, or what is the same thing, to the agriculture of Cuba."*[78]

GOVERNAR LOS ESCLAVOS: SLAVERY AND LABOR

In the *Discurso*, Arango is chiefly concerned with justifying the slave trade and the use of slaves as the necessary means to valorize the property and investments of Cuban *hacendados*. He devotes less attention to justifying slavery as an institution.[79] In 1811, he emphasized the "immense profit (*utilidad*) that all branches of our national industry have drawn from devoting the negroes to the service of all of our rural estates. . . . The magnificent products of this service and its prodigious influence are to be seen not only in the progress of the island, but in that of the slave trade and the national marine. . . . [W]ithout negro slaves, there would not be colonies."[80]

Arango presumes a racialized labor force. He refers to negroes rather than to slaves and regards them as particularly suited to agricultural tasks (*faenas campestres*) in the hot climate of Cuba.[81] Though he describes them variously as ignorant or barbarous, he regards their condition as unfortunate, wretched, and sad. In his eyes, they are fellow humans who, in their dependent state, are deserving of protection. He argues that negroes are slaves who do not have civil status (*persona civil*). For that reason, they are more deserving of greater compassion and greater protection by law and humanity.[82] At the same time, caution and vigilance were necessary, especially when the planters of Cuba had the example of the Saint Domingue uprising before them.[83] In a good slave system, Arango insists, it is necessary that civil laws avoid the abuses as well as the dangers of slavery.[84] On these grounds, he constructs a justification of Cuban slavery by contrasting it with the French slave system:

The French looked at the slaves as beasts, and the Spanish looked at
them as men. The principle of those [French] masters and even their
slave legislation has always been excessive vigor, to inspire in their
slaves all the fear that they can, believing that only in this manner is it
possible for a single white to govern a hundred negroes in the middle
of the forest and in the midst of such heavy and continuous tasks. . . .
None of the resources that the negro lacks in the French colony are
missing in our colonies as much because the laws give them to him as
because the masters are careful to observe them because of their utility. The slaves of Havana find themselves today with all the assistance
and satisfactions (*bienes*) that the happiest [slaves] in the world can
obtain, and our civil laws have balanced perfectly the two extremes,
that is, the abuses of the owners and the development of insubordi-
nation and insolvency of the slave.[85]

Arango here places himself in a long tradition that seeks to contrast the
mild character of Iberian slavery with the harsher practices of northern
European powers. Yet for the purposes of this argument, it is perhaps more
interesting to examine how conceptions of property, interest, slavery, and labor
shaped Arango's program of economic development. As part of his project to
increase the productive efficiency of Cuban plantations, Arango sought to
lower the costs of maintaining slaves and obtain more work from them, but
without increasing their suffering through maltreatment or overwork. His goal
was to promote an economical method of "governing" slaves (*metodo de gobernarlos económicamente*). This understanding of slave management combines
the Christian conception of the reciprocal obligations of master and slave,
which provided a framework for master-slave relations beginning in sixteenth-
century Brazil,[86] with a notion of the technically efficient organization of tasks.
(Rafael de Bivar Marquese has argued that by the end of the eighteenth century
the frame of reference for the meaning of the term "*económico*" in planter discourse had shifted from the direction of the household to management of a
productive enterprise. An "economical" master is one who would constantly
seek to increase his property, treating his expenses as an investment for future
returns rather than as an expenditure.[87])Arango sought to obtain more work
from the slaves by reorganizing the distribution of tasks on each plantation in
order to eliminate disorder and confusion in the labor of the slaves. But he
intended nothing that would "increase the affliction of the most unfortunate
portion of the entire human species."[88] In addition, he sought to lower the costs

Fig. 6. *Cuban sugar mill, Ingenio San José de la Angosta*, lithograph by Eduardo Laplante. From Levi Marrero, *Cuba: Economía y sociedad*, vol. 10 (Madrid: Editorial Playor, 1983), portfolio insert III.

of supporting the slave labor force by encouraging slave provision grounds and local production of food crops.[89]

Perhaps surprisingly, Arango's conception of slave governance is combined with a conception of labor that recalls that of Adam Smith, who, of course, is generally regarded as the founder of modern liberal political economy and paradigmatic critic of slavery.[90] Arango, like Smith, conceives of labor as a material process that is not understood beyond the production of useful goods. In his view, this labor is compatible with the division of labor, technological innovation, and amelioration of agricultural and manufacturing techniques. Indeed, Arango perceives technological innovation as a material process that eases the burden of labor and increases the output of goods. "Everyone knows," he wrote, "that economy in the labor of men consists of substituting for them by machines or beasts."[91] Smith too treats labor as a natural, material process that produces useful or desirable goods, "the necessaries and conveniencies of life." Likewise, he treats division of labor (understood as the distribution of tasks among laborers) and machinery as simply technical means to improve the "productive powers of labor, and the greater part of the skill, dexterity, and judgment with which it is any where directed or applied." Their effect is to "facilitate and abridge labor, and enable one man to do the work of many."[92] For Smith, the purpose of their application is the production of a greater physical quantity of goods with a given number of workers.

> The person who employs his stock in maintaining labor, necessarily wishes to employ it in such a manner as to produce as great a quantity of work as possible. He endeavors, therefore, both to make among his workmen the most proper distribution of employment, and to furnish them with the best machines that he can either invent or afford to purchase. . . . The productive powers of the same number of laborers cannot be increased, but in consequence either of some addition and improvement to those machines and instruments which abridge labor; or of a more proper division and distribution of employment.[93]

Smith is justly famous for his critique of slavery. Nonetheless, his well-known arguments about the inefficiency of slavery flow not from his conception of the social organization of the labor process, but rather from his understanding of the capacity of the wage relation to excite the worker's self-interest. Thus, Smith argues that wages paid to the free worker stimulate the worker's "strict frugality and parsimonious attention" in managing the fund destined for replacing or repairing the "wear and tear" upon the worker rather than having to depend upon a "negligent master." In contrast: "The work of the slave is the dearest of any. A person who can acquire no property, can have no other interest but to eat as much, and to labor as little as possible. Whatever work he does beyond what is sufficient to purchase his own maintenance, can be squeezed out of him by violence only, and not by any interest of his own."[94] At the same time, however, Smith admits the progress of the French West Indian colonies is superior to that of the British and "has been entirely owing to the good conduct of the colonists . . . and this superiority has been remarked in nothing so much as in the *good management of their slaves.*"[95]

Smith's account of the sources of the prosperity of the French West Indian colonies discloses his idea of governance. Here, his emphasis on the instrumentalization of slave labor reveals the conceptual underpinnings of liberal political economy. Management or governance is a form of authority appropriate to those who are deemed incapable of subjectivity. Smith writes: "But, as the profit and success of the cultivation which is carried on by means of cattle, depend very much upon the good management of those cattle, so the profit and success of that which is carried on by slaves, must depend equally upon the good management of those slaves; and in the good management of their slaves the French planters, I think it is generally allowed, are superior to the English." Paradoxically, Smith attributes French superiority in this regard to the authoritarian state (with the clear implication that English institutions are unsuited to slavery): "The genius of their government naturally introduces a better management of their negro slaves." The slave is best protected in a society in which property and representative government are less well developed. The arbitrary intervention of the state is the best guarantee of the slave's well-being:

> The law, so far as it gives some protection to the slave against the violence of his master, is likely to be better executed in a colony where the government is in greater measure arbitrary, than in one where it is altogether free. In every country where the unfortunate law of slavery is established, the magistrate, when he protects the slave, intermeddles in some measure in the management of the private property of the master; in a free country, where the master is perhaps either a member of the colonial assembly, or an elector of such a member, he dare not do this but with the greatest caution and circumspection.

Such protection of the slave, Smith contends, induces gentle treatment. Such treatment "renders the slave not only more faithful, but more intelligent, and therefore, upon a double account, more useful. He approaches more to the condition of the free servant, and may possess some degree of integrity and *attachment to his master's interest* [my emphasis], virtues which belong to free servants, but which can never belong to a slave who is treated as slaves commonly are in countries where the master is perfectly free and secure."[96]

If Arango and Adam Smith share a similar conception of labor, the differences between them can also be understood within a common intellectual field. Albert Hirschman has eloquently demonstrated the importance of "passions" and "interests" as organizing themes of philosophical and political economic discussion during the seventeenth and eighteenth centuries. Smith, in a certain sense, represents the culmination of this tradition.[97] He generalizes the self-interested individual as liberal subject and reconciles it with social order. In his political economy wages, rent, and profit form at once the source and the mediation of individual self-interest. Economic interest is determined by the social location of the individual within the functional differentiation between land, labor, and stock as factors of production. The relation among these forms of property regulate both individual and class interests and provide the means of making them compatible with social order and the wealth of nations.

Arango's argument for the necessity of the subordination of the slave population develops within the same terms as does Smith's argument for the self-interest of the free laborer. If for Smith, wages, generalized private property, and the market allow the socialization and regulation of the self-interested worker, for Arango, racial slavery allows no such possibility:

> To open the way for a man to hope for any good is to open the door also to his forgotten and dangerous reflections about being deprived of this good [freedom]. It is certainly to arouse in him, if not outright insubordination, then lack of compliance. We need not mention the inconvenience and ills of such attitudes in slavery, seeing them repeated in all times and in all countries. In the stupidity of the Negro and the solitude of our estates lies the most necessary subordination, and all the more to be feared is anything that may loosen this unique resource, this capital defender of the existence of the whites who live with so many negros.[98]

Arango organized his defense of the Cuban planters as the defense of the interests of men of property. However, precisely because he remains within the terms of liberal thought, slaves, for him, could have no such interest. Like all men, they were possessed of natural liberty; however, for them this liberty could not be realized through property. Rather, the liberty (and property) of slaves had to be suppressed in the interests of Cuban economic prosperity. Excluded from property, slaves were defined by the absence of interest and thus were incapable of self-interested action. (Arango favored allowing slaves the *use* of plots of land to grow their own provisions and improve their material well-being.[99] However, such provision grounds are not to be confused with the conception of private property in liberal theory.) In this sense, slaves (and, therefore, slavery) remained outside the sphere of liberal political economy. Self-interest, property, and exchange could not mediate and reconcile the interests of masters and slaves: Instead, in the absence of liberal subjectivity, domination and paternalism regulate the relation between them. Without the disciplining force of property, the slave remained a dependent subject who had to be both subjugated and protected. The slave system rested upon exclusion and domination as the means of control over the enslaved. For Arango, ignorance and barbarism justified slavery, yet, in his conception, slavery could only perpetuate them.

The proximity between Arango and Adam Smith formed by conceptions of free trade, labor, and self-interest give us grounds to question the boundaries and supposed antimonies between proslavery thought and liberal political economy. These boundaries are much more permeable and problematic than the unified fields of inclusion/exclusion presupposed by the concept of ideology (base/super-structure) would lead us to believe. Emphasis on the opposition between modern liberalism and archaic proslavery thought obscures both Smith's debts to the physiocrats[100] and Arango's position within Enlightenment thought.

The point here is not to deny the differences between liberal and proslavery ideologies, but to locate the position of each within a shared conceptual field. By linking self-interest, the distribution of forms of private property (wages, profit, rent), and market exchange to provide a systematic account of social organization, Smith is able to form an internally unified and consistent political economy. From this perspective, there is a closure that allows for a strictly "economic" conception of social relations and permits formation of the discipline of political economy as a self-contained system of thought. Consequently, Smith appears as the founder of modern political economy at the same time as physiocracy is consigned to the role of precursor and placed outside of modernity.

In contrast, Arango's conception of the slave economy permits no such unified economic discourse. Beyond the more limited purpose of the *Discurso*, his discourse can only be unsystematic. In his case, productive relations rest upon slavery and racial domination for their reproduction. Such domination does not allow for either a unified system of political economic thought or the formation of individual subjectivity mediated by private property relations. Hence, it is not compatible with liberalism as ideology. Yet, such differences exist within a common conceptual field and have a historical affinity with one another. From such a perspective, the sources and internal coherence of both proslavery thought and liberalism appear more open and diverse. Differences between them no longer appear as absolute. Rather, they may be understood as opposed yet mutually formative tendencies that draw, at least in part, from the same sources. Such an approach can lead to rethinking fruitfully analytical and interpretative frameworks; it further reveals both disjunctures and new histor-ical unities. It points to the need to distinguish between political and economic liberalism as a finished, articulated ideology and the complex discontinuous discursive field from which it is constructed.

In this context, it is useful to recall Paul Gilroy's idea that slavery and race form boundary concepts that shape, or perhaps even define, modern ideolo-gies of progress and modernization. They are constituted within the historical relations of modernity, but their exclusion from consideration within it are the conditions for liberal ideologies of progress. Recognition of this exclusion allows consideration of the complex and contradictory character of modernity.[101] Here, liberal ideology veils the modernity of slavery, while slavery reveals the complexity and contradictoriness of liberalism.

CONCLUSION

In his *Discurso sobre la Agricultura de la Habana y Medios de Fomentarla*, Francisco Arango y Parreño mobilized the conceptual vocabulary of political economy and the Enlightenment to articulate a project for the transformation of Cuban economic and social life; this project rests upon the interdependence of the slave trade, free trade in Cuban agricultural products, scientific improvement of agriculture, and reform of slave management. Rather than being anomalous, each of the elements presented by Arango is interdependent and mutually reinforcing: Each presupposes the others and requires them in order to achieve its full effect. Arango's argument brings together the unrestricted supply of slave labor, free trade, and agricultural innovation in order to promote a conception of well-being based on fertility, the circulation of commodities, science, and the creation of abundance. It represents the specific formulation of slave relations in Cuba within changing conditions of world economy. It thereby calls attention to the diversity and continual historical reconstitution of slaveries in the Americas.

This proposal represents an attempt to use Cuba's productive advantages to carve out a dominant position for the island in the emerging North American and European markets. It gives theoretical expression to Cuba's shift to productive agriculture and free trade. Within this framework, Arango identifies the market as the most effective instrument to supply Cuba with both the labor and materials that it requires and the outlets for its produce. Nonetheless, the intervention of the Spanish state is necessary to secure the competitive access to markets necessary to overcome Cuba's relatively weak economic position and establish Arango's "happy equilibrium" between slave imports and agricultural exports. However, free trade in itself is insufficient to transform Cuba's economy. Its success depends upon the unrestricted development of slave labor, the reform of slave management, and the scientific transformation of agriculture. Accordingly, Arango's program and the subsequent Cuban development inspired by it, represent an original response to the economic and political conjuncture formed by the Haitian and American Revolutions, industrialization, and the transformation of world markets under British economic and political hegemony.

From this perspective, Arango appears as an Atlantic intellectual who elaborated an integral program for economic renewal that, albeit authoritarian, hierarchical, and racist, was successful. His project was to inform Cuban development at least until the 1860s and clearly helped to shape the fluid and expanding world economy of the first half of the nineteenth century. Between 1801 and 1865 Cuba imported over 600,000 African slaves as well as indentured laborers from China and Yucatán. The Cuban *ingenio* developed on an unprecedented scale through systematic and ongoing technical transformation. By the 1820s Cuba emerged as the world's leading sugar producer and its output virtually doubled every ten years thereafter. The Cuban sugar industry dominated the world market and became a key pivot in the remaking of the American plantation periphery. Yet, the very success of this project increased Cuba's dependence on sugar and slavery and exacerbated tensions and conflicts between master and slave, between groups in Cuba, and between Cuba and Spain.

In Arango's view, the policies delineated in the *Discurso* would benefit both Cuba and Spain. Even as Cuba's economic development drew it into closer relation with the United States, both as an outlet for its produce and as a market for the latter's manufactured goods and other imports, Cuba remained a part of the Spanish empire. However, such policies also implicitly redefined from within the relation between Cuba and Spain and the nature of the empire. Though Cuban planters remained vassals of the King, they could not remain colonial subjects who might be simply subordinated to the interests of the Crown and metropolitan state. Rather, by developing the planters' property and therefore their independent interest, these policies meant that, even though Spain and Cuba remained parts of an encompassing imperial political unit, the planters' relation to Spain would have to be negotiated as a relationship between separate interests within the context of a market economy.

Arango's project increased Cuba's dependence on slavery in the context of the Haitian Revolution, on the one hand, and British pressure on the international slave trade, on the other. Under these conditions, the maintenance of slave relations required the presence of a repressive force that increased protection costs as well as increased regulation of master-slave relations. At the same time, expanding and competitive commodity markets put pressure on the productivity of slave labor. Ideologies of liberalism, progress, and self-interested individualism altered the ideological space in which slavery could be both proposed and defended. Indeed, in Cuba, the growth of the sugar industry, with its brutal labor regime and harsh social discipline, undermined the very Spanish paternalism that Arango deployed to justify slavery. Finally, the remarkable growth of the sugar industry exacerbated the tensions between sugar and other sectors of the Cuban economy. It created the uneven regional and social development of Cuba and provoked the social discontinuities and antagonisms that were to manifest themselves in the Ten Years War.

NOTES

1. Francisco de Arango y Parreño, *Discurso sobre la Agricultura de la Habana y Medios de Fomentarla* (1793), in *Obras* I:114–75 (La Habana: Dirección de Cultura, 1952).

2. Dale Tomich, "The 'Second Slavery': Bonded Labor and the Transformation of the Nineteenth Century World Economy," 103–17 in *Rethinking the Nineteenth Century: Movements and Contradictions*, ed. Francisco O. Ramirez (Westport, Conn.: Greenwood Press, 1988).

3. Antonio Benítez Rojo, "Power/Sugar/Literature: Toward a Reinterpretation of Cubanness," *Cuban Studies* 16 (1986): 10–12.

4. Arango, *Discurso sobre la Agricultura*, 143.

5. Giovanni Arrighi, *The Long Twentieth Century* (London: Verso, 1994), 47–58, 159–238.

6. See, for example, Eric Williams, *Capitalism and Slavery* (Chapel Hill: University of North Carolina Press, 1944); Eugene D. Genovese, *The Political Economy of Slavery* (New York: Vintage Books, 1967); Manuel Moreno Fraginals, *El ingenio: Complejo económico social cubano del azúcar*, 3 vols. (La Habana: Editorial de Ciencias Sociales, 1978); idem, *The Sugar Mill: The Socioeconomic Complex of Sugar in Cuba* (New York: Monthly Review Press, 1976); and Gordon K. Lewis, *Main Currents in Caribbean Thought: The Historical Evolution of Caribbean Society in Its Ideological Aspects* (Baltimore: The Johns Hopkins University Press, 1983).

7. See, for instance, Lewis, *Main Currents in Caribbean Thought*, 97–98, 141–42.

8. Moreno Fraginals, *The Sugar Mill*, 60.

9. Lewis, *Main Currents in Caribbean Thought*, 144–45.

10. Ibid., 149.

11. Maria Sylvia de Carvalho Franco, "'All the World was America': John Locke, Liberalismo e propriedade como conceito antropológico," *Revista USP* 17 (1993): 32–35.

12. Juan B. Amores, *Cuba y España, 1868–1898: El final de un sueño* (Pamplona: Ediciones Universidad de Navarra, 1998), 19–20.

13. Benítez Rojo, "Power/Sugar/Literature," 9–14.

14. Francisco J. Ponte Dominguez, *Arango Parreño: Estadista Colonial Cubano* (La Habana: Imp. Molina y Cia, 1937), 5–13, 26–49; Heinrich Friedlaender, *Historia económica de Cuba* (La Habana: Editorial de las Ciencias Sociales, 1978), 157–163; Levi Marrero, *Cuba: Economía y Sociedad*, X (Madrid: Editorial Playor, 1984), 8; Maria Dolores González-Ripoll Navarro, *Cuba, La Isla de los Ensayos: Cultura y Sociedad (1790–1815)* (Madrid: Consejo Superior de Investigaciones Científicas, 1999), 145–46.

15. Francisco de Arango y Parreño, "Representación hecha a S.M. con otivo de la sublevación de esclavos en los dominios frances de la isla de Santo Domingo" (1791), in *Obras* I:111–12 (La Habana: Dirección de Cultura, 1952).

16. Arango y Parreño, *Discurso sobre la Agricultura*, 133.

17. Ibid., 143.

18. Gaspar Melchior de Jovellanos, *Informe sobre la ley agraria* (Barcelona: Ediciones de Materiales, 1968).

19. Friedlaender, *Historia económica de Cuba*, 163–64; Marrero, *Cuba: Economía y Sociedad*, 15–16; Moreno Fraginals, *El ingenio* I:73; González-Ripoll Navarro, *Cuba, La Isla de los Ensayos*, 156–63.

20. Keith Tribe, *Land, Labour and Economic Discourse* (London: Routlege & Kegan Paul, 1978); Rafael de Bivar Marquese, *Adminstração & Escravidão: Ideías sobre a Gestão de Agricultura Escravista Brasileira* (São Paulo: HUCITEC, 1999). For an analysis of the vocabulary of the *Discurso*, see Anne Perotin, "Le projet cubain des grands planteurs de la Havane: Jalons pour une lecture de Francisco Arango y Parreño (1769–1839)," in *Mélanges de la casa de Velázquez*, X (Paris: Édition E. de Boccard, 1974), 273–313; Marrero, *Cuba: Economía y Sociedad*, 15.

21. Ernest Lluch and Lluís Argemí, *Agronomía y físiocracia en España (1750–1820)* (Valencia: Institución Alfonso el Magnánimo, 1985), 1–120, 185–96; Friedlaender, *Historia económica de Cuba*, 161, 166–75; Raul Maestri, *Arango y Parreño: El Estadista sin Estado* (La Habana: Publicaciones de la Secretaria de Educación. Dirección de Cultura, 1937), 8, 12; Julio Travieso, "El pensamiento económico de Arango y Parreño," *Economia y Desarollo* 10–11 (Oct.–Dec. 1970): 139–140; Franco Venturi, *Italy and the Enlightenment: Studies in a Cosmopolitan Century* (New York: Columbia University Press, 1972), 180–224, 265–91; Jose Carlos Chiaramonte, *La crítica ilustrada de la realidad: Economía y sociedad en el pensamiento argentino e iberamericano del siglo XVIII* (Buenos Aires: Centro Editor de America Latina, 1982), 33–66, 105–78; idem, *Pensamiento de la Ilustración: Economía y sociedad iberoamericanas en el siglo XVIII* (Caracas: Biblioteca Ayacucho, n.d.), xii, xxviii–xxxiv.

22. Arango, *Discurso sobre la Agricultura*, 115.

23. Francisco de Arango y Parreño, "Primer papel sobre el comercio de negros" (1789), in *Obras* I:79 (La Habana: Dirección de Cultura, 1952).

24. Francisco de Arango y Parreño, "Oficio acompañando copia de la representación sobre la introducción de negros, y corroborandola con razones muy sólidas" (1791), in *Obras* I:108 (La Habana: Dirección de Cultura, 1952).

25. Arrighi, *The Long Twentieth Century*, 80–81.

26. Ibid., 82–83.

27. Arango, *Discurso sobre la Agricultura*, 117–18.

28. Francisco de Arango y Parreño, "Representación de la Ciudad de la Habana a las Cortes" (1811), in *Obras* II:185 (La Habana: Dirección de Cultura, 1952).

29. Arango, "Primer papel sobre el comercio de negros," 79.

30. Francisco de Arango y Parreño, "Instrucción que se formo D. Francisco de Arango cuando se entrego de los poderes de la Habana y papeles del asunto" (1788), in *Obras* I:77 (La Habana: Dirección de Cultura, 1952).

31. Ibid.

32. Arango, "Primer papel sobre el comercio de negros," 79.

33. Ibid., 80.

34. Ibid.

35. Ibid., 83.

36. David R. Murray, *Odious Commerce: Britain, Spain and the Abolition of the Cuban Slave Trade* (Cambridge: Cambridge University Press, 1980), 11.

37. Francisco de Arango y Parreño, "Representación manifestando las ventajas de una absoluta libertad en la introducción de negros, y solicitando se amplie a ocho la prórroga concedida por dos años" (1791), in *Obras* I:97–102 (La Habana: Dirección de Cultura, 1952).

38. Arango, "Representación manifestando las ventajas," 97–98.

39. Ibid., 101.

40. See David McNally, *Political Economy and the Rise of Capitalism: A Reinterpretation* (Berkeley: University of California Press, 1988), 226–28.

41. Arango, "Representación manifestando las ventajas," 102.

42. Ibid., 101–2.

43. Compare Adam Smith, *An Inquiry into the Nature and Causes of the Wealth of Nations* (Chicago: The University of Chicago Press, 1976) I:98–110, 124–30.

44. Arango, *Discurso sobre la Agricultura*, 74.

45. Arango, "Representación manifestando las ventajas," 98–99.

46. Ibid., 99.

47. Arango, "Instrucción que se formo D. Francisco de Arango," 78.

48. Ibid., 77; compare Jovellanos, *Informe sobre la ley agraria*, 112.

49. Arango, *Discurso sobre la Agricultura*, 118–19.

50. Ibid., 123; compare Smith, *An Inquiry*, I:385.

51. Arango, *Discurso sobre la Agricultura*, 127–29.

52. Ibid., 122–23, 135–36.

53. Arango, "Instrucción que se formo D. Francisco de Arango," 77.

54. Ibid., 77–78.

55. Arango, *Discurso sobre la Agricultura*, 139–40.

56. Ibid.

57. Ibid., 140.

58. Ibid., 126–27; Francisco de Arango y Parreño, "Respuestas de D. Francisco Arango a los reparos que se hicieron a su 'Discurso sobre la agricultura de la Habana'" (1793), in *Obras* I:175–203 (La Habana: Dirección de Cultura, 1952), 180.

59. Arango, "Respuestas de D. Francisco Arango," 187.

60. Arango, *Discurso sobre la Agricultura*, 124–25.

61. Ibid., 135–36.

62. Ibid., 136.

63. Ibid.

64. Ibid., 136–37.

65. Ibid., 164–65; see González-Ripoll Navarro, *Cuba, La Isla de los Ensayos*, 198–205.

66. Arango, *Discurso sobre la Agricultura*, 156–57; Moreno Fraginals, *El ingenio* I:106–7.

67. See Moreno Fraginals, *El ingenio* I:131–33.

68. Arango, *Discurso sobre la Agricultura*, 136–38.

69. Arango, "Instrucción que se formo D. Francisco de Arango," 77; Juan B. Amores, "Francisco de Arango y Parreño: La transición hacia la modernidad en Cuba," *Actas del XI Congreso Internacional del Asociación de Historiadores Latinoamericanistas Europeos* (Liverpool, 1996), II:512–13.

70. Catherine Larrère, *L'invention de l'économie aux XVIIIe siècle* (Paris: Presses Universitaires de France, 1992), 175–76.

71. Jovellanos, *Informe sobre la ley agraria*, 129–36.

72. Marcel Bitar Letayf, *Economistas españoles del siglo XVIII: Sus ideas sobre la libertad del comercio con Indias* (Madrid: Ediciones Cultura Hispanica, 1968), 187–88.

73. Arango, *Discurso sobre la Agricultura*, 168–69.

74. Larrère, *L'invention de l'économie*, 212.

75. Arango, *Discurso sobre la Agricultura*, 142–43.

76. Ibid., 140.

77. Arango, "Instrucción que se formo D. Francisco de Arango," 77.

78. Arango, *Discurso sobre la Agricultura*, 115n. (Emphasis mine.)

79. Arango, "Representación de la Ciudad de la Habana a las Cortes," 185.

80. Ibid., 184–85.

81. Ibid., 184.

82. Amores, "Francisco de Arango y Parreño," 511–12.

83. Arango, *Discurso sobre la Agricultura*, 167–68.

84. Arango, "Representación de la Ciudad de la Habana a las Cortes," 185.

85. Arango, "Representación hecha," 110–11.

86. Jorge Benci, *Economia cristã dos senhores no governo dos escravos* (1700; Sao Paulo: Grijalbo, 1977); André João Antonil, *Cultura e opulência do Brasil por suas drogas e minas* (1711; Paris: IHEAH, 1968), 111–17, 131–53.

87. Marquese, "Adminstração & Escravidão," 113–14.

88. Arango, *Discurso sobre la Agricultura*, 138, 154.

89. Ibid., 138–39, 154–55.

90. See, for example, Eric Williams, *Capitalism and Slavery* (Chapel Hill: University of North Carolina Press, 1944), 107.

91. Arango, *Discurso sobre la Agricultura*, 126.

92. Smith, *An Inquiry*, I:1, 7, 11, 292, 297, 364.

93. Ibid., I:292, 364.

94. Ibid., I:90, 411–12.

95. Ibid., II:99–101. My emphasis.

96. Ibid.

97. Albert O. Hirschman, *The Passions and the Interests: Political Arguments for Capitalism before Its Triumph* (Princeton: Princeton University Press, 1977).

98. Arango, "Representación de la Ciudad de la Habana a las Cortes," 182.

99. Arango, *Discurso sobre la Agricultura*, 125.

100. Tribe, *Land, Labour and Economic Discourse*, 8–109; McNally, *Political Economy and the Rise of Capitalism*, 209–57.

101. Paul Gilroy, *The Black Atlantic: Modernity and Double Consciousness* (London: Verso, 1993).

CHAPTER THREE

VISIONS OF EMPIRE AND HISTORICAL IMAGINATION IN PUERTO RICO UNDER SPANISH RULE, 1870–1898

Astrid Cubano-Iguina

On 10 October 1868 the Spanish authorities in San Juan ordered the arrest of the renowned teacher and writer José Julián de Acosta y Calbo. He was unjustly suspected of participating in the conspiracy leading to the Lares revolt, a rebellion for independence that had begun seventeen days earlier in the mountainous interior of Puerto Rico, and had been almost immediately suppressed by swiftly mobilized troops. While in jail (first in the dungeons of El Morro, and shortly after in the district jail of Arecibo, where the interrogations on the Lares insurrection were taking place), Acosta wrote an essay titled *Horas de prisión*. Deprived of the company of his wife, children, and friends, and most of all, deprived of his books, Acosta explains, he counted only on memory to aid him in these reflections. Thanks to the marvelous power of this "magician" (the memory), he was not alone but in the sympathetic company of the thoughts and deeds of many of the greatest men of humanity.[1]

The "memory" evoked by Acosta in this short essay transports him through mountains and valleys, from Switzerland to the vast American continent with de Saussure, Bello, and Humboldt.[2] Not a single reference to the Spanish tradition appears, except for an allusion to the injustices of Francisco Bobadilla, the King's envoy sent to judge the irregularities of the Columbus administration in the early phase of the Antillean conquest. Finally, his memory rests on the "grave and heroic generation of 1776 in the United Colonies, proclaiming through the authorized voice of Washington, that the violation of their rights was the only cause of the conflict." Rebellion had nothing to do with taxation; it had everything to do with "rights." These facts and names, he adds, "submerged me in a series of reflections about the influence of the Anglo-Saxon race on the march of civilization."[3]

One year before these events, Acosta had been chosen to be a member of the Spanish Academy of History because of his erudite notations and comments on

Fray Iñigo Abbad y Lasierra's eighteenth-century *Historia geográfica, civil y natural de la isla de San Juan Bautista de Puerto Rico*. He was the first Puerto Rican to receive that honor, which represented the culmination of successful years of studying and traveling in Spain, France, and Germany. Acosta had initially traveled to Spain to study physics and mathematics, completing his degree in 1851. This achievement was made possible by a scholarship he had received from the colonial government.

Acosta's career as a teacher, liberal political leader, and abolitionist in the years following the Revolution of 1868 in Spain, and as an *asimilista* in the 1880s proposing the complete institutional and political integration of Puerto Rico with Spain, was justly rewarded by the monarchy with the granting of the *Gran Cruz de Isabel la Católica* (1886), one of the greatest honors granted to statesmen in the service of the Crown. Throughout this time, the one aspect that stands out in Acosta's impeccable political career is his proven loyalty to Spain and his commitment to Spanish liberal traditions.[4]

In view of his political career of relentless loyalty to Spain, Acosta's embittered and somewhat contradictory reflections of 1868 are revealing. The resentments that mediated the text of 1868 arose from a perception of violations of individual rights that led Acosta to pessimistically view his supposedly "Spanish race" as lacking the fundamentals of a liberal tradition, and to consider the "Anglo-Saxon race" as the hallmark of civic rights and freedom. This negative view contrasts sharply with the pragmatic and moderate approach mediating other instances of Acosta's liberal politics.

Acosta is a good point of departure to explore voices from a "frontier" of empires that was being drawn throughout the nineteenth century. As the easternmost of the Greater Antilles, Puerto Rico had been traditionally considered the "key to the Indies," an outpost of the Spanish empire, remaining as such even after the Wars of Independence broke out in South America and the fortified post at San Juan served as a base of Spanish military operations.[5] Two decades later, the United States was perceived not only as a commercial power in the region but also as an expansionist force, especially after the war with Mexico and the absorption of most of the northern Mexican territory in 1848.[6] The Antilles, including Puerto Rico, were expected to play a similar role in the late-nineteenth-century imperial designs of the U.S. as naval bases in the desired sea routes of the Caribbean and toward the Pacific.[7] During this period, contemporary policy makers and political commentators were turning the Spanish Antilles into a southern frontier of the United States.

In the nineteenth century, after the Spanish imperial system disintegrated, a new Puerto Rico had been taking shape as a sugar and coffee colony of Spain.

The booming coffee and sugar export economy strengthened the island's role in the Atlantic system. By mid-century, the North American market absorbed about two-thirds of the island's sugar production, which furthered strong commercial and cultural ties with the United States. Sons of the island's wealthy landed families went to North American universities, and merchants frequently traveled for business or education. By then, the possibility of annexation of the Spanish Antilles of Cuba and Puerto Rico to the United States had been widely discussed, though repeatedly rejected, in Madrid and in Washington. It was a well-known alternative, though it depended ultimately on the approval of the U.S. Congress. The importance of this condition should not be underestimated.

In the last quarter of the century, coffee sold in European and Cuban ports became Puerto Rico's most valuable export crop, while sugar production declined. Even so, there was increasing awareness in the colony of the particular interest certain sectors of the North American government had in the Antilles. Certain traits of the authoritarian Spanish monarchic military regime still prevailed in late-nineteenth-century Puerto Rico, although partial modernization of the political system had been granted with the abolition of slavery and the organization of partially representative political institutions and processes. Educated men, either native-born or Spanish immigrants, increasingly participated in the political discussions.

Late-nineteenth-century writers in Puerto Rico presented Spain, which they viewed as their political and cultural metropolis, and the United States, a highly valued commercial partner and a political model, as alternative sources of authority and power. They looked at the past from a similarly dual standpoint, constructing opposite poles and creating a space for negotiation with the colonial government. The imperial reference was a constant trait of their discourse. Native leaders (with a few exceptions) forged a Puerto Rican identity without contemplating a project of independent nation-state building, especially because they believed the island was too small and lacked the "strength" to be on its own, while the possibility of joining Puerto Rico to the other Antilles lacked support and raised great racial, cultural, and political fears. Their historical writings narrated the story of a national being (based on an idea of ethnic cohesiveness and on a geographical imaginary) in a constant counterpoint with the larger international scope.

In this essay I will examine some of their historical and geopolitical statements. They were nourished on the established paradigms of the Atlantic world, and produced texts written from a frontier, which I am depicting as a discursive contested space where a variety of power negotiations were taking place.[8] Local writers had competing empires in mind as they developed their scripts of praise, distrust, or resentment for both metropolitan centers of power. Their national narratives developed simultaneously and not unconnectedly. They were also engaged in very specific and concrete power struggles within the colonial society and in developing narrative affinities across national boundaries.[9]

Clashing Empires in the Press

The idea of the nineteenth-century Hispanic Caribbean as a frontier of clashing empires has been a constant in old and new historical syntheses of the region, especially those concerned with Cuba, or with the Dominican Republic of the 1860s. The study of Luis Martínez-Fernánadez constructs the Hispanic Caribbean of the mid-nineteenth century as a scenario of diplomatic tensions between imperial powers of the North Atlantic, without ignoring the importance of these tensions in the shaping of general political tendencies within the islands, especially with regard to issues concerning the slave system.[10] The historiography of inter-imperial tensions in the late nineteenth century focuses on the Cuban wars and the conflicts leading to them. Spain no longer appears as the power doomed to disappear, a determinist and polemical view put forth repeatedly since the end of Spanish rule in the Antilles.[11] Puerto Rico did not become a theater of war until the very end of the century in the Spanish-Cuban-American War. My work will concentrate precisely on the years preceding the U.S. invasion of Puerto Rico (roughly 1870–1898) when the idea of "clashing empires" filled the imagination of the educated public. I will attempt to show that this idea was also a discourse, in the sense of a text written to influence behavior, dominate "others," and exercise power.[12] Writers participated in reshaping and reproducing the polarizations that they themselves were part of and submitted to. In doing this, they framed the public debate in what can be labeled a "discourse of negotiation."

Feelings far more complex and profound than consciously articulated political ideas were at stake. Visions of empire were deeply intertwined with notions of culture. In 1865, a native writer had succinctly stated the crossroads that local liberals had reached; on the one hand there were those wishing to conserve the "glorious traditions of the Latin race," and on the other there were "the partisans of Protestant propaganda and admirers of the North American civilization."[13] It is worth exploring the meanings and uses of these paradigms in the forging of Puerto Rican identity by educated inhabitants of the colony.

The racialized and determinist terms in which the discourse of negotiation is deployed, as seen in texts like that of Acosta, deserve attention. Similar racialized arguments were used also in Spain, where a distinguished liberal statesman such as Emilio Castelar could interpret Spain's mission in America as counteracting the influence of the "Saxon race."[14] Clearly inserted in the nineteenth-century mainstream of Western culture, the racialized and determinist character of most local statements about empires and political systems can also be viewed as a strategy that facilitated the attempts of local liberal writers to subvert the otherwise depressing discourse of "Anglo-Saxon" superiority, and to make it work to their own advantage in specific situations. It also confirms the elite's entanglement in local power relations. They seemed to feel the need to ratify established paradigms and hierarchies that, after all, confirmed their position of power as a white or nearly white elite, above the majority of the inhabitants of the colony.[15]

The use of the term "race" to refer to persons of Spanish ancestry in either Spain or America was being proposed in Puerto Rico at least since mid-century, and is seen as closely related to the Spanish efforts to recuperate its economic and cultural influence in the former Spanish colonies of America. In 1853, the newspaper *El Ponceño* comments on the chaotic political conditions of Mexico: "We are united to them by ties of blood and common beliefs and cannot allow the extermination of our own race."[16]

For Spanish immigrant writers residing in the colony, the "race-war" argument came in handy to promote the idea that Spain represented a bulwark against domination by an alien Anglo-Saxon race; they used it frequently, especially in the early 1870s when the war in Cuba exacerbated tensions between the United States and Spain, and U.S. President Ulysses Grant made explicit assertions of his commitment to annexation of the Dominican Republic to the Union.[17] It is important to note, however, that the same conservative Spanish newspaper that interpreted these events in the context of a "race-war," appreciated the role of the United States as a trading partner of the Antilles and, in other instances, commented that relations between Spain and the United States were developing excellently.[18] It occasionally argued that the United States needed the continuation of Spanish political domination in Cuba. Furthermore, the same newspaper regularly advertised a Jesuit school in Alabama admitting white males between the ages of 9 and 15, or published an article in praise of the work ethic represented by Benjamin Franklin.[19]

Fears of absorption by an "alien race" were not an exclusive argument of the Spanish residents in the colony. Reformist native-born leader José Pablo Morales, who viewed the possible uniting of Puerto Rico to the United States as tantamount to suicide for the local elites, confided his pro-Spanish feelings in a letter he wrote to José Julián Acosta, in which he undoubtedly rephrased older arguments of the Cuban writer José Antonio Saco.[20] In 1876 Morales wrote that Puerto Ricans were Spaniards, "entirely and completely" by ties of duty, legal rights, convenience, and affection.[21] The liberals gathered around the newspaper *El Clamor del País* in 1883 (at that time owned by the liberal entrepreneur José T. Silva, and later by Salvador Brau) redefined the meaning of being Spanish. They rejected the historical stereotype of Spain as the intolerant Catholic oppressor of liberties. They wished to identify, not with historical Spain, but with "the Spain of today," firmly placed on the road to liberal reforms.[22]

Other reformists engaged in finding a Spanish liberal tradition with which they could identify eventually chose "Dos de Mayo" and the "Himno de Riego" as icons of historical Spanish liberalism. Salvador Brau celebrated the historical landmark of "Dos de Mayo" (the popular uprising against Napoleon's invasion of Spain in 1808), and even stated that there had been another "Dos de Mayo" in Puerto Rico when "blacks and whites, planters and slaves" all lifted up their machetes to defend Spanish rule in Puerto Rico against the British attack of 1797.[23] A San Juan newspaper, on the other hand, chose the "Himno de Riego" or the symbol used to remember the liberal military coup (*pronunciamiento*) led by the then-Commander and later General Rafael de Riego against the absolutist Ferdinand VII in 1820, and stated that the enthusiasm created in the island upon hearing this hymn was comparable to the one created in dancing *La Borinqueña*, the musical piece already considered a symbol of Puerto Rican identity.[24]

Attraction and repulsion were expressed in historical terms. The Monroe Doctrine was a frequent allusion, never fully explored in historical analyses, but categorically used as symbol of North American expansionism and, conveniently, as a negotiating piece. It was the argument that Luis Hernández Arbizu, the Puerto Rican deputy to the Cortes of 1869, used to convince the Spanish deputies of the need to grant the expected political reforms in order to stop the "always increasing progress of the Monroe Doctrine."[25] Attempts to negotiate abounded also on the occasion of President Grant's speech on reassuming the presidency on 4 March 1873. In this speech Grant offered a determinist interpretation of the U.S. role as the "guiding star" of republicanism in the world and regretted the refusal by Congress to admit the Dominican Republic into the Union on the grounds that excessive extension of the national territory would entail a risk of weakness and destruction. A liberal San Juan newspaper fully reprinted its text, without comments, suggesting either a silent approval, or a tacit message to those Spanish politicians who blocked political reforms in the colonies that they were pursuing a dangerous course.[26]

Among autonomists, who founded a party in 1887, eventually the largest political force of the colony, the priority was to show adhesion to Spain by denouncing the expansionist intentions of the United States. These politicians, constantly accused by the powerful Spanish Party in the colony of being under-cover separatists and annexationists, adopted the strategy of expressing con-cern about U.S. expansionist intentions, clearly rejecting any suspicion of annexationism. The "North American colossus," a name given to the United States since the 1870s, had to be portrayed as an absorbing power to be feared and closely watched. North American intentions in Haiti (attempting to get Môle Saint-Nicolas), in the Dominican Republic (conspiring to obtain the Samaná Bay), and, finally, in the acquisition of Saint Thomas, were discussed and analyzed as instances of an expansionist impulse.[27] The examples of Mexico, "its territory dismembered by the ambition of the colossus," and of Nicaragua, where this "dangerous neighbor had created difficulties," were brought to confirm the perils facing the "weaker Latin republics" and the pre-cautions that should be taken against "the nation of Monroe."[28]

The name of "North American colossus" was changed in the working-class newspaper *Ensayo Obrero* to "colossal Republic" with a dramatic change in meaning, and to "great Republic" in *El País*, a San Juan newspaper advocating republican or antimonarchical ideals in the context of Spanish politics, owned by José Celso Barbosa, a black medical doctor educated in the United States.[29] Organized laborers were aware of the strength of working-class movements in the United States. Barbosa, an antimonarchical journalist, was attempting to represent the interests of the urban poor, mobilized as consumers in the face of the rising prices of imported foodstuffs of the 1890s. Spanish protectionism was a barrier between consumers and cheaper imports from the United States. Thus, *El País* frequently displayed admiration for the North American way of life and downplayed the United States as a threat to the island.

Newspapers followed closely a discussion held in 1896 in the Senate regard-ing the Monroe Doctrine. *El País* reprinted the text of Senator M. Davis justify-ing the main tenets behind the doctrine and proposing that the United States revive such principles. The editorial included no further comments, obviously wishing to let readers reach their own conclusions.[30] Similarly, in another article discussing U.S. acquisition of Saint Thomas, *El País* expressly refrained from the panicky attitude characterizing other reviews of the event, using the occasion to demand that Spain establish a free port in Puerto Rico in order to withstand the competition that the new nearby U.S. free port would represent.[31]

As inadvertent collaborators from abroad in the myth of the American dream, the journalists of *El País* described the U.S. as a place where all inhabi-tants had opportunities of betterment. The population of the United States was even described as "the best nourished and the happiest people in the world."[32] But the antimonarchical and radical *El País* was not alone in this attitude. Contradictorily, the conservative and pro-Spanish *Boletín Mercantil* also recited from that script by writing on behalf of Benjamin Franklin's work ethic, or by claiming that social mobility was accessible equally for the "less talented" and less educated segments of the population in the United States.[33]

However, many other articles transmitted fears of propertied groups in describing the U.S. legal system as "libertine" and the North American people as "dangerous."[34] *La Prensa*, a liberal newspaper of Mayagüez, depicted the North Americans in a more positive light as a strong people, capable of fierce competition because they were "active, intelligent and rich."[35] The fears went beyond the economic sphere to include possible undermining of the norms of the patriarchal family defended by educated men, as well as challenges to the Spanish language and the religious beliefs, all of which were sources of pride. Although some newspapers described with positive undertones the enormous advances of U.S. women in the public life of that country (praising the fact that it was done "without producing confusion of the functions of both sexes"), these pieces of information were undoubtedly an instrument for the construction of difference and a cause for misgivings among the educated male population of the colony.[36]

The conservative Spanish residents through their *Boletín Mercantil* furthered those fears with an article devoted to describing the way racism created tensions that were eroding the supposedly modern and successful North American Union. By contrast, continued the *Boletín*, in Spain the people of color were appreciated as good sons, deserving members of the Hispanic family.[37] The conservatives also noted, in their discussion of the possibility that certain U.S. interests would want to annex Cuba, that a Philadelphia newspaper had published an article that expressed alarm at the thought of annexing a territory of Spanish or African culture, where people did not speak English and were unprepared to be North American citizens. Furthermore, rephrased the *Boletín*, the article stated that the Cubans were effeminate, had a sickly aversion to all effort, were morally deficient, and were incapable of fulfilling the duties attached to citizenship.[38]

The anxieties expressed by the liberal lawyer Rosendo Matienzo Cintrón are revealing. If the United States occupied Puerto Rico, he pondered, "the vigorous strength of this young Saxon nation" would force Puerto Rico to assimilate "the source of life" from the mother country Spain. Otherwise, Puerto Ricans would be "pauperized" and condemned to disappear by virtue of "natural selection."[39] Making Spaniards out of the Puerto Rican population thus seemed an advisable strategy for the "regeneration of the race." Even working-class leaders shared in the discourse for regeneration, as was evident in an editorial in the newspaper *Ensayo Obrero* alluding in a tone of defeat to "*huestes enfermizas*" ("our sickly followers") and stating the need for the laboring people to "regenerate."[40]

The making of Spaniards in Puerto Rico required improved public education and cultivation of loyalty to Spanish national symbols. Spain was providing public education at a slow pace, with illiteracy in the colony at 85 percent of the population, not too distant from the percentage registered for the Peninsula. For autonomists the ideal conditions for education would be created once native leaders were allowed to administer the colony. Adhering to the Spanish "race" meant for them not only subscribing to a biological hierarchy above the native darker groups. It also entailed promotion of the Spanish language, to which writers, evidently, felt deeply attached, shared customs and family values, and even an attachment, albeit distant, to Catholicism. With this concept of turning inhabitants into their definition of "Spaniards," the native writers subverted determinist racism to promote a more optimistic and empowering discourse favorable to their projects of hegemony in the local sphere.

If fear of the "Northern colossus" was displayed and directed to serve specific needs, praise of North American qualities was used accordingly, as a model to be followed. Journalists paid attention to surprisingly minute details of North American political life. For example, a liberal newspaper commented on the 1871 message of the governor of the state of New York to the legislature and praised his good administration and behavior.[41] The United States became the model of a good system of public education in an article published in 1876 by a journalist criticizing a recent agreement of the Provincial Deputation. This representative body, interested in cutting expenses in the colonial budget, had reduced the salaries of certain categories of teachers.[42] Another newspaper praised the behavior of "colored men" in the states. It described the great expectation created by an exposition of black culture that was about to begin in New York, commenting that this was due to the "constant study and dedication of colored men in that rich country."[43]

An enormous amount of detail about the North American people was observed at a distance and without judgment. Readers of an article titled "The Electric Executioner" were informed that the state of New York had eliminated capital punishment by hanging, replacing it with electricity. Another titled "A Polyglot State" showed surprise that the last message of the governor of Minnesota was printed in ten different languages, so that the various immigrants that made up the population of that prosperous state could read it.[44]

The unmerciful materialism of North American society was an important paradigm taking shape toward the end of the century. By 1888 an editorial in *El Clamor del País* was establishing a "difference" by stating: "the North Americans are more realistic than us." The word "Yankee" became synonymous with "ambitious."[45] By the end of the century, the autonomist Mariano Abril was confirming what was already a cliché among Puerto Rican writers: the myth about the North Americans being a soulless people interested only in merchandise.[46] Spain was, by opposition, a model of idealism, the adjective "heroic" appearing in most apologetic statements about the "mother" country.

This trend, however, was attenuated by other more positive perspectives on North American culture. Even the critical eye of *La Democracia* (known for its emphasis on the myth of the "dangerous neighbor") was bound to counteract its effects by recalling something similar to the "American dream," another of the leading myths of the time:

> Given the well known proverbial egotism of the Yankees, our race is unable to understand certain eminently humane manifestations of that colossus. . . . The Yankees are, nonetheless, generous and flexible in the face of human misery, and this aspect of that great nation has to be studied inside its territory to be convinced of its truth by seeing the innumerable institutes devoted to beneficence, and in the face of its real cosmopolitism, by virtue of which it opens its arms and offers bread and home to immigrants, who lacking either abandon the land of their grandparents and knock at the door of that glorious American nation.[47]

In general, it is worth noting how ambivalent opinions could be. Taking this condition of the discourse of empire into account could prove rewarding for understanding shifting alliances in the late nineteenth century. Paul Nelson Chiles, in his 1942 doctoral dissertation, attempted to classify opinions according to political party (liberal or conservative) loyalties, and tried to find consistent alignments according to the economic, political, and cultural nature of the matters discussed. This type of approach to the study of the press in Puerto Rico rendered good results, but as Chiles acknowledged in the introduction to his work, even conservative Spaniards residing in the colony printed "friendly articles" about the United States.[48] Alignments were too fluid and tended to escape any attempt at establishing a fixed classification.

WRITING HISTORY: FROM INTERNATIONAL TO NATIONAL NARRATIVES

The writers' gaze at the past was many times international in scope and expressly political in its intentions. Historical paradigms confirmed the exemplary role attributed to the United States. A liberal journalist in Mayagüez presented a series of famous examples in history of the damaging effects of absolutism and compared them to the "greatness, power, glory and joy" seen in the United States, resulting from liberal doctrines and freedom. The fact that these doctrines when applied to the South American republics failed to create a similar effect (a historical argument that was very dear to the conservative writers of the colony because it proved to them how inadequate liberal doctrines were for the "Latin" race in America) was due to purely individual actions, to "the abuse of rulers usurping the rights of the citizen," acting as tyrants disguised as republicans.[49]

Evolutionist historical proposals were used in the 1890s to establish the ideals of a slow pace of political change and the inevitability of freedom and fully democratic institutions in the future. This is the conclusion of a series of articles by J. Contreras Ramos compiling the major moments in universal history: "Maybe the twentieth century will see the birth of the democratic monarchy or the conservative republic, as the logical and natural antecedent of the federative form. This perhaps will be the last evolution of our history."[50]

In this lengthy piece, Contreras gathers most of the salient motifs of the dominant discourse. He justifies the Spanish conquest of America by stating that the indigenous race was an inferior race, while the conquering race was superior.[51] The absolutist monarchy fulfilled a progressive mission in creating the modern nationalities.[52] The Declaration of the Rights of Men was the most brilliant page written after the Gospel.[53] The United States was the cradle of freedom and that nation's commitment to these ideals had allowed for its impressive progress: "[T]he history of its advances seems like a dream." But, regretting that materialist ideals have dominated North American society, Contreras adds that nowadays in the Anglo-Saxon America the "golden calf is adored."[54]

Working-class newspapers reproduced evolutionist historical schemes; their determinism, however, was a guarantee that social justice was at the end of the road of progress. Their firm belief in the power of what was intended to be a counter-discourse did not always succeed in breaking with ruling-class schemes:

> The despotic Roman Empire was followed by the monarchies softened by the charitable spirit of Christianity, and these were followed by constitutional monarchies and besides these, the modern republics

which have returned power to the people, the only sovereign that one day will rule the world. . . . The governments have to let loose, so to speak, without delays because the issues that agitate the people can be solved in the soft terrain of reason.[55]

Working-class writer Juan Williams paid special attention to (among other icons such as Toussaint L'Overture, the leader of Haitian independence) the epochal events taking place in the "land of Washington and Lincoln," as for him this was the beginning of a crucial process in the history of the working class. He, of course, had received this knowledge from native middle-class teachers and mentors, but was undoubtedly able to select from alternative views.[56] In choosing to highlight this type of event, workers negotiated with local autonomist leaders who were definitely interested in counting on their support.

In the convergence of autonomists and working-class leaders, the key historical icon was Rafael Cordero, the mid-nineteenth-century mulatto teacher and artisan in whose school black and white, rich and poor children of the neighborhood in San Juan could equally receive an elementary education for free. Symbol of the multiracial identity and cross-class alliance that were being constructed, and honored equally by middle- and working-class writers (some of whom had been his students), the figure of Cordero was not omitted from the historical landmarks of Juan Williams, along with the "great laborer of Maguncia, Guttenberg, to whom we owe our current progress and freedom," Benjamin Franklin and others.[57] For the autonomist middle-class historian Salvador Brau, however, it was important to mention in his biography of Cordero (at a conference in the Ateneo Puertorriqueño) that, as opposed to Toussaint or Dessalines, Cordero did not redden the pages of Puerto Rican history with blood, but brightened it with a charitable spirit.[58] Thus, nation-building narratives, with their inner class tensions, were inseparable from the international frame of mind in which writers seemed to operate.

The historical events of the Spanish conquest and colonization of Puerto Rico also captured the attention of the educated public. All through the second half of the nineteenth century, a relatively large group of native writers of geography textbooks to be used in public (namely, municipal) and private schools, had engaged in establishing a very basic factual framework concerning the history of the Spanish presence in Puerto Rico. In the parts concerning local geography, their historical protagonist was the island of Puerto Rico, always depicted as a "province" of Spain. The "people" of Puerto Rico occasionally emerged in these writings as a historical actor composed of a mixture of Spanish, Indian, and

African "blood" and customs.[59] In these, as in many other instances, the foundational historical paradigm was Fray Iñigo Abbad y Lasierra's eighteenth-century study of the conquest of the island of Puerto Rico (based on the chronicles of Herrera and Oviedo) and of the racial components and customs of the population. This seminal work was a product of enlightened reformist attitudes under the rule of Charles III.[60] The edition annotated by José Julián Acosta in 1866, along with prior literary romantic and *costumbrista* narratives, all joined in to create the imaginary ethnic prototype of the *jíbaro*, the Puerto Rican peasant.

Evidently interested in compiling and verifying knowledge about the role played by the island of Puerto Rico in the events of the Spanish and international histories with which professionals were familiar, native amateur historians, such as the medical doctor Cayetano Coll y Toste, practiced careful research and reading of chronicles and documents. The interest in the history of the Spanish conquest was particularly stimulated by the colonial government's official celebrations in 1892 of the fourth centennial of the discovery of America, and in 1893 of the island of Puerto Rico, which generated further debate and reflections. Coll y Toste himself related how the functionaries in charge of placing a commemorative monument on the exact site where Christopher Columbus's expedition had disembarked, asked him to present convincing proof of his theory on the subject, for the exact location was a matter of heated debate among several other professional and amateur historians. Coll y Toste engaged in a rigorous exposition establishing one location by contrasting different sources and cautiously deploying logical deductions. His essay was prized and published in 1893 in the form of a book titled *Colón en Puerto Rico*.[61]

Historical research more or less based on current methods and with scientific claims was being developed in a semiprofessional manner by other native writers such as the public functionary and journalist Salvador Brau.[62] Considered the initiator of Puerto Rican historiography, Brau did not publish his *Historia de Puerto Rico* until 1904. But the compilation of documents and the establishment of facts through debate had been taking place since the mid-nineteenth century.[63] Some of the key interpretive paradigms were created by the eighteenth-century work of Fray Iñigo Abbad y Lasierra. Certain aspects of the imaginary frontier separating the subjects of the King of Spain from the libertine northern foreigners occupying and attacking the Antilles had been initially drawn in this foundational work of 1782. The English attack of 1797 was thus interpreted in that tradition, as a foreign intrusion followed by a decisive defense of local authorities and native population, all fighting together to preserve Spanish rule in Puerto Rico. The date remained as a historical landmark.[64]

History writing was defended on the grounds of exploring the Puerto Rican peculiarities as a province of Spain. This is the message conveyed by the liberal Spanish journalist Manuel Fernández Juncos in the prologue of the 1878 historical-geographical description of the island written by a native-born member of the Spanish army in the colony, Manuel Ubeda y Delgado. Fernández Juncos was surprised to see that in Puerto Rico "there were educated youngsters who knew fairly well the history and geography of other countries, but ignored completely that of their native land."[65] Manuel Elzaburu Vizcarrondo advanced a similar argument in a conference about the relationship of history with literature, read in 1888 in the *Ateneo Puertorriqueño*, which he then presided. He argued that the provincial peculiarities of Puerto Rico had to be captured in its literary history, as was being done in other Spanish provinces. Historians had to look at literature to discover the essential characteristics of the period they wished to study. A complete Puerto Rican bibliography of literary works had to be compiled, and this task, argued Elzaburu, had only just begun with the auspices of the *Ateneo*. The local government had to provide support by creating placements for librarians and archive personnel, as provincial governments did in the Balearic and the Canary Islands.[66]

However, government support was concentrated on the commemoration of Columbus's voyages. Thus, in the 1890s, Christopher Columbus turned out to be the most generally revered figure, even in working-class newspapers.[67] More pro-Spanish texts also honored Queen Isabella and took pride on the "Latin race," while a more critical writer used the occasion to recall that the most meaningful aspect of the discovery of America was that it was the land of Washington and Bolívar.[68]

In a collection of essays commemorating the centennial of the discovery of Puerto Rico promoted by the *Revista Puertorriqueña*, the native woman writer Fidela Mateu de Rodríguez wrote an essay titled "¡Pobres Indios!" expressing guilty feelings about being Spanish, a descendant of the exterminators of the indigenous population of the island.[69] In making this incursion into the public discussion, Mateu was incorporating a new style in the expression of feeling and attempting, from a feminine vantage point, which had previously been excluded from the public sphere, to participate in current democratizing movements. A male writer introduced Mateu to the readers in a patronizing manner. Even so, it is interesting that she was bringing into the public sphere, in a blunt and perhaps naively straightforward manner, a nostalgic attitude toward the extinct indigenous population, constructed as an "otherness" from a Spanish point of view.

The indigenous population acquired a different meaning in the more scientific gaze of naturalist Agustín Stahl. The "mysterious race" (in the words of Stahl) had become the object of interest of writers seeking to establish a prehistoric area of knowledge with greater precision. Stahl and Coll y Toste, another well-known expert in classifying stone objects (publishing his book *Prehistoria de Puerto Rico* in 1897), attempted to understand Indians according to universal prehistorical knowledge accepted at the time and to place Puerto Rico within that wider context accordingly. They were, at the same time, as Christopher Schmidt-Nowara has keenly observed, marking a territory, making a connection with a remote non-Spanish past that allowed for a Puerto Rican national perspective or claiming a physical place prior to the Spanish presence.[70] However, it seems clear that in their historical imagination, Spain and "civilization" in general eventually took the lead, especially whenever the very same writers changed focus to contemplate the recurrent image of the clashing empires.[71]

Ana Roque, a schoolteacher and writer of a geography textbook, participating in the commemorations of 1893, constructed a revealing map of loyalties. She conciliated loyalties to Spain and to Puerto Rico, all within a liberal universal framework. On defining the word *patria* she thinks first in "our brothers" all over the "Universe," second in Spain, "the heroic nation that makes us proud of great deeds, and protects us with its flag, in the noble Mother that gave us her language, customs and culture." Finally, she thinks of Puerto Rico as "the splendid region, the piece of Castilian land" where she was born.[72]

The implications and meanings of being Spanish were, in one way or another, the main preoccupation in the historical reflections of middle-class intellectuals. Mostly concerned with current demands for political change, Salvador Brau delved into materials serving as proof of the island's authentic loyalty to Spain, which made it deserving of a more liberal regime. His excellent piece titled "Lo que dice la historia" is a bitter series of letters of 1893 that were published in his newspaper *El Clamor del País*, and republished by a group of Puerto Ricans in Madrid when legislators imposed a more restrictive electoral law on Puerto Rico than the one granted to Cuba. The Spaniards justified this discriminatory policy on the grounds that Puerto Rico had a larger number of small landowners and taxpayers, and, therefore, the quota of land tax paid to be enfranchised had to be higher than that of Cuba in order to keep the number of voters in a similar proportion to the total population. In these articles Brau reproaches the Madrid authorities for their ignorance of the history of Puerto Rico and gives a fairly detailed recounting of occasions in which the islanders had demonstrated that they were as good and loyal as any other Spaniard. During the wars of independence in the continental colonies, for example, he pointed out that the island's loyalty was not due to a lack of opportunities to rebel:

> It is not that [Puerto Rico] lacked revolutionary suggestions; it is not that the circumstances restrained parricidal intentions; it is not that the gusts of the tempest did not reach its coasts. It is that in the idiosyncrasy of our people, blind love for the native soil and the persevering cult of the [Spanish] nationality appear historically confounded in a single sentiment, which not even the most painful deceptions have been able to pry apart.[73]

Interestingly, in interpreting the booming illegal trade with foreigners of the earlier colonial centuries, Brau alludes to the whiteness of the population to justify their rights as Spaniards. He first explains that contraband was not the inhabitants' fault, lacking other means to fulfill their needs for clothing and agricultural tools. Second, the process worked to the benefit of the colony because in their relations with foreigners, the natives "procured the selection of the European race by means of marriages of their daughters with the maritime merchants, bringing them to reside in the country, though never consenting to pretensions harmful to the nationality which, as a sacred inheritance, they had received from their progenitors."[74] This allusion confirms the persistence of "whitening" projects and racist concerns, and the inclination to use such racist arguments as negotiating tools to obtain concessions from metropolitan statesmen, even when a multiracial identity was considered politically more advisable.

Since his works represent the foundation of a long process of historical reflection in Puerto Rico, Brau's text deserves attention. History and political negotiation were inseparable in the colony, and racist discourses were interwoven with reflections on the past. The politics of the native educated elites, though committed to the ideal of universal male suffrage and a multiracial Puerto Rican identity, entailed a hierarchy of races inseparable from their own class perspective.

Conclusions

The Puerto Rican elite expressed diverse visions of empire. Some expressions reveal pride in their Spanish or partially Spanish ancestry, in their sharing the official language and religion of Castile. This allowed them to claim rule over the native population, and to endeavor through education to make them fit in civilized imperial designs. But scripts were extremely adjustable to the leading historical and geopolitical paradigms of the time, which deployed a binary schema of competition between the United States (or the Anglo-Saxon race) and Spain (or the Latin race). Although the opinions varied depending on the specific goals pursued, these sometimes contradictory statements can be read as integral parts of a very malleable discourse of negotiation. Writers in Puerto Rico were able to distribute praise and reproach at will, in accordance with specific goals. Not one single view managed to acquire a decidedly authoritative status.

Both Spain and the United States were directly or indirectly depicted as multicultural nations capable of containing the Puerto Rican nationality. The word "national" was reserved for the "larger" consciously chosen Spanish nationality, and after 1898 it was conveniently applied to the United States. The script had an inseparable coda signaling the strength of local identity and the claims of exclusive domain. At the same time, in the discursive constructions of the Puerto Rican identity a universal dimension is usually present, signaling a conscious wish to participate in modern cosmopolitanism, possibly inserted within the local discussion by way of the Spanish Krausist movement.[75] The general dynamic is that of the interplay between distrust for foreign influence and fear of isolation, the latter more pronounced in women's and workers' texts.

The writing of history in Puerto Rico adhered to international paradigms in the nineteenth century. Building the historical subject of the people of Puerto Rico was a conscious endeavor of men and women writers not necessarily linked to a rejection of the "Spanish nationality." However, the reading of these texts acquires new meaning if read with a different code, namely that of the social tensions contained in the prevailing class, ethnic, racial, and gender hierarchies. Nation-building narratives then operate as the native writers' claims of domain and exclusiveness over a territory easily defined in geographical terms as the "island." These claims deployed through ethnicity, in the face of Spanish-born "intruders" occupying offices and jobs in the colony, for example, or out of fears of women breaking out of the domestic sphere imagining abstract "universal" equality, or workers developing an imaginary universal brotherhood of laborers. In their political projects local writers negotiated with popular groups, strategizing to keep a balance between their awareness of the importance of popular support in modern politics (for late-nineteenth-century standards), and the need they perceived for tutoring those groups as inferior beings waiting for the benefits of "civilization." They thus shared a long list of values and meanings with the imperial representatives.

The effects of the symbolic fray of words as far as empire policy is concerned might have been limited. Perhaps of greater significance was the enormous impact this ambiguous play with words "from the frontier of empires" had on the making of the Puerto Rican nationality, by stimulating a continuous process of redefinition and strengthening of identity. While the political imagination of the time was filled with all sorts of reflections about clashing empires and Puerto Rico's role in the conflict, many other issues remained locked out of public discussion. The question of identity and the relations to the great empires monopolized a large fragment of the public sphere. Thus, considered within the colonial territory, the negotiating discourse had an undoubtedly empowering effect on local elites by postponing other tensions.

NOTES

1. Jaime Alberto Solivan de Acosta, "Don José Julián de Acosta y Calbo," I:23 in *Escritos de don José Julián de Acosta y Calbo*, 3 vols., ed. Jaime Alberto Solivan de Acosta (Carolina: First Book Publishing of Puerto Rico, 1995–97); Lidio Cruz Monclova, *Historia de Puerto Rico (siglo XIX)*, 6th ed., 3 vols. (Río Piedras: Editorial Universitaria, 1970), I:463.

2. He undoubtedly refers to the Swiss explorer and scientist Horace Bénédict de Saussure, to the Venezuelan writer Andrés Bello, and to the German geographer Alexander von Humboldt.

3. Translation of "me sumergieron en una larga serie de reflexiones sobre la influencia de la raza anglosajona en la marcha de la civilización." José Julián Acosta, "Horas de prisión," in *Escritos*, I:65–69, esp. 68.

4. Acosta had devoted time to the study of the life and ideas of Jovellanos, one of the founders of the reformist current of thought in eighteenth-century Spain. See "Jovellanos" (unpublished manuscript), Colección Acosta, Centro de Investigaciones Históricas, Universidad de Puerto Rico.

5. See Aida R. Caro Costas, "The Outpost of Empire," 9–24 in Arturo Morales Carrión, *Puerto Rico: A Political and Cultural History* (New York: W. W. Norton, 1983); María Rosario Sevilla Soler, *Las Antillas y la independencia de la América española (1808–1826)* (Sevilla: Escuela de Estudios Hispanoamericanos-Consejo Superior de Investigaciones Científicas, 1986).

6. Luis Martínez-Fernández, *Torn between Empires: Economy, Society, and Patterns of Political Thought in the Hispanic Caribbean, 1840–1878* (Athens: University of Georgia Press, 1994), 20–21.

7. For a brief discussion of the main U.S. imperialist theses, see María Dolores Luque de Sánchez, *La ocupación norteamericana y la ley Foraker (la opinión pública puertorriqueña) 1898–1904* (Río Piedras: Editorial Universitaria, 1980), 23–25.

8. For a discussion on the concept of "frontier" and the need to consider the "interimperial dimension," see Jeremy Adelman and Stephen Aron, *Forum Essay*. "From Borderlands to Borders: Empires, Nation-States, and the Peoples in Between in North American History," *American Historical Review* 104 (June 1999): 814–41.

9. See Stuart Hall, "When was 'The Post-Colonial'? Thinking at the Limit," 242–60, esp. 257, in *The Post-Colonial Question: Common Skies, Divided Horizons*, ed. Ian Chambers and Lidia Curti (reprint; London: Routledge, 1998).

10. Martínez-Fernández, *Torn between Empires*. For an older work (1942) depicting local views on the United States, see Paul Nelson Chiles, *The Puerto Rican Press Reaction to the United States, 1888–1898* (Reprint edition by Arno Press, 1975).

11. A writer of 1899 used the metaphor of Cuba and Puerto Rico standing over "an inclined plain" necessarily leading to freedom from Spain. Enrique J. Marques, *Cuba y Puerto Rico* (Puerto-Rico: Imprenta de *El País*, 1899). See a critique of the determinist views in Christopher Schmidt-Nowara, *Empire and Slavery: Spain, Cuba, and Puerto Rico, 1833–1874* (Pittsburgh: University of Pittsburgh Press, 1999), 6.

12. For a brief theoretical article on the power of discourse, see Pedro Cardim, "Entre textos y discursos: La historiografía y el poder del lenguaje," *Cuadernos de Historia Moderna*, Universidad Complutense, Madrid, 17 (1996).

13. José Pablo Morales, "Ideas de un jíbaro sobre la reforma" (manuscript, 1865), Colección Acosta, Centro de Investigaciones Históricas, Universidad de Puerto Rico, Río Piedras.

14. The text reads as follows: "We are not only a European power. We are also an American power. . . . The Latin race needs us. It needs Spain to counteract the impetus of the Saxon race." Extract from a speech in the Spanish Cortes at Madrid, reproduced sympathetically by the prestigious *Boletín Mercantil*, in an article entitled "España en América," 8 February 1871.

15. See the inferiority of the "mixed" and dark races discussed in an article reprinted from *El País* in *El Clamor del País*, 14 April 1888.

16. *El Ponceño*, 8 January 1853.

17. See, for example, *Boletín Mercantil*, 28 November 1873.

18. Ibid., 20 January 1871; 9 November 1892.

19. Ibid., 24 January 1875; 7 March 1875.

20. Morales, "Ideas de un jíbaro."

21. José Pablo Morales, *Misceláneas históricas* (San Juan: La Correspondencia, 1924), 53.

22. *El Clamor del País*, 13 November 1883.

23. Salvador Brau, *Ensayos (Disquisiciones sociológicas)* (Río Piedras: Edil, 1972), 168.

24. *La Correspondencia*, 28 August 1892, quoted by Manuel Alvarado Morales, "Idea acerca de Estados Unidos de América en los periódicos *La Correspondencia* y *La Democracia* (1890–1898)" (M.A. thesis, Department of History, University of Puerto Rico, 1975), 86.

25. Cruz Monclova, *Historia*, II:127–28.

26. *El Progreso*, 6 April 1873.

27. The name "colossus" appears in the conservative Spanish newspaper of San Juan, *Boletín Mercantil*, as early as 14 December 1873, and again in the autonomist newspaper of the 1890s, *La Democracia*. See, for example, 21 November 1894; 26 February and 2 March 1896.

28. *La Democracia*, 28 March 1895. The idea of autonomy as a means to avoid absorption of the Spanish Antilles by the United States was proposed by the Spanish republican leader Rafael María de Labra. See Alvarado Morales, "Idea acerca de Estados Unidos," 72–73.

29. *Ensayo Obrero*, 19 December 1897; *El País*, 4 January 1896.

30. "La Doctrina Monroe," *El País*, 6 February 1896.

31. "Sobre la venta de Saint Thomas," *Id.*, 22 February 1896.

32. *El País*, 23 January 1896.

33. *Boletín Mercantil*, 10 February 1882.

34. *La Democracia*, 21 November 1894.

35. *La Prensa*, Mayagüez, 19 February 1880.

36. Ibid. See also the article "La actividad de los Norte-Americanos" in *La Prensa*, 29 July 1880.

37. "Qué contraste," *Boletín Mercantil*, 19 August 1887.

38. *Boletín Mercantil*, 16 June 1889.

39. Quoted in Luis M. Díaz Soler, *Rosendo Matienzo Cintrón: Orientador y guardián de una cultura* (San Juan: Instituto de Cultura Puertorriqueña, 1960), 2 vols., I:142–43.

40. *Ensayo Obrero*, 19 December 1897.

41. *El Progreso*, 3 February 1871.

42. *La Prensa*, Mayagüez, 14 December 1876.

43. *El Clamor del País*, 2 June 1888.

44. Ibid.

45. See, for example, *La Correspondencia*, 16 July 1891.

46. *La Correspondencia*, 19 June 1898.

47. *La Democracia*, 18 March 1895.

48. Chiles, *The Puerto Rican Press*, viii, 96–97.

49. "Contra el supuesto abuso de la libertad," *La Razón*, 15 October 1870. See another reproduction of the historical beginnings of liberal regimes in the United States when "Washington signed the famous Federal Constitution of 1774" in *La Razón*, 3 January 1873.

50. *La Ilustración Puertorriqueña*, 10 February 1893.

51. Ibid., 25 December 1892.

52. Ibid., 10 March 1893.

53. Ibid., 25 November 1892.

54. Ibid., 25 January 1893.

55. *Justicia*, 25 March 1894.

56. See, for example, Juan Williams, *Hojas de palma: Colección de artículos enciclopédicos* (Ponce: Biblioteca Popular, Imp. El Telégrafo, 1895), 7.

57. Ibid., 61.

58. Brau, "Rafael Cordero," 31 October 1891, *Ensayos*, 159.

59. See Marta E. Vázquez Santos, "La enseñanza de geografía política de Puerto Rico durante el siglo XIX : 1852–1898" (M.A. thesis, Univeresity of Puerto Rico, 2001).

60. See Fray Agustín Iñigo Abbad y Lasierra, *Historia geográfica, civil, natural de la isla de San Juan Bautista de Puerto Rico* (Río Piedras: Editorial Universitaria, 1979), 85–89.

61. See "Epistolario del Dr. José G. Padilla: Carta al Dr. Coll y Toste referente a su libro Colón en Puerto Rico," 8 de abril de 1894, *Boletín Histórico de Puerto Rico* 10 (1923): 330–31; "Puertorriqueños Ilustres: El Padre Nazario," *Boletín Histórico de Puerto Rico* 11 (1924): 181–84; *Boletín Histórico de Puerto Rico* 13 (1926): 15.

62. For the labeling of this period's historical works as scientific, see Isabel Gutiérrez del Arroyo, *Historiografía puertorriqueña* (San Juan: Instituto de Cultura Puertorriqueña, 1957).

63. See Alejandro Tapia y Rivera, *Biblioteca Histórica de Puerto Rico* (Puerto Rico: Imprenta de Marquez, 1854).

64. Coll y Toste wrote a rigorous historical essay in 1892 (recognized by the Sociedad Económica de Amigos del País in 1897 on the event of the centennial of the attack) using that date as one of the landmarks in the evolution of the "Puerto Rican civilization." See Cayetano Coll y Toste, "De la civilización de Puerto Rico en 1797, desde el punto de vista moral y material, y breve estudio comparativo entre el estado de cultura de aquella época y el actual," *Boletín Histórico de Puerto Rico* 1 (1914): 162–79.

65. Manuel Fernández Juncos, "Prólogo," in Manuel Ubeda y Delgado, *Isla de Puerto Rico: Estudio histórico, geográfico y estadístico de la misma* (Puerto-Rico: Tip. Boletín Mercantil, 1878).

66. Manual Elzaburu Vizcarrondo, "Una relación de la historia con la literatura," in *Prosas, poemas y conferencias* (San Juan: Instituto de Cultura Puertorriqueña, 1971), 214–26.

67. See *Revista Obrera*, Ponce, 19 November 1893.

68. *La Correspondencia*, 12 October 1892.

69. Fidela Mateu de Rodríguez, "¡Pobres Indios!" *Revista Puertorriqueña: Album del Centenario de Puerto Rico*, 1893.

70. Christopher Schimdt-Nowara, "Conquering Categories: The Problem of Prehistory in Nineteenth-Century Puerto Rico and Cuba," *Centro Journal* 13 (spring 2001): 5–21.

71. A well-known and many times quoted passage by Coll y Toste is the one stating his recollection of the day Spanish authorities handed the city of San Juan to the North American military forces in 1898. He watched the ceremony from the balcony of his house and recalled to have had a struggle in his conscience between "his Latin heart" and his "Saxon head." *Boletín Histórico de Puerto Rico* 6 (1919): 29–32, esp. 31.

72. Ana Roque, "Patria," *Revista Puertorriqueña. Album del Centenario de Puerto Rico*, 1893.

73. Salvador Brau, "Lo que dice la historia," *Ensayos*, 170.

74. Ibid., 167.

75. See J. López-Morillas, *El krausismo español* (México: Fondo de Cultura Económica, 1980).

CHAPTER FOUR

"SPAIN AND AMERICA: ALL IS ONE"
Historiography of the Conquest and Colonization
of the Americas and National Mythology
in Spain c. 1892–c. 1992

Antonio Feros

INTRODUCTION

*I*n a collection of essays published in 1887, *Heregías: Estudios de crítica inductiva sobre asuntos españoles*, Pompeyo Gener wished to help Spaniards reflect upon their own and other identities by offering his views on nationalism and nation building. Among his ideas are some that are particularly important for the topic of this chapter and, in general, for the topics addressed in this volume. First, according to Gener, *nation* must be understood not as "socially and historically" constructed but as a natural and timeless creation. Each nation, he claims, has its natural "essence or spirit," which is present from the very beginning and which remains unaltered in the face of historical, racial, and political processes and experiences. Second, all nations are the result of an aggregation or mixing of various "races," at least in the moment of their actual formation. Third, nations do not need to be constrained within the borders of a self-contained territory. There are some conditions—language and religion, for example—that made and make possible the creation of "empires," which in time become "empire-nations" composed of several territories in various continents. Gener believes that Islam, Buddhism, and Christianity, especially its Catholic branch, are "universal religions" that naturally need to expand and to convert others, thus becoming the bedrock of empires. In the Spanish case, language and religion, indeed, helped to create an "empire-nation" composed of territories in Europe, America, and Africa, all of them sharing one language, one religion, and the "Spanish essence" due to the racial miscegenation that took place in each of the territories that formed Spain. Equally important is that, even if some of these territories became independent to form a particular "state"—the American territories formerly under Spanish sovereignty, for example—their inhabitants continued to be an essential part of a "transnational" Spanish community. Fourth, the "idea" of Spain, or better still, the awareness among a people that they were members of a nation called Spain, existed at least from the end of the fifteenth century, and coincided with the completion of the so-called "*Reconquista*" (reconquest) of the Iberian peninsula against the Moors. Fifth, Gener believes that there were three important moments, all of them characterized by confrontations against other peoples and nations, that helped develop a clear meaning of Spanishness: the already mentioned "Reconquista" against Muslim communities in the Iberian peninsula; the "wars sustained to colonize the New World"; and the war of resistance against the imperial Napoleonic army.

Pompeyo Gener also reflected upon who had more influence in the nation-building processes, and, although he acknowledged the role played by governments, he believed that the most important means to help people identify themselves as members of a nation are "chronicles, histories, poems, symphonies, statues and monuments." In Spain some chivalric heroes and rulers conquered territories, defeated enemies, and created the laws and institutions that made possible the persistence of the nation. But historians, poets, and chroniclers "created the national spirit, unified all groups and kingdoms, and wrote their history," thus helping to construct the conscious Self of a nation called Spain.[1]

Gener's conceptions are important here because they clearly convey contemporary views about the concepts and processes that made Spain similar to but also different from other "nations." Some of these views are also important because in time they became the keystones of both the dominant official and scholarly imperial narrative in nineteenth- and twentieth-century Spain: that both nation and empire had multiethnic foundations; that the Spanish nation cannot be understood without its imperial past, and vice versa; and that for a nation to truly exist it needs to be conceived in histories, poems, and public representations. This essay addresses these and other views on the construction of Spanish national history. More specifically, it discusses an essential chapter in national history and the invention of Spanish nationalism: views, from inside and outside academia, on the Spanish conquest and colonization of America, since the late nineteenth century. In other words, the purpose of this chapter is to analyze the genesis of a Spanish imperial and colonial narrative, how different interpretations were made uniform to create a master narrative, and how this master narrative acted as a cultural and political unifier of the peoples in the Iberian Peninsula.

In a book that aims at analyzing the various historiographical paradigms that have dominated the study of Spanish colonialism in the Americas and the responses of some Latin American countries to their colonial pasts, it seems important to recover the origins and foundations of these various paradigms. In this essay, the aim is to reconstruct the creation of a paradigm that many historians have identified simply as a reaction to the so-called Black Legend, thus creating the White Legend of Spanish imperialism.[2] Indeed, modern scholars have analyzed the literature on the Spanish empire published in Spain or by Spanish authors after 1880, first, as a response to foreign critiques against Spain's policies and actions in its American colonies, a reaction that has its origins in the eighteenth-century "dispute over America" and the controversies during the movements of independence in Hispanic America,[3] second, as a post-colonial attempt to engulf the independent nations in Hispanic America into agreeing to recognize Spain as the civilizing fatherland and the leader in the struggle against the United States of America's imperialism; and, third, as an attempt at legitimating the "neo-imperial" ideology of Franco's regime.[4] There is no doubt that all these intentions and goals played a role in the development of a specific imperial narrative in modern Spain. After all, historical narratives, to use Sara Mills's words, "do not occur in isolation but in dialogue, in relation to or, more often, in contrast and opposition to other groups of utterances."[5]

It is argued here, however, that the Spanish master narrative on the conquest and colonization of the Americas created since the late nineteenth century was not only a defensive reaction to foreign attacks. The ultimate aim of the Spanish imperial narrative was, in effect, to serve the process of nation building by trying to uncover all experiences, moments, and theories that made clear the existence of a unique Spanish Self shared by all regions, and by all racial, social, and political groups that were part of the Spanish empire from the sixteenth to the nineteenth century. In other words, this imperial and colonial narrative appeared as a central chapter in the process of constructing Spanish nationalism,[6] and the centrality of such endeavor is, I believe, what gave this narrative its power and continuity. If there is something that needs to be emphasized, it is that during more than a hundred years there were no important challenges or critiques to the hegemonic view of Spain's imperial past, and that, at least from the late nineteenth century to the late twentieth century, liberal and conservative scholars and governments basically agreed upon the central components of this imperial narrative. And this happened, it is important to remember, during a period dominated by the existence of contrasting views on the past, present, future, and meaning of Spain,[7] and also by armed conflicts (remember the Spanish Civil War, 1936–1939), in which contenders defended at least two radically different perspectives on Spain and its "essence." In other words, if since the 1870s there were various and conflicting views on the identity and the history of Spain as an Iberian nation, there was, however, only one view about the identity of Spain as a global empire.

I have divided this essay into two different sections. One, "Legends," covers the late nineteenth century until the 1930s, the period of systematic construction of a mythology about the history of Spain as an imperial and colonial power. The second part, "Histories," discusses books and articles published after 1940, a time characterized by the continuity of the discourse discussed in the previous section, but also by the creation and institutionalization of the history of America as an academic discipline. As we shall see, there were not many differences between both periods regarding the basic components of the master imperial narrative, but there were some variations in the arguments used to legitimate it. During the first period, unable to agree upon the history of Spain as a nation, scholars and the various Spanish governments needed to find moments, deeds, enterprises that could be identified as "Spanish" (as opposed to Castilian, Catalan, Galician, liberal, or conservative), and nothing better—to use again Pompeyo Gener's words—than "the wars sustained to colonize the New World" and the three centuries of Spanish presence in America that followed them. In the second period, the institutionalization of the "History of America" made it possible to defend this imperial narrative as an "objective truth" based not on counterfeit data but on genuine and internationally credited "scientific" research.

Some preliminary words and statements are, however, necessary. In her book *American Pentimento*, Patricia Seed has written that historians "are not yet trained to examine critically differing national and regional expectations of narratives, themes, and subjects in the writing of comparative history. Yet such a step is necessary for history to transcend national boundaries."[8] As I understand her words, what historians should do is not to escape from national history—however defined—but to make every effort to understand the particular processes, contexts, and ideas that made it possible for each community to imagine itself as a separate, different, even exceptional entity with its own distinct history. What is important here, therefore, is not so much to declare once again that all nations are "imagined communities," or that all of them followed one or another nation-building "model." Rather, what matters in this essay is to identify and understand the "differing [Spanish] expectations of narratives." This is not an essay in comparative history, and indeed our point of departure rejects the existence of a "shared European mentality"[9] that allegedly made all experiences similar. Nations were viewed as different and were diversely historicized,[10] and the same should be said about empires, which were based on different discourses, ideologies, and aims, and responded to an enormous variety of changing conditions.[11] In addition, historians are now paying attention to the existence of different European concepts and perceptions of non-European populations, the role played by racialist theories to identify and classify them, and the contrasting political and intellectual consequences of these different discourses.[12] When confronted with the work of those who discussed Spanish imperial history, we find that in Spain the main approach was not the defense of racial superiority and therefore the defense of a racialist concept of Spanishness. In general, Spaniards advocated the idea of "mestizaje," both "cultural" and "biological," between all ethnic groups involved, voluntarily or forced, in the colonization of America. These views became the foundation of one of the most persistent myths or legends in the Spanish colonization of the Americas: that all Hispanic societies are in essence racial democracies.

Legends

Discussions on the character and history of the Spanish empire began well before the nineteenth century, but they never crystallized into a well-structured and encompassing narrative. There were, indeed, hundreds of books, articles, and pamphlets vindicating Spanish colonialism in the Americas, but in general Spanish scholars did not worry about writing a history of the Spanish empire, or tried to integrate the imperial experience into the history of the "nation."[13] As Carolyn Boyd has written, "most authors were content to observe that Spain had brought 'civilization' and religion to the New World, and had received little economic benefit in return."[14] Things began to change after the 1870s, coinciding with the so-called "Restauración," a political movement led by Antonio Cánovas del Castillo aimed at creating a conservative regime.[15] Political stability, claimed the leaders of this movement, was required not only "to restore more traditional (i.e., monarchical and centralizing) forms of government," but also to recover the true Self of the nation. This is what explains why so many general histories of Spain were published during this period, and an increase in the number of commissions by the crown and other public authorities (the Parliament, the Government, and professional institutions) of paintings and sculptures representing individuals and events that epitomized this Spanish self.[16] Equally important is that, most probably influenced by the proximity of the fourth centenary of Columbus's first voyage, and the colonial crisis Spain had to confront in Cuba, Puerto Rico, and the Philippines (1868–1898), some institutions, especially the Royal Academy of History, started to pay more attention to the need of writing the "true" history of Spain in America.[17]

Before scholars were able to put together a narrative of the history of Spain in the Americas, however, they needed to develop, first, a clear understanding of the specificity of the Spanish nation and, second, to produce a well-reasoned explanation of the virtues of colonization in general and Spanish colonization in particular. The first task was assumed by Antonio Cánovas del Castillo, the architect and leader of the Restauración, in an influential lecture he gave in 1882, entitled *Discurso sobre la nación*,[18] which included, if not a highly original theorization of the Spanish nation, certainly a detailed set of ideas that helped other intellectuals to couple national and imperial Spanish history. First, Cánovas believed that a nation does not need to be bounded territorially and defended the idea that there were a few "super nations" integrating many peoples from various territories located on more than one continent. One of these "super nations" was the Spanish or Hispanic, integrated by peoples in the Iberian Peninsula and Spanish America. Based on this idea, Cánovas characterized the wars of independence in Spanish America not as a war to free colonies from a "tyrannical" metropolis, but a "civil war among Spaniards."[19] Equally important, Cánovas alleged that the only way to unify peoples of different cultures, races, languages, and religions was the Spanish way, which did not rely on brutal conquest, but on the construction of a spiritual brotherhood. In this sense, Cánovas emphasized Spaniards' conviction in the common origins of all human races and that the only differences among them were physiological, the result of secular adaptations to dissimilar natural conditions.[20]

If Cánovas offered a very positive view of Spain as a transatlantic and multiracial nation, Maldonado Macanaz offered a highly articulated examination of Spanish colonialism, which he viewed as the most perfect colonialism in the history of humankind.[21] Colonialism, according to Maldonado Macanaz, was both "divine and human," meaning that texts identified as sacred (the Bible) and what he calls "modern philosophy" order humans to "multiply and populate the earth," and therefore to expand. Nothing is more dignifying for a nation, he claims, than "to discover islands and unknown lands, establish prosperous settlements, teach and civilize savage populations."[22] As other authors before and after him, Maldonado also upholds Catholics' belief in the common origins of all humans: "we are all brothers and equal in God's eyes,"[23] also insisting that this belief is what truly differentiates Spanish from English colonialism. The Anglo-Saxon race, for instance, does not like to live among peoples who have different customs, and certainly does not promote any kind of racial and ethnic assimilation; on the contrary, "according to the level of resistance they encounter from the natives, Anglo-Saxons limit themselves to two possible options: they exterminate all natives or oppress them."[24] Against this grim picture of Anglo-Saxon attitudes toward the colonized, Maldonado represents the

Spanish colonial system as one based on higher moral grounds because it employed humanitarian and paternalistic methods to civilize "savages." Maldonado claims, for example, that Spaniards encountered in America a population that was scattered across diverse tribes, whose number was smaller than claimed by foreigners, and who were naturally contrary to work. Despite these obstacles, Spain triumphed in its attempts to civilize and modernize them, without having to use "any kind of tyranny and without having to exterminate these inferior races." Spaniards were always against the enslavement of the natives, who otherwise were treated as "minors" and therefore had the fundamental "right" to be protected against violent colonizers, but also against themselves and their natural instincts. The humanitarian principles extended to the ways Spaniards acted toward African slaves. As happened with Native Americans, African slaves received a treatment that was "much softer, [more] humane and liberal than the treatment they received in the French and the British colonies"; Spaniards, for example, baptized all slaves, let them marry among themselves and kept their families united, let them rest on Sundays and main holidays, and permitted them to change masters if they were mistreated.[25] The reason behind this humanitarian behavior was that the aim of Spain was not the exploitation of the colonized but their civilization, or better still, their transformation into Christians and Spaniards.[26] But to make this possible, Maldonado wrote, cultural and religious programs were not sufficient, and Spaniards also demonstrated that to truly civilize and modernize these peoples it was necessary that the metropolis promote "the mixture or fusion of colonizers and colonized" through the creation of cities where all of them could live together and, more important, intermarry thus promoting biological, and not just cultural, miscegenation.[27] At this point it is important to remember that this "cult of mestizaje," which became prominent after the 1850s, was a fundamental piece in the creation of a Spanish imperial and national narrative, although it also affected other disciplines. As Joshua Goode has written, between "1880 and 1923, racial theorists had forged an identity whose main buttress was Spain's history of multi-ethnic contact. Racial strength was rooted in the proficiency of the Spanish race to fuse the different groups that had coexisted in the Iberian Peninsula . . . [and therefore] the task of the Spanish sciences was to trace the history of racial fusion."[28]

   This view of Spanish colonialism became common among Spanish politicians and intellectuals, from the left and the right, in the last decades of the nineteenth century. José Ferrer de Couto, a man of conservative political ideas and a defender of slavery, shared his views with, for example, two of the most active liberals of the period, Rafael María de Labra and José del Perojo.[29] Labra, a formidable intellectual who defended the autonomy of Cuba before 1898, believed that colonizing is the "most serious and grandiose responsibility a people can bear upon itself, and nothing is more magnificent and attractive in the history of humanity than those nations that have the right to be called great colonizing nations." It is these societies that are in charge of carrying the "torch of civilization" to all peoples on the earth.[30] No other nation, Labra writes, could claim better credentials than Spain, a nation that did not exploit other peoples, but constructed societies with "the same spirit and blood," and made so many sacrifices to help other peoples that "no one could deny Spain the first place among all colonizing nations."[31]

This defense of colonialism proved essential in the process of revision of the history of Spain in America that gained momentum around 1892 coinciding with the acts organized to commemorate the fourth centenary of Columbus's first voyage (1492–1892).[32] During the commemorations of this centenary, as Bernabeu Albert has indicated, there were a large number of patriotic demonstrations and exaggerated claims about the significance of 1492 and the role of Spain in the history of the world,[33] but there were also attempts to offer a more scholarly view of Spanish colonialism in the Americas. This was evident in a series of lectures organized by the Ateneo of Madrid, the most important scholarly and cultural institution outside academia in Spain, and a few conferences and international meetings, especially the IX Congress of Americanists organized by, among others, the Royal Academy of History. The themes of the sessions of the IX Congress of Americanists, for example, indicate that the organizers designed a program aimed at demonstrating that the impact of Spain on the world was positive, both economically and culturally. Even more important were the themes discussed in the section on "anthropology and ethnology" in the same meeting, designed to demonstrate, first, that the population before the discovery was less numerous than claimed by Spain's "enemies"; second, that before the arrival of Spanish conquistadors and colonizers the various "Indian" races who inhabited America were in decline, and that it was the action of Spain, protecting Amerindians and promoting miscegenation, that had allowed the conservation of an important number of them.[34]

The speakers in the Ateneo discussed similar themes, making evident that Spanish intellectuals had been already able to agree on the general characteristics of Spain's colonialism in America.[35] What is important to remark is that we are not yet talking about a "professional" narrative of the Spanish empire and Spanish colonialism, but rather the construction of a first frame composed of basic principles, many of them defending Spain's activities against what these authors and Spanish authorities viewed as an unjustly negative history of the Spanish conquistadors' deeds promoted by foreigners. Four of the conferences delivered in the Ateneo de Madrid give us a clear idea of the topics Spanish intellectuals and officials were interested in highlighting. Enríquez de Aguilera y Gamboa spoke about the viceroyalty of Mexico, to insist upon the idea that colonialism should not be viewed as an act of force but as an act of mercy, a duty not a right, especially when the aim was "to save other peoples from barbarism and savagery," as Spaniards did in Mexico, a society ruled by tyrants who sacrificed their subjects and allowed cannibalism.[36] The anthropologist Manuel Antón y Ferrándiz, in turn, claimed that the first true anthropologists were the sixteenth-century Spaniards who truthfully described the new lands and peoples they encountered in America, and who believed, unlike Enlightened "anthropologists" such as the Comte de Buffon and his followers, that all races are equal and that if some of them were less developed this was due to adverse natural environments, not to their inferior intellectual capacities.[37] The member of the Royal Academy of History, Antonio María Fabié, reminded his audience that by reading Las Casas's writings many could think that Spaniards brought to America violence, murder, and larceny, but that before judging them one should remember that the principles that guided sixteenth-century conquistadors were not the ones that predominated in Fabié's times. Everybody should take into consideration, he remarked, that in the same conditions all Europeans, past and modern, "conduct themselves not just like sixteenth-century Spaniards, but more cruelly."[38] In his lecture offered on 18 February 1892, Manuel Pedregal contended that Spaniards found in America large populations and that, contrary to English and French colonizers, their aim was to Christianize the Indians, whom they always treated as brothers and protected against destruction and annihilation by implementing the most progressive and humanitarian set of laws in the history of colonization.[39]

The defeat of Spain in 1898 in its war with the United States of America and the loss of Spain's last colonies in the Americas and Asia (Puerto Rico, Cuba, and the Philippines) made the need to rewrite the history of Spanish imperialism even more urgent, if only as a defensive move to counter the jingoist campaign organized in the United States, in which Spain was represented as a backward country responsible for the lack of modernization in Latin America and the Caribbean islands.[40] What is important to highlight here is that after 1898 everybody thought that it was vital for the nation to write a more comprehensive narrative of Spanish colonialism in the Americas. The themes and arguments were very similar to those developed in previous decades, but now there were more rigorous attempts to write a general vision of this period of Spanish history.[41] It is not necessary to analyze all the authors who wrote about the Spanish empire after 1898; a few of them should suffice, although discussion here will refer to themes to avoid repetitions. The writers to be considered are Julián Juderías, the author of the first systematic response to the so-called Black Legend; Rafael Altamira, the real promoter of "hispano-americanism"; and Jerónimo Bécker, one of the first authors who published a general compendium of Spanish colonial history in the Americas. None of them was strictly speaking a professional historian, but their works profoundly influenced the views of later generations of historians, the ones who would help to create and would control the discipline of Spanish American history after the 1930s.

After 1898 it is easily discernable that the aim of Spanish authors was to break down the components of the Black Legend, while creating alternative black legends against other European and U.S. colonialisms. No one conducted a more systematic attack against the latter than Juderías in *La leyenda negra*, originally published in 1917 and republished several times throughout the twentieth century.[42] Juderías, a literary historian, was the first author to offer a systematic rebuttal of the Black Legend and the first one to present it as a deliberate, negative campaign orchestrated by the enemies of Spain since the late fifteenth century. As in many other cases, Juderías's *La leyenda negra* is, indeed, a self-congratulatory and apologetic text that nevertheless helped put together an alternative paradigm regarding the history of Spanish colonialism. Juderías dedicates one of the chapters (chapter 6) to rebut attacks against Spanish colonialism in America, the deed, according to him, that should be understood as the one that truly represents the essence of the "Spanish race." His aim was, however, not only to refute the various components of the Black Legend, but also to find the philosophy that was behind the Spanish colonization, which Juderías summarized by saying that the Spanish monarchs viewed their role in America as a "divine mandate" to propagate the Christian faith and to educate and civilize the hordes of "savages" and "barbarians" that Hernán Cortés and other conquistadors encountered in the Americas. It is true, he conceded, that in the beginning some natives were mistreated, but these exceptional cases occurred against the wishes and orders of the Spanish rulers.[43] The Spanish colonial system stood in sharp contrast with those sponsored by the Dutch, French, English, and North Americans. In the territories these nations colonized, natives lost their lives, lands, and dignity, and on many occasions they were simply exterminated.[44] To find this truth, he writes, it is sufficient to read Rudyard Kipling's novels, whose characters seem to have only one mission in life: "to destroy all the natives."[45]

Responses to Spain's enemies were accompanied by the creation of a more systematic Spanish legend, now aimed at portraying the positive aspects of the Spanish colonization of the Americas. Perhaps the most important author of this period was Rafael Altamira, a republican, who as professor at the University of Madrid was in charge of teaching courses on the history of the political and civil institutions in Spanish America. Besides his academic duties, Altamira also became the founder of "hispano-americanismo," and in many of his numerous publications he presented a consistent, thorough, and nuanced narrative of the Spanish empire in America, insisting upon the themes and perspectives already discussed by previous authors.[46] The defeat of Spain in 1898 moved him to dedicate all his conferences and publications "to rectify the legends, misunderstandings, and calumnies" about Spain's history. His work, he stressed, was therefore guided by a "patriotic vindication" of his nation; as a true liberal, his duty was to censure the errors and limitations of his nation, but as a scholar he was compelled to uncover the truth about the various and competing versions of the history of Spain.[47]

Like many of his contemporaries, Altamira was also concerned with the various ideas on nation and race, because he believed they were essential to understand conflicting views of the past. For Altamira, a nation is not the product of a single, racially homogenous people. Actually, he believed that "pure races" did not exist and therefore nations were not constituted on racial uniformity among all their members. All existing peoples were the result of a complex and variable mix of various races. A nation comes into existence as a result of common "interests and passions" among originally diverse peoples, even if they live in different territories and continents. The factor that gives essence to a nation is, therefore, a shared history, ideas, goals, and education.[48] These ideas and beliefs did not preclude Altamira from affirming that there were differences between peoples, that total equality between nations was impossible. As a liberal, Altamira believed that colonialism existed precisely as a result of these inequalities, and, indeed, he defined colonialism as the necessary "social tutelage" that superior peoples had to exert upon their inferiors.[49] He also believed that Spain had always been truthful to this liberal concept of colonialism,[50] and as a result he asserted that Spain never created an empire—a metropolis exploiting conquered and marginal colonies—but a "transatlantic nation," with all the parts sharing the same "spiritual matrix."[51] Altamira also proposed a research agenda that became central for those working after the 1930s. There were three main components of this research agenda. The first was to recover the moral and philosophical principles that guided the conquest and colonization of the Americas—what were the actual intentions, aims, ethics, and legal principles that the Spanish government, religious orders, and conquistadors claimed to be defending. Second, scholars were urged to study the errors and imbalances of a colonial administration that, "even if it was not perfect, was the best under the standards accepted by all early modern nations and even by today's nations." Third, Altamira called for the reintegration of the history of the conquest and colonization of America into national history. The conquest and colonization of the Americas was the event that gave prestige and power to Spain, made the Spanish nation different and exceptional, and demonstrated that Spaniards are able to triumph against adverse conditions.[52] To take this research agenda to the full, Altamira also advised other Spanish authors to avoid becoming annoyed by those still using the Black Legend against Spain, because "we modern Spaniards cannot take responsibility for what our ancestors did."[53]

Jerónimo Bécker, like Juderías a literary historian and politically more conservative than Altamira, in his work *La política española en las Indias (rectificaciones históricas)*,[54] insists upon the same topics, and in many ways it reads as a copy of Juderías's *La leyenda negra*. The importance of Bécker's book is that it was commissioned by the Royal Academy of History to be presented as the official version of the history of Spanish colonialism in America at the "Congreso de Historia y Geografía Hispanoamericana" that took place in Seville in 1921. Like Altamira and others, Bécker proclaims that the history of Spanish America must be viewed as part of the history of the "Spanish nation," and that the colonization of America was a "national and patriotic enterprise" conceived to create new provinces of a unique "Nation."[55] Thus, although the American territories are referred to sometimes as "colonies," he writes, in reality they were "kingdoms" or "regions" with the same rights and laws as the regions and kingdoms in the Iberian Peninsula, while their inhabitants— Amerindians, "peninsulares," Creoles, and mestizos—were, from a juristic point of view, equal to peninsular Spaniards.[56] Throughout the book, Bécker makes very general and patriotically charged observations about the actions of the various Spanish governments to educate the natives, to protect them from "violent" conquistadors, while defending that Spaniards were the first ones who criticized the enslavement of Africans and other peoples.

HISTORIES

During the 1930s and especially after 1940, Spanish intellectuals interested in the history of Spain and Spanish America had to confront new challenges and contexts. One was the product of political changes within the Iberian Peninsula. The victory of General Franco in the civil war that affected Spain from 1936 until 1939 gave new urgency to the recovery of Spanish imperial discourses and history. By presenting himself as a newborn savior of Catholic Spain and the true inheritor of traditional virtues and political goals, Franco opted to adopt the symbols and imperial theories of the early modern Spanish monarchs, including a vindication of Spain as the architect of America and as leader of "hispanidad."[57] There were, however, other challenges or changes that neither Franco nor the Spanish intellectuals were able to control or avoid. One of them was the development of anti-imperial doctrines and movements, and the increasing influence of "indigenism." In the case of the Spanish imperial history, these movements, unlike the Black Legend, questioned not so much the past in itself, but the present circumstances of the peoples and countries previously subjected to Spain, thus stating that everything that was currently wrong in Latin America was the result of Spanish colonialism.[58] In this new political context the main critique by non-Spanish historians of the dominant imperial narrative discussed above was to state that it was constructed by taking into consideration only the general "principles and philosophies" that allegedly had served as guides for royal officials and colonizers. Anti-imperial critics, however, viewed general laws and, especially, the so-called Christian values and principles with disdain, preferring to analyze and discern real colonial practices. In this context, many Spaniards believed that to legitimate the Spanish legend of the conquest it was necessary to turn to the "science" of history; the aim was now to demonstrate that the humanitarian principles that guided Spanish policies in the Americas were truly implemented in practice; that the existence of a large "mestizo" population was not the result of the predatory behavior of colonizers and conquistadors but the result of an official agenda aimed at transforming the Americas into Spain's twin sister; and that the policy of concentrating the indigenous population in newly built villages had nothing to do with exploiting the natives as a workforce, but expressed the genuine commitment of the Spanish Crown to protecting its American subjects.

The importance of putting history at the service of national and imperial myths was already evident in the conclusions of the "II Congreso de Historia y Geografía Hispano-Americanas," held in Seville in 1921. The fifth final resolution adopted by the congreso states that history is crucial to make possible the "spiritual communion of the entire Hispanic race," and asked national governments to promote the study of the "history of Spain, and of the conquest, colonization and emancipation of the American continent."[59] Historians had as their duty to accumulate as much archival information as possible but, at the same time, to write popular history in order—in the words of Gregorio Marañón, the most influential nonprofessional historian in the first three decades of Franco's regime—to create "living legends."[60]

But even this type of history required a compromise by the Spanish government to promote the institutionalization of the discipline of American history and provide funds to publish as many primary sources as possible. Efforts to fully allow the development of the History of America as an academic discipline came to fruition precisely after 1940, immediately following the victory of Franco.[61] Before, there were only a few officially supported initiatives designed to give the history of America academic prestige. Besides the Royal Academy of History, in theory responsible for writing the official history of Spanish America, there were not many other institutions aimed at promoting research and teaching on the conquest and colonization of America by Spain. In the beginning of the twentieth century the government made the decision to create two chairs in the University of Madrid, one in Arts and Sciences specifically geared toward covering the history of America, whose holder was Antonio Ballesteros, the other in the Law School on the institutional history of Latin America, whose holder was Rafael Altamira. This situation remained unchanged until the late 1930s, when Américo Castro attempted to promote the history of America from within the Centro de Estudios Históricos, a research institution sponsored by the Republic, an initiative accompanied by the creation of a journal dedicated to the history and culture of Latin America, *Tierra Firme*.[62]

Franco's victory brought important changes in this terrain. First, the history of America was incorporated as an independent discipline within the structure of the new Consejo Superior de Investigaciones Científicas (CSIC), an ambitious institution created to promote research in all fields and disciplines. Historians of America, both Spanish and foreigners, were invited to take part in the activities of the Instituto Gonzalo Fernández de Oviedo (the section in charge of American history within the CSIC), and to publish their works in the official journal of the institute, *Revista de Indias*, whose first issue was published in 1940. In 1944 the government allowed the creation of two independent departments of American history, one in the University of Madrid, and the other in the University of Seville. The department in Seville, like the Instituto Fernández de Oviedo, also received funds to create and maintain its own scholarly journal, the *Anuario de Estudios Americanos*, whose first volume was published in 1944. In the years after 1945, and especially after 1975, Spanish governments permitted the creation of many other departments of American history, although the groups in Madrid and Seville, with the addition of the Catalan group in the 1960s, remained by far the most influential.[63]

The belief that the History of America was an independent discipline and that it fully deserved inclusion in the academic world helped to change the language used by those who defended the actions of Spain during the three hundred years of colonialism; it also helped to promote a more ambitious research agenda and a commitment to display scholars' findings to a larger public beyond academia. The intentions and the new research agenda were clearly stated in several articles published in the *Revista de Indias*. In the opening remarks to the journal's first issue, for example, Antonio Ballesteros reminded his readers that God himself had selected Spain to discover America, to immediately assure that America has a personality, an essence, that was fundamentally Spanish. The Spanish empire was not formed to pursue material interests but was aimed at the expansion and transmission of Hispanidad. Manuel Ballesteros Gaibrois best articulated the aims of these professional historians in an article he published in 1949, also in *Revista de Indias*. This and other journals, he affirmed, wanted to publish original research articles in order to demonstrate that the existing narratives on the Spanish empire were the result of an "objective and scientific" analysis of the American realities. The analysis of the archival documents, for them the only witnesses of the past, were going to be complemented by the publication of reviews on books addressing the history of Spain and Latin America, reviews that, Ballesteros promised, will be harsh to those who despise the truth of Spanish colonialism; everybody needed to know, he wrote, that if the reviewers disagreed with some of the books published outside Spain, this was due not to their patriotism but to "methodological differences and the reviewers' love for the veracity of the original documents."[64] In the words of another of the leaders of this new generation of Spanish Americanists, Miguel Herrero, "the duty of Spanish historians was, using new and modern research methods, to construct the history of the invasion of America by the Spanish culture, analyzing, fixing, and detailing every single event, law, institution, and name" involved in this history.[65]

With these principles and agenda as their guides, the Americanists of the 1940s and 1950s started to publish with intensity unknown until then, making the history of Spanish America one of the most popular disciplines. It was during the 1940s and 1950s when some of the most important and influential works on the history of the Spanish conquest and colonization of the Americas were published, and, even more important, this febrile activity also translated into the publication of numerous general works. Indeed, one of the main lacunae in the previous period was the inability of Spanish intellectuals to offer a more comprehensive view of the period of Spanish dominance in the

Americas,[66] a situation that changed after 1940. There were two especially important attempts in the 1940s and 1950s. The first one was Manuel Ballesteros Gaibrois's *Historia de América*,[67] viewed by Gregorio Marañón as "the newest and more perfect vision of America."[68] In this work, addressed to an "educated readership and university students," Ballesteros offers a very optimistic view of the state of and interest in the history of America in Spain. After a historiographical introduction he embarks upon a study that goes from the description of pre-Columbian America to the situation of the various American nations in the twentieth century, while paying special attention to the history of colonial America from a comparative perspective. As a summary of his views, Ballesteros claims that what made Spanish colonization of the Americas special was that Spanish colonialism was uninterested in wealth; rather, it was both "patriotic," because colonizers wanted to create new Spains and extend the sovereignty of the Spanish monarchs, and "Catholic," because the principal goal of the conquistadors was to disseminate Christianity.[69]

Even more important was the publication in 1956 of a collective volume appropriately entitled *El legado de España a América*,[70] a very important book in which some of the leading Americanists from Spain and Spanish America offer a succinct but powerful synthesis of some of the topics that were central to the Spanish conceptualization of the colonial history of America: population and customs, including racial miscegenation as an officially sanctioned policy that resulted from and reinforced the lack of racial and ethnic prejudices in Spain (Barón Castro); the use and dissemination of the Spanish language as a symbol of the brotherhood between Spaniards and Americans (López Estrada); the rich cultural production in the Americas thanks to the efforts of the Spanish monarchy (Ramón Ezquerra); the implementation of a modern and specifically American legislation, the so-called *Leyes de Indias* (José María Font); the principles that guided the system of education in colonial America, a system that attempted to integrate all inhabitants of the Americas (Constantino Bayle); the surge of a specific Spanish American literature (López Estrada); and the importance of the economic development of the Americas thanks again to the measures taken by the Spanish Crown (José Tudella).

Like the "old history," this "new history" of Spanish America was constructed upon a defense of Spanish imperial doctrines and practices, which several authors discussed and vindicated during the first years of the 1940s. Jaume Vicens Vives[71] stated that a world confronted by wars of universal scale needed a new kind of imperialism but not the "materialistic and violent" one represented by Britain and the United States, but one he defines as "classic and

Mediterranean" represented by Rome and Spain, in which predominates the "spirit over the economy and where the unity of the various peoples is achieved through moral affinities and not through violence and oppression."[72] This idealistic view of the Spanish empire, and its value in the twentieth century, was further sustained by a series of works, many of them written by foreign historians who were amply accepted by the Spanish establishment—like the North American Lewis Hanke and the Mexican Silvio Zavala—insisting on the righteousness of the general principles that guided the Spanish conquest and colonization of the Americas. Lewis Hanke, for example, argued that the foundations of Spanish colonization included the principle of protecting the indigenous population against the individualism of the conquistadors, and that "racist" and "callous" conceptions of the Native Americans were in Spain rather marginal. Silvio Zavala's works were even more influential and better received by Spanish historians, who praised them as models of objectivity and scholarship; Zavala was a historian, they claimed, never influenced by contemporary politics (in explicit reference to the ideological enemies of Franco), a sharp critic of the Black Legend, and, more importantly, a recognized "indigenist" and "anti-racist."[73] The importance of using Zavala as a model for the newly founded objectivity in the study of the ideological foundations of the Spanish empire could be understood by following the publication history of one of his books, *La filosofía política en la conquista de América*.[74] First published in Mexico City, with a laudatory introduction by Rafael Altamira, in 1947, it was then republished in 1963 by the UNESCO, and finally reedited in 1992 as part of the celebrations for the Fifth Centenary of Columbus's first voyage, with a significant title: *Por la senda hispana de la libertad*. In this and other works, Zavala claimed that the actions of Spain in the Americas were not exercises in conquest, but in civilization.[75]

A vindication of Spanish colonialism, of its singular nature, also provoked the publication of countless works studying the legislation and institutions (*"encomiendas," "reducciones," "protectores de Indios"*) that were believed to be fundamental to understand and exculpate the accomplishments of Spain in the Americas, as nothing else than "indigenism" in its purest form. Constantino Bayle, for example, published in 1945 *El Protector de Indios*, first as an article and a few months later as a book,[76] arguing that this institution was created by the Spanish Crown to protect "weak Indians" against the conquistadors' greediness. One of the most criticized institutions of Spanish colonization in the Americas, the "encomienda," had also its historian, Carmelo Viñas Mey, who in *La sociedad americana y el acceso a la propiedad rural*,[77] presented the existence of the encomiendas as a proof that religious, not economic, aims were behind this derided institution, while claiming that the encomienda also helped the modernization of the peoples of Spanish America, by providing them with the work ethic and the individualistic ideologies that made possible the development of capitalism.[78]

To demonstrate that the Spanish monarchy's policies and initiatives were aimed at protecting the natives, and that their situation in the twentieth century had nothing to do with the colonial past, Manuel Ballesteros added two new sections in *Revista de Indias*, one called "Historia indígena," the other "Indigenismo," where he commented on articles published in foreign "indigenist" journals, which he criticized as being guided by anti-Spanish sentiments.[79] His efforts culminated with the publication of a book, *Indigenismo americano*, in which he and his collaborator, Julia Ulloa, argued that Amerindians' sufferings increased dramatically after the wars of independence in the early nineteenth century, and that, overall, the situation of the Indian population was better in Spanish America than in the United States of America.[80]

Conclusion

Between 1970 and the 1990s hundreds of articles and books appeared underlining the positive aspects of Spanish colonialism in the Americas, a "deed," Spaniards were told, the entire nation should be proud of and celebrate. Indeed, even the death of Franco and the transition to a new political system could not deflate this view of the Spanish imperial past. The history of America produced in Spain went beyond political parties and ideologies to be a part of a shared concept of "nation," or better still, a fundamental part of Spanish nationalism. This is not to say that no one wrote critically of the history of Spanish colonialism in the Americas. The *Revista de Indias*, for example, published in 1953 an excellent article by Juan Friede in defense of Bartolomé de las Casas, by then well integrated in the dominant imperial and colonial narrative, in which the author argues that Spanish colonial policies and the debates over the Indians were attempts by the Spanish authorities and elites to find "the juristic principles that could legitimate (not 'moralize' as some prestigious Americanists assert) the conquest, the enslavement of the Indians, the *encomiendas*, the imposition of financial tributes and other institutions" that produced not the acculturation, Christianization, and civilization of the Indians, but "their almost complete annihilation."[81] But these criticisms were few and rare,[82] and the political transition from Franco's dictatorship to constitutional monarchy and democracy seemed to have been truly smooth in the terrain of the history of America. It is, for example, rather symptomatic that the *Revista de Indias* did not hesitate to publish an article by Mario Hernández Sánchez-Barba, which is nothing less than an attempt to connect and legitimate the dominant vision on the history of Spain in America with the new political context by using the words of King Juan Carlos I.[83] Equally important is to underline again the idea that historians who otherwise had contrasting political views shared identical visions of the history of Spain in America, as could be easily perceived by comparing the work of Salvador de Madariaga[84]— a liberal historian who lived in exile in Oxford and Switzerland from 1939 until 1977—and the work of a more conservative historian, José Manuel Pérez Prendes.[85] Prendes's vivid description of what he calls "colonialismo indiano" perfectly summarizes the views shared by a majority of his contemporaries:

> [Spanish colonialism in the Indies] provoked serious demographic alterations (decreasing of the Indian population, introduction of Blacks, establishment of mestizaje); forced important ecological changes; and extracted and appropriated enormous amounts of material resources. But at the same time, Spain proclaimed the freedom of all human beings (Las Casas and Sandoval are the symbols of this movement); conserved and protected Indian cultures, translating many of their languages into Spanish; Spaniards inserted themselves into America through their mix with natives; introduced products, plants and farming methods in order to minimize ecological damage, and [the Spanish governments] invested in the Americas many of the rents and profits extracted from the colonies in religious, cultural and social welfare.[86]

What these similar visions indicate is that the history of Spanish colonialism in America was not and is not simply an academic matter; rather it has been and is a "national" or, better still, a "state" concern. In other words, it has constituted itself as an essential element of the "Spanish national character." To challenge the imperial and colonial narrative analyzed in this chapter involves not only questioning the memory of the Spanish past but disputing how Spaniards view themselves today. As Pierre Bourdieu wrote, "The construction of the state is accompanied by the construction of a sort of common historical transcendental, immanent to all its subjects."[87] The history of America produced in Spain, popular or academic, is one of the best proofs of this practice. During the last decades many of the elements that, according to Spanish intellectuals, shaped the so-called Spanish character have disappeared or lost their appeal; religion, language, territorial and political unity, all have been questioned within the Peninsula by the recognition of religious freedom, the existence of other official languages in addition to Castilian, or the construction of a semifederal state. Only the legend of Spain in America remains intact. Spanish governments—both federal and regional—still consider October 12 a crucial day to celebrate, and in fact October 12 is almost the only holiday observed in all regions. Clearly emblematic was the celebration of the Fifth Centenary of the "discovery of America" in 1992, a series of events, publications, commemorations, and conferences sponsored by local, regional, and national authorities all over the Peninsula. Equally important is the constant use of the idea of "racial democracy," or the defense of Spain as a nonracist society, a discourse created in order to defend Spanish colonialism in the Americas, and used by contemporary Spaniards to defend themselves when accused of mistreating immigrants from Africa or, paradoxically, Latin America. The Spanish "paradigma," the one constructed throughout the last hundred years, has defied all political, social, religious, and historiographical changes. It has proven to be as resistant to new research as the North American legend of the "Conquest of the West." Ronald Wright's words on this paradigm could easily be applied to the Spanish *paradigma* on the conquest and colonization of America:

> Perhaps no other modern nation is such a prisoner of its mythology, or so needs to be. The United States views itself as a beacon of freedom planted on virgin soil, where great wealth has been built up by honest sweat of pioneer brows. Certainly, many Americans have toiled hard, but the ultimate source of their prosperity—their "start-up capital"—was the theft of a continent and the destruction of the millions who lived there. . . . Unabashed historical amnesia (as Carlos Fuentes has called it) is essential to America's utopianism. White America can live with itself only if it forgets the past.[88]

Notes

1. Pompeyo Gener, *Heregías: Estudios de crítica inductiva sobre asuntos españoles* (Barcelona: F. Fé, 1887), 46–47 and 33–38.

2. On the Black Legend and Spanish responses since the sixteenth century, see Ricardo García Cárcel, *La leyenda negra: Historia y opinión* (Madrid: Alianza Editorial, 1992).

3. On the origins of this polemic, see Antonello Gerbi, *La disputa del Nuevo Mundo: Historia de una polémica*, trans. Antonio Alatorre (1955; Mexico City: Fondo de Cultura Económica, 1993); Jorge Cañizares-Esguerra, *How to Write the History of the New World: Historiographies, Epistemologies, and Identities in the Eighteenth-Century Atlantic World* (Stanford: Stanford University Press, 2001).

4. See, for example, Mark J. van Aken, *Pan-Hispanism: Its Origin and Development to 1866* (Berkeley: University of California Press, 1959); Fredrick B. Pike, *Hispanismo, 1898–1936* (Notre Dame: University of Notre Dame Press, 1971); Lorenzo Delgado Gómez-Escamilla, *Imperio de papel: Acción cultural y política exterior durante el primer franquismo* (Madrid: C.S.I.C., 1992); and Christopher Schmidt-Nowara, "After Empire, After Franco: A Dialogue with Josep M. Fradera on Spanish Colonial Historiography," *Bulletin of the Society for Spanish and Portuguese Historical Studies* 25, 3 (2000–2001): 2–14.

5. Sara Mills, *Discourse* (London: Routledge, 1997), 11. On the Black Legend and Spanish responses since the sixteenth century, see García Cárcel, *La leyenda negra*.

6. On the topic of Spanish nationalism, see the articles collected in the special issue of *Ethnic and Racial Studies* 24, 5 (2001), dedicated to Iberian identities; see especially the introduction by M. K. Flynn, "Constructed identities and Iberia," 703–18.

7. The best studies are Carolyn P. Boyd, *Historia Patria: Politics, History, and National Identity in Spain, 1875–1975* (Princeton: Princeton University Press, 1997); and José Alvarez-Junco, *Mater Dolorosa: La idea de España en el siglo XIX* (Madrid: Taurus, 2001).

8. Patricia Seed, *American Pentimento: The Invention of Indians and the Pursuit of Riches* (Minneapolis: University of Minnesota Press, 2001), xi.

9. Ann Laura Stoler and Frederick Cooper, "Between Metropole and Colony: Rethinking a Research Agenda," in *Tensions of Empire: Colonial Cultures in a Bourgeois World, ed.* Frederick Cooper and Ann Laura Stoler, (Berkeley: University of California Press, 1997), 35.

10. On this theme regarding Spain and Latin America, see for example, Mónica Quijada, "Qué nación? Dinámicas y dicotomías de la nación en el imaginario his-panoamericano del siglo xix," *Cuadernos de Historia Latinoamerica* 2 (1994): 15–51; Andrés de Blas, "Introduction" to Antonio Cánovas del Castillo, *Discurso sobre la nación*, ed. Andrés de Blas (1882; Madrid: Biblioteca Nueva, 1997); José Luis Abellán, "Introduction" to Angel Ganivet, *Idearium español [1897] y El porvenir de España [1912]*, ed. José Luis Abellán (Madrid: Biblioteca Nueva, 1996); José Alvarez Junco, "La nación en duda," in *Más se perdió en Cuba: España, 1898 y la crisis de fin de siglo*, ed. Juan Pan-Mantojo (Madrid: Alianza Editorial, 1998), 405–75; and Christopher Schmidt-Nowara, "The Specter of Las Casas: José Antonio Saco and the Persistence of Spanish Colonialism in Cuba," *Itinerario* 25, 2 (2001): 93–109.

11. Anthony Pagden, *Lords of All the World: Ideologies of Empire in Spain, Britain and France, c. 1500–c. 1800* (New Haven: Yale University Press, 1995); Seed, *American Pentimento*; Jeremy Adelman and Stephen Aron, "From Borderlands to Borders: Empires, Nation-States, and the Peoples in Between in North American History," *American Historical Review* 104, 3 (1999): 813–41; and Christopher Ebert Schmidt-Nowara, "Response" to Jeremy Adelman and Stephen Aron, *The American Historical Review* 104, 4 (1999): 1226–28.

12. Patrick Wolfe, "Land, Labor, and Difference: Elementary Structures of Race," *American Historical Review* 106, 3 (2001): 866–905.

13. José Arias Miranda in his *Examen crítico-histórico del influjo que tuvo en el comercio, industria y población de España su dominación en América* (Madrid: Imprenta de la Real Academia de la Historia, 1854), for example, complained about the lack of a genuine

and comprehensive history of the Spanish colonization of America, and affirmed that it would be impossible to write good Spanish history without including in this narrative the history of Spanish America (46–62).

14. Boyd, *Historia Patria*, 85–86.

15. See José Alvarez Junco and Adrian Shubert, eds., *Spanish History since 1808* (London: Arnold, 2000), part 2, "The Restoration, 1875–1914"; and Christopher Schmidt-Nowara, "Imperio y crisis colonial," in *Más se perdió en Cuba*, 31–89.

16. Carlos Reyero, *La pintura de historia en España: Esplendor de un género en el siglo XIX* (Madrid: Cátedra, 1989).

17. Ignacio Peiró Martín, *Los guardianes de la historia: La historiografía académica de la Restauración* (Zaragoza: Institución "Fernando del Católico," 1995), 98–101.

18. Antonio Cánovas del Castillo, *Discurso sobre la nación*.

19. Ibid., 22, 72.

20. Ibid., 80–81.

21. *Principios generales del arte de colonización* (Madrid: M. Tello, 1873). The origin of this book was the creation of a department within the University of Madrid to train the members of the civil service who were to serve in the Philippines. Maldonado Macanaz was the holder of one of the chairs and was specifically in charge of teaching the history of colonialism, a task he intended to do by comparing English and Spanish colonialisms, which he viewed as antithetical. I used the second edition published in 1875, which is almost identical to the 1873 edition.

22. Ibid., 22–32.

23. Ibid., 93–96.

24. Ibid., 97.

25. Ibid., 150–58.

26. Ibid., 201–3.

27. Ibid., 205–13.

28. Joshua Seth Goode, "The Racial Alloy: The Science, Politics and Culture of Race in Spain, 1875–1923" (Ph.D. dissertation, University of California, Los Angeles, 1999), 2.

29. José Ferrer de Couto, *América y España consideradas en sus intereses de raza, ante la República de los Estados Unidos del Norte* (Cádiz: Imprenta de la Revista Médica, 1859); Rafael María de Labra, *Política y sistemas coloniales: La colonización en la historia*, 2 vols. (Madrid: A. de San Martín, 1876); and José del Perojo, *Ensayos de política colonial* (Madrid: Imprenta de M. Ginesta, 1885).

30. Labra, *Política y sistemas coloniales*, 1:51.

31. Ibid., 2:84.

32. Michel-Rolph Trouillot, *Silencing the Past: Power and the Production of History* (Boston: Beacon Press, 1995), chap. 2; Salvador Bernabeu Albert, "El IV Centenario del descubrimiento de América en la coyuntura finisecular (1880–1893)," *Revista de Indias* 44 (1984): 345–66; and idem, *1892: El IV Centenario del descubrimiento de América en España: Coyuntura y conmemoraciones* (Madrid: C.S.I.C., 1987).

33. See, for example, the introduction of Juan Valera, one of the most influential intellectuals of the time and a very popular novelist, to the first issue of the official journal of the commemorations, *El Centenario*, in which he claims, repeating the words

used by some sixteenth-century Spaniards, that the "discovery of America" by Columbus was the most important event in the history of humanity, only surpassed by the birth and death of Jesus Christ; *El Centenario* 1 (1892): 5.

34. Justo Zaragoza, "Programa del IX Congreso de Americanistas," *Boletín de la Real Academia de la Historia* 21 (1892): 220–24; Justo Zaragoza was the General Secretary of the congress.

35. Ateneo de Madrid, *Conferencias dadas en el Ateneo de Madrid sobre el Descubrimiento de América* (Madrid: Sucesores de Rivadeneyra, 1892). Each lecture has it own page numbers.

36. Enríquez de Aguilera y Gamboa, Marques of Cerralbo, "El virreinato de México," delivered on 24 May 1892, in *Conferencias dadas*, 7–17.

37. Manuel Antón y Ferrándiz, "Antropología de los pueblos de América anteriores al descubrimiento de América," delivered on 19 May 1892, in *Conferencia dadas*, 7–15.

38. Antonio María Fabié, "El Padre Fray Bartolomé de las Casas," delivered on 25 April 1892, in *Conferencias dadas*, 14.

39. Manuel Pedregal, "Estado jurídico y social de los indios," delivered on 18 February 1892, in *Conferencias dadas*, 9–11.

40. For an example of this literature, see Henry Charles Lea, "The Decadence of Spain," *The Atlantic Monthly* 82 (1898): 36–46.

41. On the 1898 conflicts, how they influenced Spanish intellectuals and reflections about the past and the future of the nation, see Carlos Serrano, "Conciencia de la crisis, conciencias en crisis," in *Más se perdió en Cuba*, 335–403; and Javier Varela, *La novela de España: Los intelectuales españoles y el problema español* (Madrid: Taurus, 1999).

42. Julián Juderías, *La leyenda negra: Estudios acerca del concepto de España en el extranjero* (1917; Barcelona: Araluce, 1943).

43. Ibid., 132.

44. Ibid., 137, 370, 382–83.

45. Ibid., 384. See also Angel Ganivet, *Idearium español [1897] y El porvenir de España [1912]*, 60–83, 125; and Alfonso Posada, *Instituciones políticas de los pueblos hispano-americanos* (Madrid: Hijos de Reus, 1900), 23–25, 37–38, 60–66.

46. On Altamira see Rafael Asín Vergara's introduction to his edition of Rafael Altamira, *Historia de la civilización española* (Barcelona: Crítica, 1988); and Boyd, *Historia patria*, chap. 5. Although he was a very prolific author, here we will consider only three of his works: *Psicología del pueblo español* (1902; Barcelona: Editorial Minerva, 1917); *España en América* (Valencia: F. Sempere, 1908); and his "Prologue" to Charles F. Lummis, *Los exploradores españoles del siglo xvi: Vindicación de la acción española en América*, trans. Arturo Cuyás (Barcelona: Araluce, 1916).

47. Altamira, *Psicología del pueblo español*, 14–15. Altamira believed that some aspects of the Black Legend were true, which brought him to congratulate Charles Lea for his studies on the Spanish Inquisition, and on the Spanish treatment and expulsion of the Moriscos (see Altamira's letters to Charles Lea [1901–1908], in Henry Charles Lea Papers, Folder 24, University of Pennsylvania Library), but he also believed that, in general, attacks against Spanish colonialism in the Americas were utterly wrong.

48. Altamira, *Psicología del pueblo español*, 46–50.

49. Ibid., 51–52. On this topic, see for example Bhikhu Parekh, *Rethinking Multiculturalism: Cultural Diversity and Political Theory* (Cambridge, Mass.: Harvard University Press, 2000), esp. 40–47; and Uday S. Mehta, "Liberal strategies of exclusion," in *Tensions of Empire*, 59–86.

50. Altamira, *España en América*, 103.

51. Ibid., 24.

52. Altamira, "Prologue to Lummis," 14 and 33. See also Cesáreo Fernández Duro's review of Edward Gaylord Bourne's *Spain in America (1450–1580)*, in *Boletín de la Real Academia de la Historia* 46 (1905): 361–63.

53. Altamira, *España en América*, 104–5.

54. Madrid: J. Ratés Martín, 1920.

55. Ibid., 22–24.

56. Ibid., 24–25.

57. See Delgado Gómez-Escamilla, *Imperio de papel*; in the 1940s several authors published books on the Spanish imperial theories and practices. See, for example, Jaume Vicens Vives, *España: Geopolítica del estado y del imperio* (Barcelona: Yunque, 1940); Ricardo del Arco y Garay, *Grandeza y destino de España* (Madrid: Escelicer, 1942); Ricardo del Arco y Garay, *La idea de imperio en la política y la literatura españolas* (Madrid: Espasa-Calpe, 1944); Juan Beneyto Pérez, *España y el problema de Europa: Contribución a la historia de la idea de imperio* (Madrid: Editora Nacional, 1942); and Eleuterio Elorduy, *La idea del imperio en el pensamiento español y de otros pueblos* (Madrid: Espasa-Calpe, 1944).

58. See Jacques Lafaye and James Lockhart, "A Scholarly Debate: The Origins of Modern Mexico—Indigenistas vs Hispanistas," *The Americas* 68, 3 (1992): 315–30; and Jeremy Adelman, ed., *Colonial Legacies: The Problem of Persistence in Latin American History* (New York: Routledge, 1999).

59. Jerónimo Bécker, "Conclusiones del II Congreso de Historia y Geografía Hispano-Americanas celebrado en Sevilla en mayo de 1921," *Boletín de la Real Academia de la Historia* 79 (1921): 85.

60. Gregorio Marañón, "Prologue" to Manuel Ballesteros Gaibrois, *Historia de América* (Madrid: Pegaso, 1946), xiii.

61. On Spanish historiography and the teaching of history in general during this period, see Boyd, *Historia patria*, chaps. 7–9.

62. This short summary on the situation of the discipline of American History in Spain before 1940 is taken from Manuel Ballesteros Gaibrois, "La moderna ciencia americanista española," *Revista de Indias* 10, 37–38 (1949): 579–95; Manuel Ballesteros, "Los comienzos de un Instituto y de una revista," *Revista de Indias* 49, 187 (1989): 545–53; and José Alcina Franch, "Testimonio: El 'americanismo' de los años 40," *Revista de Indias* 54, 201 (1994): 265–71.

63. Ibid.

64. Ballesteros, "La moderna ciencia americanista española," 589.

65. Miguel Herrero, "Para la historia de la cultura hispanoamericana," *Revista de Indias* 1, 1 (1940): 191; and Ramón Ezquerra Abalía, "Los primeros tiempos de la 'Revista de Indias' (1939–1949)," *Revista de Indias* 49, 187 (1989): 558. See also Ballesteros, "Los comienzos de un Instituto y de una revista," 558.

66. See, for example, Carlos Pereyra, *Historia de América española*, 8 vols. (Madrid: Editorial "Saturnino Calleja," 1920–26), vol. 1:9, 11.

67. Manuel Ballesteros Gaibrois, *Historia de América* (Madrid: Pegaso, 1946).

68. Ibid., xi.

69. Ibid., 182.

70. José Tudella, ed., *El legado de España a América*, 2 vols. (Madrid: Pegaso, 1954).

71. Jaume Vicens Vives is considered the historian who led the historiographical revision that took place in Spain after the 1950s; see Schmidt-Nowara, "After Empire," 2–14.

72. Jaume Vicens Vives, *España: Geopolítica del estado y del imperio*, 159 and 211. See also Ricardo del Arco y Garay, *Grandeza y destino de España*; and *La idea de imperio en la política y la literatura españolas*.

73. See the reviews by F. Mateo and Richard Konetzke of two of Zavala's books, *Servidumbre natural y libertad cristiana según los tratadistas españoles de los siglos xvi y xvii*, published in Buenos Aires, 1944, and *Ensayos sobre la colonización española en América*, originally published in the United States by the University of Pennsylvania Press in 1943, in *Revista de Indias* 7, 23 (1946): 141–46.

74. Silvio Zavala, *La filosofía política en la conquista de América* (Mexico City: Fondo de Cultura Económica, 1947).

75. The terms used by Spanish historians to defend Spanish imperialism and colonization came to the surface in a very interesting debate that took place in 1954 between Spanish and Latin American historians. Some historians and institutions from Latin America (for example, Ricardo Levene, historian and president of Argentine's National Academy of History), asked their colleagues in Spain and other countries to change the name "colonial America" to refer to the period of Spanish domination in America, and select something more "neutral and unprejudiced," such as "the period of Spanish government" or, even better, "the pre-national period." Reports of this debate were published in *Revista de Indias* 15, 55–56 (1954): 154–80.

76. Constantino Bayle, *El Protector de Indios* (Seville: Publicaciónes de la Escuela de Estudios Hispano-Americanos de la Universidad de Sevilla, 1945); it was first published in *Anuario de Estudios Americanos*, 1945, 1–180.

77. Carmelo Viñas y Mey, *La sociedad americana y el acceso a la propiedad rural* (Madrid: n.p., 1944).

78. Carmelo Viñas y Mey published in 1930 a book entitled *El estatuto del obrero indígena en la colonización española* in a series edited by Rafael Altamira, a book in which Viñas y Mey asserted that the Spanish legislation in the Americas was the most progressive of the times because it was based on the idea of equal rights between Spaniards and Indians, who were in addition legally protected against all iniquities committed by the former.

79. See, for example, *Revista de Indias* 12, 45 (1951): 607–13.

80. Manuel Ballesteros Gaibrois and Julia Ulloa Suárez, *Indigenismo americano* (Madrid: Ediciones Cultura Hispánica, 1961).

81. Juan Friede, "Fray Bartolomé de las Casas: Exponente del movimiento indigenista español del siglo xvi," *Revista de Indias* 14, 51 (1953): 28, 30.

82. Of all the articles, for example, published by *Revista de Indias* to celebrate the fiftieth anniversary of the journal, only one author, Juan Gil, offered a critical view of the Spanish historiography on the Americas (Juan Gil, "Historiografía española sobre el descubrimiento y descubrimientos," *Revista de Indias* 69, 187 [1989]: 779–80).

83. "El concepto de comunidad hispanoamericana en los discursos del Rey D. Juan Carlos I de España: Análisis valorativo y de síntesis," *Revista de Indias* 61, 165–66 (1981): 337–57.

84. Salvador de Madariaga, *Auge y ocaso del imperio español en América* (Madrid: Espasa-Calpe, 1977).

85. José Manuel Pérez Prendes, *La monarquía indiana y el estado de derecho* (Madrid: Asociación Francisco López de Gomara, 1989).

86. Ibid., 20–21.

87. Pierre Bourdieu, "Rethinking the State: Genesis and Structure of the Bureaucratic Field," in *State/Culture: State-Formation after the Cultural Turn*, ed. George Steinmetz (1991; Ithaca: Cornell University Press, 1999), 68.

88. Ronald Wright, "Review of Patricia Nelson Limerick's *Something in the Soil: Legacies and Reckonings in the New West*," *Times Literary Supplement*, 9 February 2001, 9.

PART TWO

Colonial Pasts and

National Presents

Fig. 7. De Anza Motor Lodge,
Albuquerque, New Mexico.
Photograph by Christopher Schmidt-Nowara.

Introduction

Christopher Schmidt-Nowara and John Nieto-Phillips

*I*n his landmark monograph, *The Past Is a Foreign Country*, historian David Lowenthal explains that the manufacture and deployment of "the past" is very much a function of "the present." Put otherwise, the way nations (not to mention empires) choose to define their historical trajectory says much about the historians and the times in which they live. This assessment certainly holds true when one considers how Spanish colonialism has been envisioned and reimagined over the past century.[1]

Reading Antonio Feros and José del Valle's essays together allows us to track the continuities and ruptures in historical discourse before and after 1898 and the elaboration of hispanismo as a dominant paradigm. A key feature of hispanismo is language; for language—and, more precisely, distinctions between Castilian and Latin American Spanish—came to embody the ambitions of Spain toward its former colonies. We intentionally say Castilian or Spanish because as both Feros and del Valle argue, hispanismo was not only an outward-looking ideology crafted in response to decolonization but also an inward-looking one intended to counter and silence, especially in the twentieth century, the aspirations of Catalan, Basque, and Galician nationalists. Here is a particularly revealing example of the fusion between colonial (and postcolonial) initiatives and the internal politics and cultures of the European metropolis discussed by Cooper and Stoler.

Jeremy Adelman's study of two of the major figures in Latin American historiography—José Manuel Restrepo and Bartolomé Mitre—introduces a discordant note in this *hispanista* concert. Indeed, creole nationalisms form one of the major challenges to hispanismo's hegemonic pretensions; they are the Black Legends to its White. However, as Adelman carefully shows, the anti-Spanish roots of Latin American patriotic ideologies are complex and varied: Restrepo and Mitre differed greatly from one another in describing the origins and prospects of their nations. What they did share, however, was openness to broader Atlantic-world trends. Like the North American George Bancroft and the Frenchman Jules Michelet, Restrepo and Mitre modeled their national histories on Exodus: Colombians and Argentines, like the Americans and the French, redeemed themselves by revolting against European empires and the old regime, though Adelman notes that they faced the future with less certainty than their U.S. and French republican counterparts.

Other corners of the postcolonial Americas, such as the southwestern United States, proved more fertile soil for hispanismo, though for motives quite distinct from those of Ramón Menéndez Pidal and other Spanish intellectuals, as John Nieto-Phillips suggests. Amid a rising tide of anti-Mexican sentiment, Anglo civic boosters reimagined their new environs as a pastoral escape from the ills of industry and urban blight; they recast the savage west as a Spanish Southwest, where memories of Spanish colonialism still lingered among the adobe mission ruins of California, or the Spanish Pueblo architecture of Santa Fe. The imagined Spanish past—the munificent White Legend—proved a potent marketing tool, but it was equally a means of recharting the racial landscape toward political ends.

Sam Truett picks up on the ramification of this approach to Spanish colonial history in twentieth-century North American historiography by examining the work and career of Herbert Eugene Bolton. Bolton wrote very much in the key of Charles Lummis and other early historian/boosters of the Southwest, casting figures like Coronado as old world knights-errant wandering through the new. However, Bolton was a far more rigorous scholar who worked in numerous archives, theorized the institutional history of Spain in the Americas, and exerted tremendous influence on the teaching and writing of Spanish American and U.S. history from his position at Berkeley. Nonetheless, Truett shows that despite Bolton's impact on the profession, his idea of "Greater America" fell on deaf ears in the earlier twentieth century. This curious failure leads Truett to reflect on the changing political and paradigmatic conditions of U.S. historiography and to contemplate when and why scholars are sometimes willing to look beyond national borders and why at other times they cleave more closely to nation-building projects, questions that have become all the more pertinent since our original meeting in New York in September of 2001.

NOTE

1. David Lowenthal, *The Past Is a Foreign Country* (Cambridge: Cambridge University Press, 1985).

Fig. 8. Awarding of the Príncipe de Asturias Prizes. Courtesy of *Hola* (Madrid) num. 2935, 9 November 2000.

CHAPTER FIVE

SPANISH, SPAIN, AND THE HISPANIC COMMUNITY
Science and Rhetoric in the History of Spanish Linguistics

José del Valle

SPAIN, LATIN AMERICA, AND THE LANGUAGE OF ENCOUNTER

On 9 November 2000 the Spanish variety magazine *Hola* published a large two-page group photograph taken a few days earlier at the Prince of Asturias awards ceremony. At the center of the picture stands the impressive figure of Prince Felipe escorted by all the honorees. To his left, past Cardinal Marini, we see a radiant Víctor García de la Concha, the veteran University of Salamanca professor and current director of the *Real Academia Española* (henceforth *RAE*). Behind them, covering the multilevel podium installed for the solemn occasion, stand the directors of all the American Academies of the Spanish language. The smiles and air of satisfaction they display are not unwarranted: The Asociación de Academias de la Lengua Española has just been handed the "Premio Príncipe de Asturias de la Concordia." The symbolic value of the event as well as the power of its photographic documentation in *Hola* should not be overlooked: the Spanish Crown had just publicly knighted the linguistic nobility, had honored them for their contribution to harmony and peaceful coexistence. The Latin American intellectual class had been granted (and had gracefully accepted) the honor of standing behind the Spanish prince and the *RAE*'s director, proclaiming the successful institution of Spanish as the foundation for pan-Hispanic harmony.

Since the creation of the Instituto Cervantes in 1991 and the modernizing overhaul of the *RAE* throughout the nineties,[1] it has become clear that under

---

The part of the present article that analyzes Ramón Menéndez Pidal's linguistic ideas was first published as part of chapter 5 in *The Battle over Spanish*, edited by José del Valle and Luis Gabriel-Stheeman. I thank Routledge for allowing me to reproduce portions of that book.

the skin of Spain's linguistic diplomacy beats the heart of this nation's renewed interest in building solid bonds with Latin America[2]—an interest that, I suspect, is not unrelated to the growing economic presence of Spanish corporations in that continent, and to the possible reluctance of some Latin Americans to acquiesce to the former metropolis's new economic and maybe even cultural hegemony.[3] We should not be surprised then that efforts to promote Spanish, public displays of loyalty to it, and statements of friendly cooperation have proliferated during the last decade of the twentieth century: after all, the justification of the new transatlantic interest (whatever its nature may be—cultural, economic, political) and of the type of relationship with the former colonies that is being fostered (no matter how cozy and harmonious it may now seem and how sincere the efforts may actually be) is bound to encounter some of the hurdles posed by a common history that includes the violence of conquest, war, and colonization.[4] As we will see, the tension between the Black Legend of Spanish exploitation and the White Legend of Spanish benevolence—to which Chris Schmidt-Nowara refers in the introduction to this book—still has a determining influence not only in the present configuration of the "comunidad iberoamericana" and the narratives that shape its historical development, but also in the elaboration of the linguistic image and language history from which the dominant conceptualization of the pan-Hispanic community draws its legitimacy.[5] In fact, it is my contention that one of the principal goals of Spain's contemporary language policy—grounded, as I will argue below, in the linguistic roadmap designed by the founding father of Spanish Philology, Ramón Menéndez Pidal (1869–1968)—is to cleanse the uncomfortable memories of this nation's colonial past.

Movements in the ideological fault line of colonial history still shake, at times, the grounds on which the idealized pan-Hispanic community of the future is being constructed. The realm of language—of its cultural history—has been witness to episodes that clearly illustrate the bumpy coexistence of, on the one hand, a spirit of linguistic unity and, on the other, nagging reminders of the price paid (or to be paid) for such unity. Some contemporary language scholars have been shockingly candid in their endorsement of the White Legend and in their view of colonization as a *mission civilisatrice*. In 1991, for example, Manuel Alvar (1923–2001), distinguished Spanish philologist and dialectologist, and director of the *RAE* between 1988 and 1991, unequivocally stated his views on what the role of Spanish and Hispanic culture should be in the modernization of Latin America:

> Mexico knew better than anybody else the value of having a language
> that unifies, that liberates the indigenous communities from their

backwardness and misery. . . . Saving the indian, the redemption of the indian, the incorporation of the indian, as they used to say, is nothing but de-indianizing the indian, incorporating him into the idea of the modern state, in order to use him in projects of national solidarity, and in order to extend to him the benefits of belonging to that same society. . . . The path to freedom runs through hispanization.[6]

Of course, such bluntness, such candid return to the barbarism/civilization dichotomy of nineteenth-century nation-building narratives, is unusual among the most visible protagonists of the public discourse on language. While Spanish is indeed praised, its alleged superiority is rarely claimed so directly. Instead, the language's higher qualities are advanced through the creation and projection of a linguistic image that links it to two highly appreciated values of modern democratic societies: harmonious coexistence and economic progress. In this image, Spanish is the crucial element that enables and encourages cultural intercourse among Hispanic nations and that guarantees the creation of a commercial community. García de la Concha—the RAE's current director—formulates the first of these values as he equates Spanish with an inalienable link among all Hispanic nations, with the common fatherland that engenders superlative harmony: "It is really exciting to see how the language is functioning as a place of encounter and not simply as a channel of communication. The language provides us with a common fatherland in superlative harmony" (quoted in El País on 7 September 2000).[7]

Yet, even apparently harmless figures of speech used in the design of the linguistic image may have serious consequences if uttered in a context (linguistic as well as extralinguistic) that triggers a movement at the cultural fault line and the consequent release of the tension between the White and Black Legends. On 23 May 2001, in a brief speech at the Cervantes Prize award ceremony—echoing García de la Concha's description of Spanish as "lugar de encuentro," or place of encounter—King Juan Carlos I made the following statement: "Our language has never been an imposed one; instead, it has been a language of encounter. No one was ever obliged to speak Castilian; different peoples and nations, through their free will, chose to make the language of Cervantes their own."[8] Of course, Basque, Catalan, and Galician nationalists protested immediately and vigorously; and the Casa Real—overwhelmed perhaps by the forceful reaction and by the possibly fatal consequences of the incident for Juan Carlos's image in Spain's periphery—quickly and clumsily responded: the King was referring to America!

As these episodes indicate, the task of Spain's linguistic diplomacy is not an easy one. Language plays a central role in the arduous undertaking of forging alliances with Latin American intellectuals, consolidating Spain's prestige and leadership, harnessing the notion of pan-Hispanic community, and, ultimately, earning widespread acceptance of Spain's allegedly legitimate presence in the former colonies. As anticipated above, throughout the 1990s and up to the time when these lines are being written, the Spanish government and language policy agencies—with the financial support of corporations such as Telefónica and PRISA—have engaged in the promotion of a simple but well-designed language ideology[9] that, using the unity of the language as a centerpiece, focuses on building a sense of community among all Hispanic nations and strives to promote the advancement of Spanish businesses in language-related markets.[10]

SPAIN'S POST-COLONIAL PRESTIGE AND "*LA BATALLA DEL IDIOMA*"

While, unquestionably, this language policy has received massive institutional support only at the end of the twentieth century, the policy itself—or rather, the ideology that it espouses and promotes—is not in the least new. In fact, the roots of its articulation are to be found at the previous turn of the century: in a period straddling the *Desastre* of 1898; at a time when language-based nationalisms developed in Spain's periphery, and when the new Latin American nations still struggled with their own nation-building ventures; in days of bitter debate over the status of science and scientific research in the country's universities. These *desastres* must have created an acute awareness of the fact that control of the cultural market—to use Pierre Bourdieu's term—was now more difficult than ever. The new historical and political circumstances had caused the emergence of powerful competing paradigms for the development of a historical account of Spain that legitimized contending views of its future. Thus, the time was ripe, it seems, for the establishment of cultural (and of course political) institutions that would seriously undertake the liberal national project. It was in this context that the historicization of the Spanish language, that is, the development of a legitimate (i.e. institutionally sanctioned) historical-linguistic narrative—a linguistic paradigm, as it were—took place. Broadly coinciding with the spread of hispanismo, an impressive government-sponsored cultural, intellectual, and scientific project was launched: the Centro de Estudios Históricos. From the Centro, and under the mentorship of Ramón Menéndez Pidal, emerged the Madrid School of linguistic and philological studies, which would consolidate the dominant language ideology by grounding it simultaneously in the powerful foundations of science and in government-sponsored cultural institutions.[11]

Throughout the nineteenth century, the academic and intellectual prestige of Philology grew as a result of the increase in the wealth of data available to scholars and the development of more precise methods for the description and classification of languages.[12] The progressive focus on their formal dimension—mainly their morphology and phonetics—resulted in the birth of Linguistics as an independent academic discipline, which, due to its rhetorical and methodological association with the natural sciences, as well as its emphatic commitment to accuracy and rigor, became surrounded, from the early stages of its development, by a halo of superiority vis à vis the Humanities, of which it had been a historical ally.

However, the scientific isolation of language—its total formalization—was difficult to accomplish: Language is just too sticky with associations, too closely interconnected with history, literature, or philosophy. Ironically, a purely scientific description of language demanded the total detachment of this deeply human phenomenon from precisely human will. Therefore, while developments in Linguistics were moving the discipline closer to the natural sciences—at the price of "dehumanizing" its object of study—language continued to be closely associated with certain social movements and continued to be a crucial cultural artifact and political instrument in the life of human groups.

Scholars of nationalism, for example, agree that language was (and is) a central element in the cultural repertoire available to the conceptualization of nation, to nationalist discourses, and to academic analyses of their birth, character, and social function. De Blas Guerrero has expressed this opinion unequivocally: "Of all the cultural elements that participate in the origin, development and transformation of nationalist movements and ideologies, none has been more important than language."[13] Eric Hobsbawm also places language at the center of his account of nationalism. In his view, in the development of nineteenth-century liberal nationalism, three criteria—in addition to the threshold principle—were used in order to determine whether a given territory was a legitimate candidate for nationhood:[14] "Historic association with a state, . . . a long-established cultural elite, possessing a written national literary and administrative vernacular, . . . and a proven capacity for conquest."[15] For Hobsbawm, therefore, in the liberal version of nationalism the link between language and nation was established, but not as emphatically—not even in the same terms—as it would be after 1880. To be clear, language was indeed used as a defining factor; however, due to the obvious material advantages that would derive from its knowledge, its acceptance as a symbol and a model for verbal behavior by all national subjects was taken for granted. The presence of other languages—regional languages—within the confines of the nation was not perceived as a threat: "The national heterogeneity of nation-states was accepted, above all, because it seemed clear that small, and especially small and backward, nation-alities had everything to gain by merging into greater nations."[16] In John Stuart Mill's words: "Nobody can suppose that it is not more beneficial for a Breton or a Basque of French Navarre to be . . . a member of the French nationality, admitted on equal terms to all the privileges of French citizenship."[17] But the liberal national project would be disrupted when, after 1880, a new type of nationalism emerged: In this new strand, the threshold principle was given up and language and ethnicity were placed at the very basis of the claims for nationality. Thus when, as in Spain, the new nationalisms competed with the liberal national project for the loyalty of citizens, the state would have to deploy or create institutions intended to persuade those citizens of their membership in a national, cultural, and *linguistic* whole. In this context, processes of linguis-tic standardization—not new in history—were placed at the service of nation-alist ideologies: The creation of a standard language did not suffice, and the "naturalization" of the community's linguistic homogeneity became a neces-sity. Ralph Fasold sees this naturalization of the language/community relation as a crucial—maybe *the* crucial—aspect of language policy and planning:

> I would dare to suggest that the most frequent single problem in installing a national language has nothing to do with vocabulary expansion, spelling or grammar standardization, the adequacy of the educational system or the presence of an ensconced colonial lan-guage. The biggest problem is that there often simply is no language that a sufficiently large majority of the citizens will accept as a symbol of national identity.[18]

Thus the success of these attempts at legitimizing the standard as the basis for the nation would depend, at least in part, on the credibility of the institu-tions in charge of presenting the language to the citizens as their own. It is clear, then, that the scientific prestige of Philology and Linguistics coexisted with an increased awareness of the political importance of language; this was the perfect context for the emergence of the political involvement—voluntary or not—of philologists and linguists, who became—using again Pierre Bourdieu's image—the holders of the *skeptron*, "known and recognized as being able and enabled to produce [a] particular kind of discourse."[19]

As stated above, at the turn of the century, Spain and Latin America were undergoing multiple political transformations that, to some extent, relied on language-based cultural notions and on citizenship projects in which language

education was central.[20] Therefore, the establishment of a coherent language policy, the shaping of the public discourse on language, and the exercise of control
over the institutions that produce them became a political necessity; especially
as, while Spain strove to gain national and international prestige, Spanish
became a multicentered language and the various hubs of power in the
Hispanic world—as well as within Spain—competed for protagonism within
the organization of the new postcolonial order. Carlos Rama has used "la
batalla del idioma" to refer to one aspect of the relationship between Spanish
and Latin American intellectuals in the nineteenth century:

> Throughout the nineteenth century, both in Latin America and in
> Spain—the part of Spain that cares about the intellectual life of the
> Americas—there is a constant dispute over the problems of Castilian
> and its use in America, which is an important episode in the field of
> cultural relations between both continents.[21]

One aspect of the problem was the difficult institutional relation between the
former metropolis and the former colonies in the almost immediate aftermath of
independence. In that context, the RAE represented to Latin American intellectuals a conservative and *casticista* approach to language. Julián Marías has summarized that attitude that so irritated Latin Americans in the following terms:

> The old *purists* from the previous century believed that the Spanish
> language was, at least, primarily Spanish, that our country had pro-
> prietary rights over it, or at least, privileged control. There was a
> belief—interestingly, in one of the least creative periods of its his-
> tory—that the language was created in Spain and accepted—or cor-
> rupted—in America.[22]

Some Latin Americans responded to such attitudes with expressions of distrust and even disdain for the RAE. Domingo Faustino Sarmiento's (1811–1888)
writings, of course, offer multiple examples of this negative perception:

> It is degrading for nations that have acquired such status to be wait-
> ing for the rulings—useless and inappropriate—of a powerless, disre-
> puted and lethargic Academy conscious of its own uselessness and
> lacking authority even in Spain.[23]

Fellow Argentinean Juan María Gutiérrez (1809–1878), in explaining the reasons for rejecting his appointment as "miembro correspondiente," stated to the RAE's director:

> Sir, I believe it is dangerous for a South American to accept a title granted by the Spanish Academy. Accepting it would tie me up through the powerful bond of gratitude and would demand courtesy, if not full submission to the dominant ideas of that corporation.[24]

A corporation, "cuerpo," the RAE a few years earlier had expressed its concern about the possibility that the language would become bastardized in America. To this charge Gutiérrez replied:

> Language is closely related to ideas and it cannot become bastardized in any country where intelligence is active and where there is no obstacle to progress. It will change, yes, and by changing, it will simply follow the current formed by the passing of time, which is revolutionary and irresistible.[25]

Gutiérrez's reluctance to collaborate with the Spanish institution is also found in the writings of the Peruvian Manuel González Prada (1848–1918) who, in 1888, wrote:

> There is even international servility: literary and scientific organizations tend to become dependent on the Spanish Royal Academies. Men of letters, lawyers and doctors turn their eyes, in a shameful gesture, to beg for an academic degree.[26]

Clearly, the skepticism with which some Latin American intellectual figures perceived the RAE contributed to a decentering of the language standardization process. This absence of a universally accepted institution of linguistic power and Spain's debunking as a center from which a linguistic norm could emanate caused some alarm among the educated classes—both in Spain and Latin America. One of the earliest—certainly one of the most quoted—expressions of concern about the possible fragmentation of Spanish was Andrés Bello's, made in the "Prólogo" to his *Gramática de la lengua castellana destinada al uso de los americanos*:

> But the worst of all evils, the one that will deprive us of the invaluable advantage of a common language unless we put an end to it, is the

many grammatical neologisms that are flooding and blurring a lot of what is being written in America, and that by changing the structure of the language, will eventually turn it into a multitude of irregular, licentious, and barbaric dialects, embryos of future languages that, in the course of a long process of development, will reproduce in America the dark period which in Europe led to the corruption of Latin.[27]

Bello's grand linguistic and cultural oeuvre and his language-planning efforts in Chile greatly contributed to appeasing the fears of fragmentation that he had expressed. However, such fears did not completely vanish. In 1899, Colombian philologist Rufino José Cuervo (1844–1911), in his prologue to Argentinean writer Francisco Soto y Calvo's *Nastasio*, referred to the still distant and unfortunate but likely development of new languages from the dialectal remains of Spanish. Such evolution would be, according to Cuervo, the result of three factors: dialectal differentiation (of which he was reminded by Soto y Calvo's inclusion of a glossary at the end of his book), lack of contact among Latin American countries, and the collapse of Spain as a unifying center and source of intellectual inspiration for all Hispanic nations. Spanish writer and essayist Juan Valera (1824–1905) was quick to respond—in an article published on 24 September 1900 in *Los Lunes de El Imparcial* under the title "Sobre la duración del habla castellana"—rejecting Cuervo's prediction and questioning each one of the claims on which such conclusion was based.[28] This exchange would continue for three more years in the course of a polemic in which the Colombian would try to ground his prediction in the findings of historical linguistics—a naturalistic/deterministic version of it that defined the evolving character of language in strictly natural—i.e., formalistic—terms (and that would very soon be discredited).[29] Of course, in order to justify his fragmentationist position he had to stick to the idea that the Spanish-speaking world lacked a powerful language center. Valera, for his part, continued to defend the essential unity of the Spanish language and Hispanic culture, which he saw as one and the same on both sides of the Atlantic.[30] For him, the future of the language was in the hands of its speakers, but mostly, in the hands and pens of writers and intellectuals who had the responsibility to serve as models through both their linguistic practices and their views on language. The polemic had a telling ending: In his 1903 article, Cuervo put aside all linguistic argumentation for a moment and wrote:

Valera wants Latin American nations to be literary colonies of Spain, even if, in order to supply them, he has to resort to foreign products; and, thinking that he still has the inalienable right to violent repression of the insurgent colonies, he is unable to tolerate that an American questions such possibility given the present circumstances: that makes him lose his temper and his traditional serenity. Here ends the fraternal love.[31]

MENÉNDEZ PIDAL'S INTERVENTION: THE LANGUAGE IMAGE AND LINGUISTIC SCIENCE

As we have seen, throughout the nineteenth century, just before Menéndez Pidal launched his philological and linguistic projects in the context of the University of Madrid and the government-sponsored Centro de Estudios Históricos, historical linguistics had been rapidly developing in Europe as an independent academic discipline. As Linguistics grew in academic prestige and as language matters became more and more prominent in cultural and scientific debates,[32] Spanish intellectuals experienced with much preoccupation their nation's delay in incorporating this new and successful science to their universities.[33] Their concern was not unjustified, since, as late as the beginning of the twentieth century no historical grammar of Spanish had yet been produced. It would be precisely Pidal who would fill this vacuum by publishing, first in 1904, his *Manual de gramática histórica española*, and later, in 1925, what would come to be known as his linguistic masterpiece, *Orígenes del Español*. In order to fully understand the political implications of Pidal's oeuvre, we must keep in mind that his linguistic work was not exhausted with academic writings such as the *Manual* and *Orígenes*. He also produced a number of texts intended for a wider audience of educated readers: They were popularizations of his linguistic ideas, of the conclusions he had reached in his highly regarded but less widely read philological research. The development of a popular strand in Pidal's work is consistent with his views on the social role of the intellectual (one that, as we saw earlier, had been demanded by Valera). In an interview with one of his disciples, he stated:

While some hold the idea of the race's original and fatal unfitness (source of an unjustified and deadly pessimism) others suggest that it has degenerated with time (a relative pessimism that leaves the door open for regeneration). I am even more optimistic; I do not see any degeneration. . . . The virtue and vigor [of the nation] have weakened, or rather, have become asleep and latent; but as soon as one approaches the people, one finds the live sources of energy waiting to be aroused, strengthened and channeled by leaders capable of representing the spirit of a whole people. . . . we have never lacked—and we do not lack now—great Spaniards able to take control and direct spontaneous efforts along the sure paths of national reconstruction.[34]

Thus, aware that the linguistic polemics were ultimately based in a pessimistic perception of Spain's cultural prominence and potential for leadership, he set out to dissipate any fears of fragmentation and persuade his contemporaries that Spanish was a uniform and stable language that symbolizes the historical accomplishments and the promising future of Spanish civilization. Pidal undertook this task through both his academic and his popular linguistic texts. Of course, reducing the making of the *Manual* and *Orígenes* to a political motivation would be a flagrant oversimplification and misrepresentation of the complex forces that intervened in the production process. Pidal's academic writings demonstrated a detailed and broad knowledge of the state of Linguistics at the beginning of the twentieth century and proved to be significant contributions that expanded the explanatory powers of the discipline.[35] But their scientific accomplishments must not obscure the fact that they were produced in a specific social context and under certain cultural and political conditions (see above) that may have influenced Pidal's work. The questions he set out to resolve, as well as the possible types of answers he could conceive, were very much the product of both the scientific and the political environment of his work. The relevance of Pidal's linguistic oeuvre, for the purposes of the present essay, does not derive from its standards of descriptive accuracy—which, by the way, were fairly good. In other words, the question addressed here is not whether Pidal was right or wrong (although that may be a valid and productive question in a different context). The problem that our reading of Pidal attempts to address is the identification of the cultural and political ground in which his work emerged at the beginning of the twentieth century and its relation to the circumstances in which Spain's present language policy is being deployed at the beginning of the twenty-first. In fact, the power of Pidal's popular writings—from which most examples below will be drawn—was derived from their connection with the scientific writings, the ones that actually granted Pidal the special legitimacy required to discuss language matters with appropriate authority.

As our earlier references to Bello and Cuervo's views of Spanish illustrated, the material basis for all claims that fragmentation might—or would—occur was the existence of dialectal differences within Spanish—in conjunction with the new aesthetic trend that was bringing nonstandard forms to the realm of literature,[36] and with Spain's failure to act as a unifying force. The argument was that, if the educated classes in Latin America adopted dialectal forms, new standard languages might emerge in each Hispanic nation. Pidal's stature as a linguist and philologist, his knowledge of the Spanish language in particular and of linguistic phenomena in general, was too sharp to plainly deny the existence of dialects and variation. Therefore, he faced the task of defending unity while acknowledging diversity. He responded to this challenge by opening two fronts: On the one hand, he had to argue that variation was minimal, that is, that there was not only *unity* but also a high degree of *uniformity* among Spanish dialects. On the other, he had to show that the existing variation was consistent with the life of a *normal* modern language and that in no way should it threaten its unity, diminish its value, or tarnish its image. The fragmentation polemics had shown that the availability of hard data did not determine the conclusions. Instead, the central element in the articulation of the controversy had been the divergent perceptions of the future (i.e., postcolonial) path of language standardization and the desire or interest—conscious or unconscious—to impose on the description of that path a master narrative of fragmentation or unity.

Three basic ideas pervade Pidal's popularizing linguistic writings: Spain's special loyalty to the true spirit of the language, the existing linguistic uniformity both within Spain and across the Atlantic, and the power of human institutions to control language. On Spain's special status in the linguistic landscape he wrote:

> The European type is more directly and firmly consistent with the old line of evolution; peninsular society . . . maintains more faithfully its linguistic style; . . . The American type belongs to peoples that developed after breaking away from peninsular life . . . ; peoples who feel less intensely the linguistic tradition.[37]

His firm faith in unity was based on the following:

> This fact suffices to understand that Spanish American popular speech does not significantly deviate from Castilian.[38]

> The speech of the educated in Spanish America is, if we look at its most prominent features, the educated speech of Andalusia.[39]

On the power of language planning and linguistic intervention, he wrote: "The means to spread the linguistic norm are today incredibly superior to what they used to be."[40] The effect of Pidal's intense insistence in the homogeneity of all varieties in his popularizing texts is that all descriptions and references to dialectal variation—both scientific and popular—are bound to be absorbed or overpowered by the master narrative of unity and uniformity. This is precisely one of the strategies with which he strove to neutralize the fragmentationist interpretation of dialectal variation.

In addition to insisting on homogeneity, Pidal's main goal for countering the dissident theories was integrating variation in his language image:

> The distance between general educated Spanish, which represents unity, and the popular Spanish of various regions, which represents diversity, cannot be interpreted as a process of growing divergence, whose differentiation will be such that literary Spanish will be unintelligible to the people. Instead, it should be conceived of as two wavy lines that run side by side in the same direction and whose peaks and valleys frequently tend towards convergence, often touching but without ever merging completely. The literary language is always the goal towards which popular language aspires, and, vice versa, the popular language is always the fountain in which the literary language likes to refresh itself.[41]

In order to respond to the claims of fragmentationists, Pidal resorted to a conceptualization of language in general and the Spanish language in particular that views variation—at least a certain degree of variation—as consistent with the life of a healthy and stable language. Guided by this image, Pidal's readers are more likely to perceive variation not as a wild and disruptive phenomenon, or as an inevitable symptom of fragmentation, but as a process actually controlled by the laws that govern the life of language.

But perhaps the most surprising aspect of Pidal's language image is that he manages to create a positive notion of variation: not as a lesser evil, as one might expect, but as an essential component of the language. One of the legacies of linguistic historicism is that language can only be conceived as a dynamic entity, one that necessarily evolves over time. However, in the dominant linguistic culture of modern society, variation and change are supposed to be, on the one hand, moderate and controlled, and on the other, organic, that is, internal. External influences are usually seen with suspicion and considered to be most dangerous for the preservation of the language's identity. Similarly, internal variation, while recognized as inevitable, is only accepted with great reluctance. Pidal addresses the issue of internal variation in the dialects of the uneducated classes by distinguishing between *popular* and *vulgar* speech: "The *popular* always entails the mutual understanding between the educated and the people in general; the *vulgar* a greater initiative on the part of the uneducated people."[42] Thus, external influences and vulgar forms constitute a serious threat to the integrity of the language and the culture it represents—especially if they are adopted by disloyal or unqualified members of the speech community who may somehow gain undue protagonism. Yet languages, even the healthiest ones, must change. What better source of innovation for the language than the language itself? Here resides the crucial value of dialects, of variation, of the *popular* speech represented in the lower tier: still part of the same tradition, of the same history, popular forms offer to the language "the fountain in which the standard is to refresh itself." In other words, change from within.

But there is still something missing for this linguistic picture to be perfect. As stated before, for Pidal, variation is not to be feared as long as it is subject to the laws that control the life of healthy languages; evolution—change from within—is normal as long as it is natural. But what are those laws of linguistic gravity that keep the popular language always running parallel to the standard, preventing it from making any sudden turns?

Pidal insisted that, contrary to the dominant views developed within Linguistics in the nineteenth century, language is not a natural phenomenon controlled by inevitable laws totally independent from human will. Instead, he maintained that language is a social activity, one of the traditions that define a community's identity. As such, it must be the result of a collective consensus.

In earlier work, Pidal had explained how the development of folk songs and traditional ballads is connected with human will. In the origins of these poetic compositions, we find the efforts of the human beings who created the tradition: the "patrón," the "modelo ejemplar y superior." Throughout their lives, we find the compliance of the individuals, who, in spite of their superlatively free ("libérrima") participation, maintain the tradition unaltered. Language, also a social phenomenon and a defining element of a community's identity, is subject to the same forces that explain the history of folk songs and traditional ballads:

> The language lives in a state of constant variation and essential permanence. Each speaker moulds the materials deposited in his mind by tradition . . . ; but in spite of that, the language remains with its essential identity.[43]

We see, then, that the linguistic image produced by Pidal is characterized by an essential tension—almost by an internal contradiction. On one hand, language lives in the variable actions of superlatively free individuals; but on the other, it retains its essential identity. Such conception of language contains a built-in frailty: Individual freedom, as much as it is natural, is also dangerous, since individuals may be exposed to and adopt undesirable linguistic forms. It is therefore essential for the guardians of the community's identity to keep them at bay, lest these undesirable forms generalize and enter the common patterns of linguistic behavior changing the essential identity of the language. And just as dangerous as the spread of undesirable forms is the spread of undesirable ideas about language and the culture it is supposed to represent. The excessive emphasis on fragmentationism or on the uniqueness of the American history of Spanish by linguists and intellectuals might lead to the spread of a feeling of cultural collapse and to a reaffirmation of Spain's inability to perform its leadership role.

For this very reason Pidal argues for the need to summon the loyal linguistic elite. These individuals are granted special status, since, as long as they are capable of earning the consent of the people, they can control the life of language. Therefore, for Pidal, control over a language's identity cannot be taken for granted; it requires securing the loyalty of all members of the community both to the proposed linguistic norm and to the proponents of that norm. The power of the linguistic elite to generate collective loyalty to a given language and to the culture it represents—to create the social will to preserve a certain view of tradition—is the force that maintains the hegemonic vigor of the top tier—the standard—always pulling the lower tier—the popular dialects—toward it. The future of the Spanish language and Spanish culture depends therefore not so much on *what it is* as on *what we say it is, what we want it to be.*

> While society *wants* to preserve its language, its vitality is guaranteed; and while society receives from language a given mental conformation, before, social will conformed language and continues to conform it.[44]

But who is the implicit "we" in Pidal's linguistic image? Who embodies the tradition that defines the community? Who has the responsibility of establishing the norm and safeguarding it against any possible illnesses by serving as an active model of behavior? In the Spaniard's language ideology, education and intellectual sophistication are crucial criteria for determining who is to be included in the linguistic elite. As we have seen, for Pidal, while a certain degree of variation was deemed normal in popular speech, the educated variety had to exhibit the highest possible level of uniformity. In the case of the Spanish-speaking community, Pidal insisted that the differences in the speech of the educated classes in Latin America and Spain were few; however, he saw them as constituting two separate norms and threatening the unity of the language. Therefore, in Pidal's linguistic model the socioeducational criterion did not suffice to precisely define the ideal speaker, since, by itself, it did not guarantee the level of uniformity required of the standard. In order to resolve this inconvenience, Pidal resorted to historical and geographic reasons that privilege one of the educated varieties: the educated speech of Castile:

> The etymological type [the Castilian norm], legitimized by practical and historical reasons, will *reconquer* the terrain lost to the derived type [the Latin American norm].[45]

The practical motives adduced by Pidal for the adoption of the Castilian variety as the Spanish norm—multiple homonyms caused by *seseo* and *yeísmo*—were, in reality, very few ("multitud de homonimias enfadosas que el seseo y el yeísmo ocasionan").[46] Instead, he allowed the historical reasons to carry greater weight in the justification of his choice. For Pidal, Spaniards, inhabiting the soil where the language was born, naturally had closer ties with it, and displayed stronger loyalty to its essence—as the preservation of an etymologically correct variety proves. In contrast, the American norm had emerged among "peoples that . . . feel the idiomatic tradition with less liveliness"[47] The circumstances of the colonization were such that a relative disruption of the linguistic order in America could not but be expected:

> Spain brought to America its religious institutions, its schools, universities and academies, its printing presses, its literature, its entire civilization; but the difficulties of governing such a vast territory . . . produced inevitable deficiencies in the gigantic enterprise. In the colonization, the lower classes were abundant.[48]

Once the norm has been established, its acceptance in the Hispanic community as a whole is the responsibility of the linguistic elite, who must secure linguistic control by earning the consent of the people. The construction of social consent depends on the linguistic elite's ability to create an appealing image of the language and to present themselves as the true interpreters of the community's collective will and linguistic identity: Grammarians, linguists, and philologists—as holders of the skeptron of language science—are in a privileged position to claim that title. In sum, for Pidal, the unity and dignity of the Spanish language ultimately rested on the ability of the linguistic, cultural, and political elite to control change by creating a linguistic utopia, and by selling it to the community, like "any political idea":

> It is possible to campaign for a type of linguistic usage; just as it is possible to campaign for a political, economic, legal or literary idea whose success we want; therefore an individual may powerfully influence the language of a speech community just as he can have influence during an electoral campaign: by gaining the support of others.[49]

A crucial element in Pidal's construction of his language vision, and a key strategy for guaranteeing the dominance of his language ideology, is the minimization of the value and cultural weight of the perpetrators of linguistic subversion. Sarmiento and Cuervo are the main two such figures that Pidal discredits. The Argentine's position on fragmentation is mentioned in passing by Pidal, and is easily dismissed as simple resentment in the aftermath of the bitter process of independence. However, Cuervo's fragmentationist ideas were more difficult to discard since the Colombian had presented his views at the end of the nineteenth century, long after the wars of independence. Pidal's concern with the Colombian's views had to do less with the ideas themselves than with the fact that a linguist, someone *holding the skeptron,* had produced them. The strategy that Pidal used to discredit such a well-regarded linguist—one that he himself much admired—was to create two Cuervos and deal with them separately. First, he praised the younger Cuervo, the great linguist who had gloriously worked for the unity of the Spanish language. He then went on to criticize the older Cuervo, linking his pessimistic attitude with his senility—"La naturaleza del sabio colombiano se vio minada prematuramente por los achaques de la senectud" (The nature of the Colombian scholar was prematurely undermined by the ailments of senility).[50] But the crucial criticism with which Pidal tackled Cuervo's position was the latter's conception of language, that is, the linguistic theory underlying his work. According to Pidal, "In his old days, Cuervo followed the wrong scientific path by subscribing to a theory of fatal evolution that by then was beginning to subside."[51]

Let us review briefly Cuervo's pessimistic prognosis for the Spanish language. Although Cuervo did maintain the inevitability of change in language, he never claimed that constant evolution *necessarily* entailed fragmentation. His pessimistic outlook was the outcome of his having lost faith in the ability of Spanish and Latin American intellectuals to build the necessary consensus to preserve a common standard. For the Colombian, the force that would keep the popular dialects running parallel to the educated norm was simply exhausted.

His moderately stated position on fragmentation was grounded in his view that the conceptions of Hispanic culture and attitudes toward its construction held by Spaniards on the one hand and Latin Americans on the other were outright irreconcilable. Consequently, Cuervo and Pidal—contrary to the latter's statements—did in fact share the same conception of language and disagreed only about their beliefs concerning the preservation of the common social will.

Thus, Sarmiento and Cuervo's dissent was explained away by attributing it to unique, individual circumstances: Sarmiento was angry in the post-colonial fever, and Cuervo was under the effects of a premature senility. What is the place, then, in Pidal's linguistic oeuvre, for the claims made by some Latin American intellectuals (such as Sarmiento, Gutiérrez, and González Prada) that Spain did not offer an appropriate cultural and linguistic model for the young nations? And what about the complaints by authors such as Ricardo Palma and Cuervo who, willing at first to construct a pan-Hispanic future, became skeptical as a result of the paternalistic and dominating attitude of Spaniards? In order to sustain the linguistic utopia, these claims must be dismissed and never openly addressed.

The centrality of the notion of progress in the discourse of modernity has given this mode of social organization an unquestionable future-oriented character. At the end of the nineteenth century, this modern condition must have posed a serious problem for a nation such as Spain whose greatest glory seemed to be a question of the past. Yet Pidal—displaying a lucid, intuitive understanding of the requirements of modernity—did not respond to the present crisis by simply basking in the nation's glorious history, by constructing a "monument" to its past; instead, he constantly projected national history onto the future, defining the Spanish language not only as the symbol of a great old civilization, but as an instrument that could build the bridge of progress for the Hispanic community.

In Pidal's history of Spanish, the language's association with the forces of civilization and with their universalizing tendencies was not a recent development. The language's history demonstrated the presence of Spain's—more precisely, Castile's—courageous spirit from quite early. In his historical-linguistic works, Pidal insisted that Spanish had its roots in the speech of Castile, which had emerged at a time when this kingdom, rebellious and energetic, offered its neighbors a *future*, an ambitious political project and the spirit to bring it to completion. In Pidal's linguistic oeuvre, the birth of Spanish in medieval Spain was presented as the emergence of the paradoxical combination of sociocultural stability and rebelliousness that would provide the Hispanic community with a sense of identity, with an *hecho diferencial*. The birth of Spanish symbolized the establishment of a solid identity that would give impulse to an inexorable march toward modernity.

In Pidal's language ideology, the inherently superior qualities of the dialect of Castile explained its projection not only in time but also in space, as it spread outside its original territorial boundaries. Spanish, therefore, while rooted in a specific place and time, established its truly modern nature by overcoming temporal and spatial limitations, by proving to be endowed with the superlatively modern quality of universality:

> When communication among the American Republics becomes so difficult that important businesses take a year to complete, when literary production disappears for over a century, then we may be sad about the destiny of our language, similar to that of Latin.... It is perhaps possible that Humanity will fall again into barbarism, that it will lose the *universality* of its *science* and of its *commerce*, that the airplane is forgotten and *transportation* is limited to donkeys. But we are so far from this that it is not more sensible to think about it than it is to think about the freezing of the sun or the fainting of the vitality of the human species.[52]

Entrepreneurship ("aventureros"), commerce ("comerciantes"), order ("magistrados, capitanes, tribunos"), knowledge ("pensadores") . . . catchwords of modernity, universally admired activities and aspirations that the Spanish language has made possible and that it has come to symbolize.

Throughout history, it has been customary for great political and military powers to symbolically show off their strength by building architectural masterpieces and engineering wonders. Such displays of national discipline, technological prowess, and, often, aesthetic sensibility became particularly conspicuous in modern times when technology reached an unprecedented peak and communications expanded the potential ideological impact of those awesome structures. Could Pidal's construction of an image of the Spanish language have performed a function analogous to that of those architectural and engineering feats? As a Spanish intellectual of the turn-of-the-century generations, he did not merely engage in the objective description of the language, but in the construction of a spectacular icon: glorious symbol for the nation's past and sophisticated vehicle for its race toward a brilliant future.

The task that has been handed down to us by history is not to destroy, out of neglect, the validity of this form [the Peninsular Spanish norm]; then, we must constantly bring it to a new literary perfection, with our ear always open to our brother nations . . . moving towards a future in which, more splendid, will appear the magnificent linguistic unity created on both sides of the ocean, one of the grandest human constructions that history has ever seen.[53]

The Prince of Asturias Prize for Harmony, the directors of all the Spanish language academies assembled in Spain for the occasion, and a photograph in *Hola* broadcasting this celebration of pan-Hispanic brotherhood and fruitful cooperation; how much closer can we get to Pidal's linguistic utopia?

NOTES

1. The modernization to which I refer has manifested itself in two separate but related ways. First, there has been an obvious distancing from the old "limpia, fija y da esplendor" motto. The new stated objective is the defense of linguistic unity, which is to be undertaken jointly by all the language academies, that is, by the Asociación de Academias de la Lengua Española. Second, there has been an effort to present the *RAE* as technologically up to date. These efforts seem to have been successful and Bill Gates himself, during his brief visit in 1999, gave the *RAE* his benediction: "El empresario estadounidense visita a la Real Academia Española y alaba su nivel tecnológico" (The American entrepreneur visits the Academy and praises its technological level) (*El País*, 16 October 1999).

2. Language standardization processes are conventionally considered to consist of four stages: *selection* of a variety that will serve as basis for the standard; *codification* of the standard normally in the form of dictionaries and grammars; *elaboration* of the standard so that it may be used in a wide range of communicative functions; and *implementation*. The task of language policy and planning agents during the implementation stage is crucial, since they must gain acceptance of the language by the target community. Such acceptance entails use, but also—and at times crucially—recognition of its symbolic value. By "linguistic diplomacy" I mean the agents in charge of implementing the language's symbolic value. For a detailed explanation of standardization see, for example, Robert B. Kaplan and Richard B. Baldauf Jr., *Language Planning: From Practice to Theory* (Philadelphia: Multilingual Matters, 1997).

3. The hegemonic attitude that some Latin Americans may resent was expressed by Jesus de Polanco (President of PRISA, a media and communications corporate Spanish group), when he stated that Latin America is "un objetivo político, económico y empresarial legítimo para los españoles" (a legitimate political, economic and business objective for Spaniards) (quoted in *El País*, 24 July 1995). Similarly a high-ranking Spanish official in the Economy Ministry was quoted in *The Washington Post*: "Spain understands Latin America in a way that no other country outside Latin America possibly could. . . . We have

used that to our advantage to build what we see as a long-term economic connection that is only going to keep binding us closer to Latin America" (quoted in *The Washington Post*, 14 February 2000). The recent publication of *Los nuevos conquistadores* (The New Conquistadors), by Daniel Cecchini and Jorge Zicolillo (Madrid: Ediciones Foca, 2002), illustrates the resentment to which I refer.

4. The current presence and interests of Spanish companies in the former colonies is associated with a form of late capitalism in which the development and independence of Latin American nations is in serious jeopardy. These very present circumstances also must not be understated as possible hurdles to the construction of an idyllic view of the pan-Hispanic community.

5. It is in part the purpose of the present essay to show what this dominant view of the pan-Hispanic community is and where it bases its legitimacy.

6. Manuel Alvar, *El español de las dos orillas* (Madrid: MAPFRE, 1991), 17–18. All translations from the Spanish originals are mine.

7. For his part, Juan Ramón Lodares—professor of Spanish Philology at the University of Madrid and author of the "trilogía de la lengua"—sees Spanish as the creator of an economic community: "The uncritical acceptance of the goals of nationalists, together with the political opportunism of those who insist that multilingualism—as decreed by the statutes of autonomy—is beautiful, have rendered the Spanish situation unique in the world: the jubilant disintegration of a linguistic community, which is nothing but a human community and, above all, an economic community" (quoted in *El País*, 19 May 2000). Also by Lodares see *El paríso políglota* (Madrid: Taurus, 2000); *Gente de Cervantes* (Madrid: Taurus, 2001); and *Lengua y patria* (Madrid: Taurus, 2002).

8. See the Spanish press for the week following the incident for details on the political turmoil caused by the King's speech. The speech itself can be found at http: www.casareal.es/casareal/home—Discursos y Mensajes: 23/4/01.

9. I define a language ideology as a system of ideas that integrates general notions of language, talk, and speech community with concrete views and actions affecting a given polity's linguistic identity and with the distribution of cultural, economic, and political power within that polity. For full treatments of the concept and field of "language ideologies" see John E. Joseph and Talbot Taylor, eds., *Ideologies of Language* (London: Routledge, 1990); Paul V. Kroskrity, ed., *Regimes of Language: Ideologies, Polities, and Identities* (Santa Fe, N.M.: School of American Research, 2000); and Bambi Schieffelin, Kathryn A. Woolard, and Paul V. Kroskrity, eds., *Language Ideologies: Practice and Theory* (Oxford: Oxford University Press, 1998). Also see Juan Valera, "Sobre la duración del habla castellana (con motivo de algunas frases del señor Cuervo," in *Obras Completas*, vol. 2 (1900; Madrid: Aguilar, 1961), 1036–40; and José del Valle, "Historical Linguistics and Cultural History: The Polemic between Rufino José Cuervo and Juan Valera," in *The Battle over Spanish between 1800 and 2000: Language Ideologies and Hispanic Intellectuals*, ed. José del Valle and Luis Gabriel-Stheeman (London: Routledge, 2002).

10. For how the economic potential of Spanish is being explored, see Instituto Cervantes, *El español en el mundo: Anuario del Instituto Cervantes 2001* (Barcelona: Círculo de Lectores, Plaza & Janés, 2001).

11. For Menéndez Pidal's life and work (including his tenure as director of the Centro) see Steven Hess, *Ramón Menéndez Pidal* (Boston: Twayne, 1982); José I. Pérez Pascual, *Ramón Menéndez Pidal: Ciencia y pasión* (Valladolid: Junata de Castilla y León—Consejería de Educación y Cultura, 1998); and Joaquín Pérez Villanueva, *Ramón Menéndez Pidal: Su vida y su tiempo* (Madrid: Espasa-Calpe, 1991). For the Madrid School see Manuel Peñalver Castillo, *La escuela de Menéndez Pidal y la historiografía lingüística hispánica* (Almería: Universidad de Almería, 1995); and José Portolés, *Medio siglo de filología española (1896–1952): Positivismo e idealismo* (Madrid: Cátedra, 1986).

12. See N. E. Collinge, "History of Comparative Linguistics," 195–202, and "History of Historical Linguistics," 203–11 in *Concise History of the Language Sciences*, ed. E. F. K. Koerner and R. E. Asher (Oxford: Pergamon, 1995).

13. Andrés de Blas Guerrero, *Nacionalismos y naciones en Europa* (Madrid: Alianza Editorial, 1994), 101.

14. E. J. Hobsbawm, *Nations and Nationalism since 1780*, 2nd ed. (Cambridge: Cambridge University Press, 1992). Hobsbawm sees a connection between the development of capitalism and nation building. In his view, in the nineteenth century, only communities that could foster the creation of a market for capitalist development were viable candidates for nationhood. He refers to this requirement as the threshold principle.

15. Ibid., 37–38.

16. Ibid., 34.

17. Ibid. Notice the extraordinary similarity between Mill's logic and Manuel Alvar's arguments on the need to de-Indianize the Indians as quoted above.

18. Ralph Fasold, "What national languages are good for," in *With Forked Tongues*, ed. Florian Coulmas (Singapore: Karoma, 1988), 185.

19. Pierre Bourdieu, *Language & Symbolic Power* (Cambridge: Harvard University Press, 1991), 113.

20. See for example Beatriz González Stephan, "Las disciplinas escriturarias de la patria: Constituciones, gramáticas y manuales," *Estudios* 3, 5 (1995): 19–46; and Julio Ramos, "Faceless Tongues: Language and Citizenship in Nineteenth-Century Latin America," in *Displacements: Cultural Identities in Question*, ed. Angelika Bammer (Bloomington: Indiana University Press, 1994), 25–46.

21. Carlos M. Rama, *Historia de las relaciones culturales entre España y la América Latina, Siglo XIX* (México: Fondo de Cultura Económica, 1982), 115.

22. Ibid., 128–29. Emphasis in the original.

23. Domingo F. Sarmiento, "Memoria sobre ortografía americana," 29 in *Obras completas*, vol. 4 (1843; Buenos Aires: Luz de Día, 1949).

24. C. Rama, *Historia de las relaciones culturales entre España y la America Latina, Siglo XIX*, 133.

25. Ibid.

26. Ibid., 134.

27. Andrés Bello, *Gramática de la lengua castellana* (1832; Madrid: Edaf, 1984), 33.

28. Cuervo's articles are reproduced in *Disquisiciones sobre filología castellana* (Bogotá: Instituto Caro y Cuervo, 1950).

29. For more detailed discussions of the polemic, see Guillermo Guitarte, "El origen

del pensamiento de Rufino José Cuervo sobre la suerte del español de América," in *Logos Semantikos: Studia Linguistica in Honorem Eugenio Coseriu*, ed. H. Geckeler et al., vol. 1 (Madrid: Gredos, 1981); and José del Valle, "La 'doble voz' de la ley fonética en la lingüística histórica española," in *Actas del I Congreso Internacional de la Sociedad Española de Historiografía Lingüística*, ed. Mauro Fernández Rodríguez, Francisco García Gondar, and Nancy Vázquez Veiga (Madrid: Arco Libros, 1999), 663–72.

30. See Valera's articles in Mexico's *La Tribuna*: "Colaboración de 'La Tribuna,'" *La Tribuna*, 31 August 1902, 1–2; and "Colaboración de 'La Tribuna,'" *La Tribuna*, 2 September 1902, 1–2.

31. Cuervo, *Disquisiciones*, 332.

32. See P. H. Robins, *A Short History of Linguistics*, 3rd ed. (London: Longman, 1990), 187–88.

33. See Manuel Mourelle Lema, *La Teoría Lingüística en la España del Siglo XIX* (Madrid: Prensa Española, 1968), 155–209.

34. Pérez Pascual, *Ramón Menéndez Pidal*, 147.

35. Pidal did in fact foreshadow some theoretical concepts (e.g., the social spread or the lexical diffusion of sound changes) that would become central much later in the century. See Paul M. Lloyd, "The Contribution of Menéndez Pidal to Linguistic Theory," *Hispanic Review* 38 (1970): 14–21; and del Valle, "La 'doble voz' de la ley fonética."

36. A trend that manifested itself in the *Nastasio*, the book prologued by Cuervo. See Rufino J. Cuervo, "Prólogo," in F. Soto y Calvo, *Nastasio* (Chartres: Durand, 1899), vii–x. *Martín Fierro* by José Hernández probably constitutes the most salient Latin American example. The presence of this trend in Spain is manifest in the works of José María Pereda.

37. Ramón Menéndez Pidal, *La Unidad del Idioma* (Madrid: Instituto Nacional del Libro Español, 1944), 29. Also by Menéndez Pidal, see *Manual de Gramática Histórica Española*, 6th ed. (Madrid: Espasa-Calpe, 1941); and *Orígenes del español: Estado Lingüístico de la Península Ibérica hasta el Siglo XI*, 3rd ed. (Madrid: Espasa-Calpe, 1950).

38. Ramón Menéndez Pidal, "La lengua española," *Hispania* 1 (1918): 1–14.

39. Ibid., 6.

40. Menéndez Pidal, *La Unidad del Idioma*, 23.

41. Ibid., 10–11.

42. Menéndez Pidal, "La lengua española," 5.

43. Menéndez Pidal, *La Unidad del Idioma*, 17.

44. Ibid., 9 (emphasis in original).

45. Ibid., 28 (emphasis added).

46. Ibid., 27.

47. Ibid, 29.

48. Menéndez Pidal, "La lengua española," 5.

49. Menéndez Pidal, *La Unidad del Idioma*, 18.

50. Ibid., 5.

51. Ibid., 10.

52. Menéndez Pidal, "La lengua española," 2 (emphasis added).

53. Menéndez Pidal, *La Unidad del Idioma*, 33.

CHAPTER SIX

COLONIALISM AND NATIONAL HISTORIES

José Manuel Restrepo and Bartolomé Mitre

Jeremy Adelman

INTRODUCTION

*N*ational history writing, like any other particular way of telling stories, has its history. As this volume makes clear, the Spanish Atlantic was no different than other broad culturally bound regions when it came to tying history writing to nation building. This essay explores one moment in the history of history writing in Latin America when the historical experience of a people could be plotted in the language of the nation. Until then there were histories—natural, religious, and mainly imperial. But after the "revolutions" of independence in Spanish America, it was the "national" narrative that emerged as the synthesizer. What made "Argentines" and "Colombians" common inheritors of a shared past was the catharsis of revolution that delivered them from a history they could not master as colonists, to one that they were supposed to master as citizens of nations. Furthermore, these revolutions and their immediate aftermaths that led to their first "histories," coincided with the maturation of the historian's task in the nineteenth century. For these intertwined reasons, gaining independence was a signal moment in modern historiography.

Like so many histories that tackle an "age" or "era," especially as regards "revolutions," these subjects immediately force upon historians the difficulty of unraveling the continuous from the discontinuous. Thus, the foundational accounts of national histories in Spanish America were inevitably bound up with the colonial past that the age was supposed—explicitly and self-consciously—to transcend. There were two ways in which colonialism mattered to its national progeny. First, being colonial, or creole, was the context in which a new "race" or "people" were born out of oppression. Indeed, until there were nations, there was no such thing conceptually as "colonial" history—the former created the latter in order to claim to be its logical successor. Second, if colonialism was the incubator of something new, it was also something that had to be rejected or purged in order to become something new. This was pronounced for Spanish American creoles, for whom the "Spanish" legacy was especially maligned. As a result, the colonial question was a fundamentally ambiguous and complicated one to its raconteurs. There was something in the past to reject and inherit at the same time. The ambiguous nature of colonial legacies therefore made the theme of "revolution" a central point in the making of the nation-states out of colonial ruins, for revolutions bore the double burden of having to dismantle and reconstitute political subjects at the same time. In the epic narratives of the first generation of creole historians, revolutions were privileged self-making moments; they were just as mythic, therefore, as the colonial pasts they aimed to topple.

The making of Spanish American national historiography had contexts that shaped them. In recent decades, our understandings of the economic, social, and cultural dynamics of the nineteenth century, when creoles plotted their grand stories, have changed. No longer is the first century of independence seen as one in which disorderly forces undermined the efforts of those who wanted order to perpetuate decades of "anarchy." The famous duality of "barbarism" poised against "civilization" has given way to a view of Latin American societies locked in conflicts over different models of order and citizenship. This ongoing contest over structures of the state, land, and personal freedoms was the setting in which creole historians inscribed their foundational texts. These circumstances, as we shall see, affected the way they wrote about nations' formative birth through revolution. In the bitter battles over the external and internal boundaries of the nation-state, historians took sides. Seen in this way, early narratives were partisan texts favoring one brand of order as national over other projects that got particularized. The first historians thereby waded into a debate over what was right and what was wrong for civic life and framed their narratives as more than just "invented traditions" of the past but as nation-making documents for the future.

NATIONS AND REVOLUTIONS

The event that catalyzed the formation of new communities, as well as modern historians, was the struggle, called in the 1820s "the revolution," for autonomy from imperial Spain. But when the wars for independence ended in Spanish South America, the dust did not settle. It continued to swirl through the nineteenth century as civil wars ripped up old viceroyalties. The continued struggles did not, however, dissuade the region's first historians from developing narratives for early nations as they came into being. These historians peered into the dust clouds to find clues for a past that would make sense of their turbulent present, and chart a road to a clearer future. They were part of a more general effort to tie great tales to great nations; history writing was part of, though not always reducible to, the cultural process of nation building.[1]

Spanish American writers thus worked within some historical conventions across the Atlantic world, conventions that aimed to separate what people inherited from the past from what they invented in the present to create something new in the future. Nineteenth-century historians looked to deep pasts as formative experiences for a national people coming into being. They did this by disconnecting literary and historical language from any "natural" or divine context or inspiration. History was man-made, the result of generations and centuries of piled up experience leading to a great catharsis or birth—most often a "revolution" in which a people finally recognizes what it wants in life and goes out to make it happen. In the Americas, colonial oppression was the bedrock; in the Old World, centuries of communal life under oppressive autocrats made the folk into a potential nation. Either way, revolutions enabled a potential nation to become a real one. Founding historians like Macauley, Bancroft, and Michelet conjured heroic stories of people defying tyrannical odds so that their collective national cause should triumph, liberating the nation from the caprice of aristocrats and kings.

Epic writing about revolutions was the consummate form for national narratives in the nineteenth century. These epics combined the idea of a heritage of the past and a cathartic moment of rupture and required inspired heroes to run the gauntlet between the two. George Bancroft, whose ten-volume *History of the United States* (1834–1874) provided the best example of "whig" interpretations of the American Revolution and its causes, told the story of a people dedicated to liberty. From Jamestown in 1607 to victory at Yorktown in 1781, "Americans" pursued the goals of freedom in a hostile environment and under tyrannous authorities—culminating in the despotism of King George III and the English Parliament. In this sense, the colonial legacies were distinctly ambiguous but felicitous: Life in the English empire combined freedom and oppression in sufficient balance to allow colonists to appreciate the former while increasingly resenting the latter. Thus Bancroft's epic created two heroes simultaneously: a chosen people and revolutionary prophets, exemplified by the founding fathers, capable of delivering them from the land of colonial bondage.[2] A similar two-step historical operation was at work in Jules Michelet's *Histoire de France* (six volumes, 1833–1844) and *Histoire de la révolution française* (seven volumes, 1847–1853). French historians of the Restoration and July

Monarchy shared moderately liberal and nationalist aspirations. As Bancroft saw the Americans, Michelet saw the French also as a people chosen before they knew it, if not by God then by centuries of fraternal coexistence after the decline of Roman rule over Gaul. In this sense Michelet shared Bancroft's heroic depiction of the "people" as makers of a forward-looking history. And like Bancroft, they needed a revolution to realize it.[3] Bancroft the "whig" and Michelet the "Romantic" charted the outlines for narrating revolutions and in so doing founding national historiographies for emerging republics. For the two, the "people" were heroes, and their entry onto the political stage ushered in a new era in human history. They likewise told a two-fold story of tyranny under old regimes and revolutions as redemptive struggles.

Both of these authors were mining a deeper vein in revolutionary narratives. Michael Walzer has suggested that the inner histories of revolutions are in fact accounts of the tensions and negotiations between two different groups, each with their own political capacities and aspirations. Revolutionary classes provided the energy and muscle; intellectuals or the vanguard provided the ideology and leadership. They also had very different consciousnesses, the former akin to slaves in Egypt (and thus oppression was so central in explaining "origins"); the latter like Moses, cast into exile. These two parties needed each other for the revolution to succeed—for the nation to be born. Loosely speaking, the metaphor of Exodus worked its way through the thick volumes of French and American historians. It provided a kind of metatradition for a view of national historiography at a time when historians claimed secular and scientific credentials for their craft.[4]

This was the intellectual context in which Restrepo and Mitre wrote their oeuvres. There existed models of national history writing pinned to narratives of revolutions, of human efforts to destroy old, even colonial, regimes. But it was in the entrails in the old that the elements for making the new had to be found—for as much as humanists were trying to insist that man could make his own history, they had to make it reaction to the past. For Restrepo and Mitre, this led them inevitably to locate the sources of nationhood in the experience of Spanish colonialism. But at the same time, Spanish colonialism was not easily likened to English colonialism or Gallic communitarianism. Nor were the circumstances in which these creole historians wrote their master works so conducive to uplifting narratives. In both republics, centralists fought with federalists, conservatives did battle with liberals, and across Spanish America, the basic principles of property rights were heavily contested. Revolutions had not given way to a new, monolithic order—something new, yes; a monolithic order, no. Spanish Americans, on the whole, could not easily comfort themselves with the teleology of national destinies. So, how to write accounts of nations coming into being when the nations ravage themselves in conflict? We are more familiar with the way Exodus narratives worked in the more canonic stories of France and the United States. We know far less about how people wrote about failed revolutions as formative experiences of early nationhood. How could failure be foundational? The revolution and its causes were just as important to national historiography in Spanish America, but the tales of both came to quite different outcomes in this corner of the Atlantic world.[5]

RESTREPO AND SIMÓN BOLÍVAR

José Manuel Restrepo's remarkable epic combined some of the conventions of emerging national epic writing with deeply held views of Spanish history to make sense of the tumultuous present moment in which he wrote. Born in 1781 in the province of Antioquia, Restrepo went to Santa Fé to study, and there joined the circle of young patriots associated with Caldas's *Semanario* and the *tertulerías* that buzzed with the news of world events. Like many other creoles of his middling class, he studied philosophy and law, with aspirations of becoming a man of letters and science on the eve of the crisis in 1810. The events that led northern South America from Caracas to Cartagena to rebel soon drew in the young lawyer's talents. Restrepo occupied several elected and appointed positions in the first republican periods, fled into exile during the Spanish "reconquest," and returned to become a close associate to Simón Bolívar after the Battle of Boyacá. He became the governor of Antioquia, served as deputy to the Congress of Cúcuta in 1821, and later as minister in several of Bolívar's cabinets. Indeed, as we shall see, the political trajectory of the lawyer and the Liberator were so entwined that the partnership invariably shaped the narrative of the revolution that made their careers.

Several tensions run through his epic, tensions that reflected Restrepo's ambivalent attitude toward the revolution, the event that freed Colombians but did not yield a durable constitutional order. In its multiple editions, Restrepo let his changing feelings toward the subject reframe the narrative. His first rendition, *Historia de la Revolución de Nueva Granada* (1827) was issued in Paris as ten small volumes plus an atlas. The second definitive edition appeared in 1858, much revised and corrected; the colonial Nueva Granada in the title gave way to "Colombia." The updating consisted of correcting mistakes, extending the narrative to 1830, adding much more on the Venezuelan side of the struggle, and removing some of celebratory passages about the Liberator—confessing, as he does several times in the epic, that the need for objectivity forced him to find flaws in Bolívar's character. By the 1850s, the original dream of a confederation from the Orinoco River to Potosí had clearly vanished, and in its wake followed localized feuding between rival political movements whose ideological differences resulted in persistent polarization. In effect, Bolívar's work dismantling the colonial order was not followed by a new "order." And this failure altered the tone of the epic from edition to edition. Indeed, it was the sense that political passions could not be tamed in a republican mold that shaped Restrepo's growing pessimism—and as we shall see will contrast sharply with Mitre's optimism as Buenos Aires began to exercise its hegemony over the republic for which it served as capital. Still, the massive collection remained dedicated to the Liberator, and its author never backed down from the basic claim that there would have been no revolution, merely a crushed revolt, without Bolívar.[6]

It was not only Bolívar who was the source of the ambivalence, but the "people" of Colombia. For Restrepo also respected what he felt was the underlying meaning of the struggle: the effort to master political passions and channel them into enduring republican institutions. This was the basic "spirit" of the revolution, though it, like Bolívar's valor, remained unrealized as Restrepo's story got revised through the years. His epic had a fundamental, transcendent purpose: This was to be a story of the past for the future, a saga to inspire readers later in the century, and move them with the sense of self-sacrifice at the example of creoles taking up arms and practicing politics for the first time. The efforts to "give themselves laws and institutions capable of securing liberty so that man might debate in his social condition, change his habits, his customs and his concerns . . . such are truly rare events which contain useful lessons for posterity."[7] But the change that Restrepo still yearned for remained an aspiration, not an achievement.

More than the political environment informed the writer. By the time Restrepo came to author his epic, the structures of Spanish American history already had a rough shape of their own. It conformed to a model of empire passed down by generations of writers and propagandists under the general rubric of the Black Legend: the stubborn view that Spain was locked in time to an obscurantist, counter-Reformation spirit that bound free-spirited men in the confines of submissive pietism. Then, when individualism got some free reign, it ran amok in the form of conquistadors tromping through the New World looking for glory and gold, only to leave the conquered to the mercy of friars and tax collectors. But this, as we know, was not just a framework for Spain—it also worked as a framework for European, and especially English, historiography, which preferred to tell the story of rising Atlantic grandeur with quite different registers—not of conquest, but of discovery and redemption. There were Spanish dissidents of this stereotyped image of peninsular oppression.[8] But they were drowned out. The Black Legend deeply imprinted the way in which creole writers understood Spanish colonialism, especially as creoles embraced the idea of Spanish tyranny to justify their emancipatory cause.

Restrepo's view of Spain's legacy to history—and the ways in which these legacies would shape independent Colombia—can be seen in the way the author treated colonialism. His portrayal of the colonies tells of great dynamism, but also great repression. Colombia and Venezuela were creations of an empire seeking to renovate itself by creating new viceroyalties and chartering corporations to develop the northern coast of the continent. People moved in; commerce flourished; and eventually, a printing press even began to issue newspapers. But if reforms weaned the new colonies, they also reached their limits. The outbreak of the Comunero revolt, rising defense costs, and fiscal penury thwarted any further change. Indeed, in some respects the fetters on revolutionary history were already evident in the ways the reforms failed to give colonists real room to thrive. The vast diversity of the population, its ethnic and geographic dispersal, the grip of venal colonial institutions, and the power of the Church created a much greater current driving back the waters of change. The result, by 1810, was that "the general masses of Granadinos and Venezuelans were subject to the deepest form of ignorance for three centuries, or for their entire time that the Spaniards dominated these lands."[9]

But if these people were stripped of civic capacities, traditions of self-rule and responsible government, how did a revolution happen at all? If colonialism held colonial subjects back, independence came "from powerful causes and motives." Enduring oppression is one thing; but tolerating it when the accidental occasion for rejecting it presents itself is quite another. As colonial subjects weathered the exactions and inflictions, the degree of exploitation reached intolerable levels after 1800. One class of people felt the burden of their status above all: the colonies' enlightened creoles who found the controls, peninsular monopolies, exclusions from public offices, and burdens of rising taxes to pay for distant conflicts more than they could bear. Creoles, inspired by the work of Antonio Nariño and others, got wind of "the marvelous and seductive (a word Nariño used deliberately) example of the United States of North America." Herein, however, lay a problem, for as the local creole elites began to grumble, four-fifths of the population could not read and lived outside the circle of civic society. Reading and literature—not property and wealth—demarked the boundaries of political capacities for change. The masses "were absolutely ignorant of the calls for independence and liberty, taking as an article of faith that royal authority came from Heaven, as they were instructed every Sunday by their priests."[10] Thus the powerful motives of revolt wrestled with deeply entrenched inertial factors whose strength "was no less powerful."

What sparked the revolt was an external rupture. Nueva Granada and Venezuela were not like the Thirteen Colonies, bristling with ideas of autonomy and independence on the eve of 1776. They had to be pushed by Spain's metropolitan crisis to take matters into their own hands. In effect, the colony was not ready for liberty; unlike North Americans they did not acquire a common sense of themselves as freedom-lovers shackled to an *ancien regime*. Instead, it was Napoleon's invasion of the peninsula and the ensuing struggle for political power that toppled the legitimacy of the empire and the monarchy. When Spanish troops repressed various outbursts—especially in Quito—the creole line began to harden. Thus it was that colonialism came to be shattered, not by an idea—or an imagined community—of an alternative world, but by a real crisis of an imperial world that gave birth to the idea of a nation where there was once a colony.[11]

It is important to appreciate Restrepo's sequence because herein lay much of the problem that would befall the revolutionaries. Camilo Torres, a prominent publicist and politico, issued a petition in the name of the Cabildo of Santa Fe to authorities in Seville. This document extolled all the virtues of universal freedom and equality—but improvised the ideal community before its institutional or civic existence. The language of emancipation soon invited the rabble, and its "passions," to the central square—a hitherto excluded colonial space—where, fired by "demagogues," these political novices issued "extravagant petitions" to the local assembly. In Restrepo's narrative, the emergence of the "pueblo" interjected in an already delicate situation, introducing an impassioned actor whose force would now swirl through the colonies with gathering strength. Thus the dilemma was partly the presence of politically immature actors; it was also the fallacy of idealism, that the vision of liberty itself contained the same transparent meaning for all. "This was to be feared precisely for the social dissolution it would provoke, even as far as families themselves."[12]

Lack of colonial experience in self-government meant that local self-rule without a king was a recipe for warlords and provincial jealousies. If federalism suited the United States, where local assemblies and civic cultures were the breeding ground for a political culture that respected authority, property, and the rule of law, in Spanish colonies, the same dogma had the opposite effects. The only way out of this predicament was to convene a national assembly to create a single charter—but doing this invited local voters to send demagogues as their representatives, and so the early experience with constitution making yielded to more disunion, not less. "Political leaders put their entire faith in passing naïve laws and constitutions, with no attention to whether they fit the conditions of the country; they were obsessed with writing brilliant sheets and not threatening civil liberty, when what was necessary was revolutionary vigor."[13] The false prophets of federalism were leading their flock from one barbarous condition to another. "The ignorant general mass of the population, which did not know its rights nor was interested in them, having been born and raised as slaves to a king, appreciated so little its newfound liberty."[14] Here was an Exodus narrative, in which deliverance of bonded people led to the worship not of a single God with a singular Commandment, but to multiple idols and ideological heresy.

The epic could end here as a saga foretold in the colonial structures bequeathed from Spanish Conquest and the hubris of a few wordy intellectuals. But what made this foundational story an epic was that it was unstable, open to possibilities. The fact was, possibilities kept surfacing; it was not so easy to fold colonies back into an old mold (though the Spanish government poured men and materiel into the task—at a massive human and material toll). The possibilities for novelty or freedom were not, however, the results of an indomitable spirit, as Bancroft or Michelet would have it. If anything, the spirit of the "people" constrained the future to a different kind of bondage, slavery to the passions. Restrepo's epic was not driven like other nationalist foundational narratives by a people refusing to submit wholly to their oppressors. What kept hope alive, indeed what drove the epic through its multiple volumes, was the narrative of individual heroism that almost, but never quite, compensated for the political immaturity of collective colonial subjects.[15] The hero of Restrepo's epic was Simón Bolívar. What made him so remarkable was the most perfect balance of ruthlessness and principles, a fusion that rescued the revolution from falling completely into the maw of defeat. For Restrepo, the revolution in Spanish America was quite unlike its North American and French predecessors: The struggle to overthrow the ancien regime would be much more difficult, bloody, and inconclusive precisely because its leaders not only had to drive out the oppressor and deliver their people from bondage, but also to instill a patriotic zeal among a people whose instincts were unfamiliar with freedom:

[T]he body politic, just like the physical body when it is ill, needs strong medicine to recover the vigor and freedom of its movements. This is especially true among certain peoples, like South Americans, who were educated in the lethargic dream of Spanish slavery; they lived in indolent apathy and feeble in all their potential. It was necessary to put them into action and to shake them powerfully to give their spirits the strength and energy capable of winning their independence and liberty.[16]

One kind of action trumped all others, and made Bolívar's character suited to the heroic role: revolutionary violence. Bolívar's practice of revolution on Spanish American soil was "not pursued out of a cruel or hard heart, but as a result of a system formed out of deep meditation and reflection upon the character of compatriots, and the acts which the Spanish had already committed or were inflicting in Venezuela at that time."[17] Accordingly, on 8 June 1813, Bolívar declared "war or death." A week later in the city of Trujillo, he delivered an even more blood-curdling speech: "any Spaniard who does not conspire with us against tyranny and in favor of justice . . . will be treated as an enemy and punished as a traitor of the Patria and consequently, without appeal, executed." The hero's example instilled a martial spirit among colonial folk, and even appealed to the masculinity of his novice soldiers who under empire were more eunuchs than men. Becoming a soldier meant becoming a man; becoming virile prepared men for their future duties as citizens in the republic. In this virtuous circle, Bolívar "armed a multitude of men who held aloft the flame of liberty with heroic acts."[18]

Needless to say, extolling revolutionary violence is a hard way to create historiographic heroes. And it created problems for Restrepo's claim to dispassionate objectivity. Restrepo knew that part of the appeal of George Washington was precisely his moderation; and part of the revulsion against Jacobin Terror was its wanton killing of traitors. Had the narrator boxed himself into celebrating an unlikable hero? Restrepo stepped back to ask the reader: Who is right? He who violates his own "natural—read colonial—sensibility" of compliant lassitude? Or he who, in the century of enlightenment and philosophy, "has renewed in America the bloody scenes of his very first conquest?"[19] Restrepo altered his narrative voice from dispassionate scientific observer to the partisan raconteur. The political necessity of a brutal war inspired "the spirits of Venezuelans and elevated them from their apathy and indifference." From the historian's point of view, as far as Restrepo was concerned, the options retrospectively also removed all room for doubt or indifference. After describing the final major battle at Ayacucho in 1824, Restrepo reminded readers that it took seven years for Bolívar to dismantle what the Spanish created over three terrible and dark centuries.[20]

When push came to shove, commitment to a more removed narrative of the revolution made room for commitment to the nation-building purpose of the narrative. If, as Lionel Gossman has noted of Augustin Thierry, French historians believed that history writing required separating partisan activity from the field of thought, this was a luxury that Restrepo felt that he, and the civic and political needs of his republic, could not yet afford. There was no room for relativistic debate, as if the historian were not a participant in that which he described. In this sense Restrepo's moral self-image echoed the role he gave to Bolívar as tamer of unruly passions.[21]

At first blush the identification of the martial hero with the militant historians might appear to squeeze out all other domains of nation building and history writing. Restrepo's epic can be read as a condemnation of politics, especially of the deliberative sort associated with *cabildos* and constitutional gatherings. For the most part Restrepo treats these occasions as evidence of how blind enlightened creoles were to the malign effects of Spanish colonial legacies. Yet, as Restrepo's narrative unfolds, and as Bolívar's triumphs accumulate, there remained a question: How did the Liberator deal with the lands he liberated? Behind the lines a new order had to be erected. Here is where the "imperio de la ley," or rule of law, mattered. On 5 August 1813, Caracas was liberated a second time (and it would not be the last). The next day, a victorious Bolívar entered his home city and there immediately ensued a familiar debate over whether Venezuela would be federal or centralist—now with an added complication, what would be the relationship with neighboring Nueva Granada. Bolívar did not hide his preferences—nor did Restrepo's narrative. Federalism was a recipe for disaster; a centralized union with fellow Andeans was a political necessity to forge a common alliance against Spain and to transcend loyalties to *patrias chicas* in favor of *patrias grandes*.[22] To defer deliberation for better times, Bolívar eventually argued for the creation of a centralized dictatorship to continue the work of the revolution, for it would provide a "shelter against the tempests in the arc of our Constitution."[23]

It is in his capacity as lawmaker, however, that Bolívar's heroism faltered for Restrepo. Across the Andes civilians took over the job of nation building. "Military government, a necessity in many circumstances, is intolerable when it prolongs its destructive existence beyond the era of dangers," observed Restrepo.[24] The time had come for the right words, not just martial deeds. The liberation of Spanish colonies only freed creoles from formal political bonds. After that the revolution had to be *for* something, not just against Spain. As Bolívar's role evolved he became, in Restrepo's treatment, less decisive, more vacillating, as if his military prowess could not serve the war of words. The outcome was not good for the unity of the region or for the stability of each republic. "In these circumstances," wrote Restrepo, "we believe that if Bolívar had presented a strong political character, firm and decided, he would have been capable of altering our form of government, to the content of many. But he worked in halves, advancing some times, retiring other times. This unstable behavior finally cost him public support, and he left nothing stable in his place."[25] After Ayacucho, Bolívar's weaknesses became more evident. He had grown so mistrustful of civilians that he promoted dictatorship as a universal panacea. "The impartial historian," writes Restrepo, "cannot help but doubt the policies of the Liberator." Then, when Bolívar got back to Santa Fé, he confronted local politicos, and Santander above all, and his dictatorial propensities got the better of him. He even promoted the idea of a constitutional monarchy, with himself as the candidate for the crown. In a rare footnote citing personal observation, Restrepo tells his readers "that I heard him many times express these ideas of whose exactitude and truth the Liberator was intimately convinced."[26] Bolívar's time had passed; it was now the moment for a new model of heroism. As one Santa Fé jurist told the general: "the only language which dignifies heroes is the language of free men."[27]

In some respects, we have come full circle, back to the idea of the political community of free men in its formative moment. Restrepo was unkind to those who conceived of Spanish America as capable of transcending through words, its colonial past. It, unlike Anglo America, could not so easily proclaim liberty for itself. But this did not mean that the right words had no role once formal ties were definitively broken, once the siren calls of the old regime were beyond earshot. Getting the sequence right was all the more important in such an unfertile environment. In Restrepo's eyes Bolívar was a hero charged with making a revolution out of Spanish legacies, a task that exceeded the abilities of any mortal. Restrepo, in outliving Bolívar, came to see the limitations that the past bequeathed to the future, and the deeper causes of the civil conflicts that plagued Spanish American politics. Revolutionary violence and its heroic leaders may have been necessary, but they were not sufficient for creating the legal foundations for men to be able to make history anew. The struggle for nationhood had become a war over the idea of itself. In this respect, the *Historia de la Revolución de Colombia* and its author became protagonists in this unresolved debate, with clearly partisan overtures to make the case for a nation, as David Bushnell has noted, that did exist in spite of itself.[28]

In the last instance, Restrepo's epic was a vindication of its subject, but stripped of any self-congratulatory pretenses. To be sure, Restrepo's anxieties about democracy, federalism, and the Church left open the problem of how nations would be built in spite of its subjects. If foundational epics aimed to unravel the telos of history as the realization of the nation-state, Restrepo's great work was unfinished, and necessarily so as it sought to compose a narrative of beginnings without an end in order to intervene in the ongoing struggles of post-colonial Colombia. Perhaps he hoped that readers would see in their history what they could not remember and that the tales of sacrifice and heroism would instruct them of their own abilities to rise above inherited colonial particu-larisms and appreciate the civic importance of the rule of law as a foundation for republican coexistence. Reading history could deliver the nation to itself.

MITRE'S BELGRANO

Bartolomé Mitre's *Historia de Belgrano y de la independencia argentina* was Restrepo's counterpart for the River Plate. Mitre's epic grew out of a larger proj-ect coordinated by Andrés Lamas to issue a compendium called the Galería de Celebridades Argentinas, and whose document-collecting phase began in earnest in the mid-1850s. This was an explicit effort to create a pantheon of Argentine "celebrities" as a balm for a deeply fractured country. The conjunctural setting is important: After decades of caudillo rulers, "Argentines" were now at each other's throats fighting over rival constitutional programs. Mitre, a firebrand associated with the liberal faction from Buenos Aires, had vociferously rejected the Constitution of 1853 and had supported the secession of Buenos Aires from the confederation. Thereafter, *porteños* were at war with their neighbors. Their arse-nal included more than guns and lances—they included words. Indeed, we might note one of the first contrasts between Restrepo and Mitre, that the latter exuded a stronger Romantic predilection to ascribe to words some powerful agentic possibilities, whereas Restrepo tended to view the work of *letrados* some-what mordantly. Indeed, it was Mitre's faith in words, strung together into epic narratives designed to make history, that emboldened his hyperproductivity and has made it so hard to disentangle Mitre the general from the politico and histo-rian. For while he was mining archives and furiously writing Mitre was also com-manding armies in the field and presiding over the republic, determined to coil the power of guns, laws, and histories into a powerful, if unfinished, drive to build a nation, not in spite of, but for itself.

Mitre's first edition of *Historia* came out in 1857 while Buenos Aires and the Argentine Republic each claimed to be the rightful republic, and relied on "history" to make the case for the rightfulness of the former. Like Restrepo's, this history would be partisan—but it, like Buenos Aires, would also have science on its side. In the preamble to the first edition, Mitre claimed that his motive for writing the biography of Argentina's independence leader was to create a "rational foundation for admiration" to destroy "superstition." Through the reasoned love of a hero, citizens could nurture love of a country and the reasoned principles that guide it. The aggregation of documented events lent "moral certainty" to the larger structure.[29] When the complete (final and fourth) edition appeared in 1887, it totaled four thick volumes and coincided with the triumphant emergence of the republic, thanks in large part to Mitre's own (quite bloody) pacification of the provinces.

There was, however, an essential difference between Restrepo and Mitre— for their biographies mattered in the shaping of their historic visions. Restrepo identified himself, to the point of invoking personal testimony as evidence, with the project that failed. Though his epic went through revisions, it did not essentially break with the movement, and the tragic outcome, that it sought to describe. Mitre represented a different generation. His hero, Manuel Belgrano, was long dead before Mitre could even read, freeing him from the weight of the memory of a failed project. While Belgrano died even before Bolívar, and in the midst of a savage civil war, Mitre could still afford to find redemptive features in his struggle—features that remained to be inherited for a future order. Mitre the historian, and the statesman, positioned himself as the heir of a legacy that he was destined to complete. (A point, it is worth noting, that his arch-nemesis Juan Bautista Alberdi could not resist needling. Alberdi accused Mitre of writing more than just self-serving history, but narcissistic history in which the shadow protagonist in the revolution was the author himself, destined to complete what the epic's hero could not. This charge was perhaps the biggest thorn to prick away at Mitre, who prided himself so much for his "objectivity" and archival fidelity.) Either way, the combination of the identification with Belgrano's republican cause and his scientific distance from it enabled Mitre to critique the hero while appropriating his work. By recognizing Belgrano's limitations, Mitre could transcend them—and in so doing realize the republic more fully.

There is an important logical issue here: How could the founder's failure be an uplifting tale? Why Mitre was able to identify with Belgrano without falling into Restrepo's gloomy trap, is what I want to explore right now. The difference is more than a matter of the biography of the biographer, but has to do with the multiple uses of Black Legend accounts of the colonial past in the effort to create postcolonial nations. The provinces of the River Plate were no less oppressed by Spanish policy than Nueva Granada. Spain, since Díaz de Solis's discovery of the estuary, subjected the region to commercial plundering and administrative tyranny. But there were differences to these outlying provinces: There was no existing native civilization that the Spanish could enslave and convert into more perfect automatons of empire. Instead, from the very start, a rustic type of Spanish pioneer, a "colonist," appeared on the scene. These "Spanish" Americans enjoyed rights under the monarchy, especially to represent themselves in matters of local concerns in town councils, or *cabildos*. Mitre introduces from the start of his narrative a feature of empire that was meant to reproduce the sclerotic hierarchies of the peninsula, but whose migration to the new world mutated into something else. Cabildos, far away from the oversight of imperial counselors and viceroys, acted as primitive democratic nodes for an increasingly autonomous province, demographically dominated by transplanted Europeans who evolved into "a virile race." Colonialism did not stand in the way of a homegrown democracy, "the embryo of a grotesque municipal republic," but this was a completely unintentional outcome.[30]

Unintentional because Spanish greed led to an obsession with colonial cores loaded with mines, like Lima and Mexico. Consistent, then, with the Black Legend was the incompleteness of the Spanish enterprise. Forgetting outlying districts, Spain let the River Plate become a porous province, draining the Peruvian viceroyalty of its specie and commercial bounty. Whereas monopoly trade benefited colonial cores and peninsular ports, it excluded Buenos Aires and Montevideo. To survive, these outliers had to violate colonial regulations. Contraband became the commercial bonanza of the region, and by the eighteenth century, trade routes wound their way from the pampas through Tucumán into the highlands and the silver lodes of Potosí. What is more, herdsmen and rustlers of the pampas discovered that the stocks of feral cattle provided a lucrative set of staples, jerked beef and leather, for consumption in the neighboring and thriving slave colony of Brazil. In all, a homegrown commercial society of primitive possessive individualists flourished under the noses of Spanish regulators. While other colonies suffered from the mercantilist grip of Spain, the River Plate went through a "commercial revolution." Then, when Spain finally agreed to give Buenos Aires its own commercial guild, the *consulado* (for which Belgrano would serve as the permanent secretary), the colony acquired a meeting place to deliberate over economic and social policies. A complement to the cabildo, the consulado was a place where creoles learned the art of self-government and representative practices, together helping create "public opinion."[31]

Mitre's emphasis on commerce served two functions: It evoked the sense that the colony was like other progressive colonies—a corner of an empire where subjects enjoyed more, not fewer, freedoms than in the metropole. In this sense, the River Plate could be the exception that proved the rule about the validity of the Black Legend for the rest of the Spanish world—and thus gave to the revolutionaries in the River Plate a "providential mission" to free the rest of the colonies.[32] Commerce was what made this colony so different, and therefore capable of realizing a future for other Spanish colonies (a point that would become even more pronounced in Mitre's other epic, his biography of José de San Martín, who did carry the struggle up the Andean cordillera). But commerce also had a deeper, metaphoric role: The colony was a body, and its veins coursed with trade goods. In the face of "absurd monopolies," wrote Mitre, contraband "became a normal function, like the circulation of vital blood, with agents all over half of southern America, working together for reciprocal interests."[33] The colony was born and matured within empire, the body grew, nurtured by trade and opportunity, and became aware of itself as separate, not identified with the metropolis. Creoles, "the real sons of the colonized earth, constituted the social nerve" of the region, and were the repositories of an "innate patriotism." Here was a folk with a predilection for individualism and an "instinct for independence."[34]

These everyday practices of creole life constituted the fabric of a "sociability" that stood the River Plate apart from other colonies like Peru and Mexico. In contrast to the venerable old viceroyalties, where tales of oppression, tyranny, and Black Legend fare, Buenos Aires acquired an increasingly "democratic character." And not just democratic, but also national. Indeed, early in the first volume, Mitre calls this space, anachronistically, "Argentina." What is important is that the Black Legend served to describe what Argentina was not, precisely because survival forced it to reject the cultural and institutional practices of Spanish imperialism. Just as Spain identified with absolutism and monopoly, these provinces of America were associated with illicit, but rampant, practices of commercial freedom and autonomy. The nature of commerce, conducted by independent, utility-maximizing creole merchants, provided a world of daily, prosaic interaction and a mechanism for other-regarding folk to band together—to become, in effect, a community of interests. This was just the sort of rational foundation for an incipient political community that liberals dreamed of—in the heart of the Spanish empire. Separation was therefore an "embryonic" fact long before 1810.

Thus, using the trope of the Black Legend, Mitre argued that in fact Argentine independence was as natural as any other revolution in the Atlantic world. The argument was spelled out even more forcefully in his sequel to the story of Belgrano, Mitre's second epic, *Historia de San Martín y de la independencia sudamericana*. Independence did not fall like immature fruit to the ground. He explicitly rejected "those historians who think that only external events" separated the colonies from the metropolis, ignoring the "revolutionary organism."[35] Creole freedom, in contrast to Restrepo's formulation, was not a response to the implosion of the metropolis, not a mechanical response to an external event. It was internal and "organic." In the story of Belgrano, Mitre stepped back and summarized his argument: "the argument" of this book "is the gradual development of the idea of the INDEPENDENCE OF THE ARGENTINE PEOPLE, from their origins at the end of the eighteenth century, and during their revolution, until the final decomposition of the colonial regime in 1820, in which a brilliant democracy is inaugurated, embryonic and anarchic, but which tends to normalize itself within its own organic elements."[36]

But if the revolution was so predetermined, why have one at all? What room was there for an individual hero like Belgrano if in the dynamics of this revolution was the inevitability of collective freedom? The viceregal space did not add up to an integrated nation coming into being collectively. By the time Mitre sat down to write his epic, several decades of Romantic writing had inscribed a basic duality to the "nation": it was both civilized and barbarous at the same time—each equally part of the whole. For Mitre, Buenos Aires, the civilized part, was the head atop a dormant body of the provinces. Like many of the contemporary dualized tropes of civilization and barbarism, Mitre agreed with his peers—Sarmiento, Alberdi, and the main agent for spreading Romantic work in the River Plate, Esteban Echeverría—that the city-country distinction did not efface a democratic unity. In all the provinces, Mitre argued, everyone "was equal *de hecho y de derecho*." Nonetheless, the country (where "semi-barbarism" prevailed) had to receive some political inspiration from the capital. The model was familiarly diffusionist, as the "organic sociability" of Buenos Aires radiated outward to the unconscious folk with natural democratic instincts. They were not objectively ready to force a revolution, but were ready to join one.[37] In this fashion Mitre created a two-step history of the revolution, of a new nation coming into being. The first accorded with the external history of the revolution: freeing the colony from Spain. The second was the "internal" revolution: dismantling the local colonial institutions and creating a new order. In both phases, but especially in the second, the internal drama of the revolutionary coalition would transform Manuel Belgrano from an enlightenment *homme de lettres* to revolutionary leader and statesman.

The first phase of the revolution began well before the French invasion. Indeed, its beginnings already signaled an important difference with Restrepo, for whom the colonists had to be pushed to their destiny. In the River Plate, a British invasion in 1806 acted as the handmaiden of independence. The behavior of imperial authorities (Viceroy Sobremonte withdrew with his garrison and treasury) and the successful creole commitment to self-"defense" "gave rise to a radical change in the political order of the colony." What creoles showed was their determination to protect their sovereignty, that they could protect it, and that the Spanish would not—in effect giving proof of de facto independence. It was the first—and extensively narrated and embellished—heroic act of self-definition.[38]

Two aspects of the episode deserve emphasis. The first is Mitre's concern to show that self-"defense" and affirmation transcended all classes and races. In contrast to Restrepo's deeply stratified Nueva Granada, Mitre's Buenos Aires was on its way to a race- and class-blind alliance behind the nation. In the jubilation following the British retreat, creole slave owners freed seventy slaves who (by legend at least) fought alongside their masters against the invaders. Second, the vehicle for this national unity was a martial consciousness. The creole reconquest awoke "a warrior spirit in all classes." The "armed pueblo" was born—organized into local militias—as an alternative military organization to the (cowardly) peninsular hierarchies. This was "a true military democracy, from the commander in chief to the very last soldier." In constructing a mythic military-pueblo alliance, Mitre gave institutional shape to a nation coming into being. The victory, and the civilized celebrations that followed, showed that this was "a serious and enlightened pueblo, with a consciousness and moral already formed, and was not the result of casual accidents."[39] Thus even before Napoleon's pensinsular campaign, creoles had run the gauntlet from "colono" to "ciudadano."

Thereafter, the history of independence reads like a concatenation of creole claims to sovereignty as the Spanish empire collapsed. The occasional feeble efforts on the part of royalists serve in the main to illustrate just how self-directed and unanimous the cause was—in Buenos Aires. The cabildo and the consulado, where Belgrano's leadership as lawyer and advocate for the cause of commercial freedom from Spanish mercantilism (he was the guild's secretary) first sparkled, took over the reins of power and became the primary policy-making organs of the state. By 25 May 1810, when the viceroy and the audiencia were deposed, de facto independence became a de jure reality. Thus far, the revolution's relatively pacific nature only helped exemplify the united consciousness of the people, the civilized manner in which public opinion viewed politics, and the combination of objective and subjective conditions determining self-made creole history. That there was no violent campaign against Spain did not make this any less revolutionary in Mitre's view—on the contrary.[40] But the peaceable conquest of power in

Buenos Aires did not alone determine the nation. The external revolution required ridding Spanish forces and institutions from the rest of the viceroyalty: especially from Paraguay, the Banda Oriental, and most fatefully, the Andes. In none of these theatres did the fighting go the way of creole patriots. Paraguayans at first welcomed Belgrano—now emerged as a "general"—and his expedition, but then, once free, separated themselves from the reconstituted, freed viceroyalty. The very worst came in the Andes where Belgrano—now the military chieftain of the "liberating armies"—saw victory as far as the Altiplano, only to get trounced by Spanish armies sent from Peru, losing forever the axis between the Andes and Potosí, and the port and Buenos Aires.[41]

So, the fate of the revolution and its leadership does not go well—and therefore become candidates for an epic of trial, tribulation, and eventually redemption. There is by necessity, then, more instability to Mitre's narrative than readers might have anticipated at the outset. Indeed, Mitre's second volume in the epic is a stark contrast to the first, and begins with Belgrano's return from the Paraguayan expedition (seen at first as a triumph) to a Buenos Aires wracked by discord. The original creole leadership is now embroiled in fratricidal conflict. Moreno and Alberti are dead, Berutti and French are banished, and others are in prison by the first anniversary of May 25. "The Revolution" conceded Mitre, "was devouring its sons."[42] Importantly, however, to the analysis that followed, the author treated the civil bloodshed within a framework natural to the history of revolutions, and less as the friction associated with the dismantling of a colonial order. The carnage was not a result, as Restrepo argued, of deep-seated colonial habits that proved difficult to extirpate, but was part of the natural laws of all true revolutions. In this sense he agreed with Restrepo that revolutionary violence was a necessary property of the epic, but he disagreed with the Colombian by arguing that the nation was simply immature and had to be forced to come into its own. Both historians argued that most of the violence had to do with the frictions within the revolutionary coalition. Restrepo reflected one side of Exodus paradox: that unfree people are simultaneously willing and unwilling to put Egypt behind them—that they feared their own freedom. For Mitre, the problem was not so much that people feared their freedom, but that they did not know what they were in for once delivered from their oppressors. Thus, for Mitre the real violence began as freed people grappled with the task of devising a new covenant binding rulers and ruled, and not a struggle over the old one.[43]

This brings us back to Belgrano, the creature of the old regime, leader of liberating armies, and defender of models of covenants that still carried the birthmarks of the regime in which he was reared. For what the cabildo, the consulado, and all the constitutional blueprints issued from the pens of the most enlightened of creole thinkers—from the 1813 charter to the highly centralized constitution of 1819—tended to reproduce was a reform of the old viceregal system. Rather than a new regime, a true democracy, revolutionary leaders formulated hybrids with the old. The biography of the hero Belgrano intertwined with the fate of the order he had thought possible. In 1819, as the provincial caudillos and their popular armies ripped up the countryside, repudiating the various legal charters coming from Buenos Aires and centralists, Belgrano himself was dying a slow death. The general's body was a metaphor for the forces that toppled the old regime, but that could not endorse the emerging new one. When he died in 1820, so too did the last vestiges of colonialism: the cabildo, the consulado, and centralist politics. "As this dangerous and decisive evolution over ten years unfolded, the new nation, master of its own destiny . . . buried for good the old order."[44] Accordingly, the mayhem and anarchy had its historic roles of releasing popular pent-up democratic energies to serve as the basis of the new covenant.[45]

Herein lays the basis of Mitre's optimism. For the barbarism of humanity—even those parts of humanity from whom little could have been expected in history, the provincial colonial subjects of the Atlantic's most oppressive empire—joined with, and then eclipsed, the forces of civilization. "Guided by a blind instinct of exaggerated independence, of an almost savage and brutally disaggregated individualism, the barbaric element was introduced into European civilization. . . . But without it, the democratic republic and the federation would have been two daughters of the painful birth of the Argentine patria."[46] "In the midst of this chaos, there existed the latent germs of a future life; in the most deafening part of the tempest, the insurrectionary masses did not lose sight of their great course; in the midst of this social and political decomposition, there prevailed a principle of conservation of the organism, both anterior and superior to the dissolving forces of anarchy." The destructive force, having done its necessary work, switched to a vital force, and "the brutal work modified into the definitive law of a new sociability."[47] In 1820, the foundations of a true "federation" were laid, based on universal male suffrage and the notion that the cornerstone of national sovereignty was a federation of autonomous provinces. What Restrepo most deplored, what made his anarchy interminable, was for Mitre the virtuous outcome of a necessary anarchy.

This revolution—the full destruction of the colonial order and the making of a wholly new one—was more than successful. It was a model of a true revolution.

In the final volume of the epic, Mitre stepped back from his narrative to contrast the events in the River Plate to those of the United States. If Restrepo believed that the conditions for a successful revolution had to exist even before it began, Mitre felt otherwise. For unlike Restrepo's narrative, Mitre's deployed the tropes of the Black Legend to depict what colonists struggled to define themselves against. So oppressive was the Spanish empire that colonists had no choice but to create the nation in its opposition. Thus, the Argentine revolution, in Mitre's narrative, contrasted with Restrepo's in which there was no escape from the past. But it also contrasted with the American Revolution, for Argentine creoles could not rely on imperial principles to guide them to the promised land. There was nothing akin to the rights of freeborn Englishmen; the practices of colonial sociability were in defiance of, and not conformity with, metropolitan rules. "Precisely because the Argentine revolution was a true radical revolution and not simply a mutation or normal evolution, a condition of its survival and progress was the complete destruction of the old and the creation of the new within its own organic elements; and this result could not be achieved without an appeal to all of society, and appealing to all social forces, with all their incoherence and their dangerous excesses." He observes comparatively: "This was not a merely defensive revolution vindicating traditional rights as in England; it was not a simple change of government with an anterior constitution as in the United States; it was a twin revolution, one political and the other social" to create a popular and democratic "FEDERATION" out of nothing.[48]

CONCLUSION

The experience of Spanish colonialism, according to these two founding historians, created the foundations for a postcolonial order. Both agreed that colonialism determined postcolonial possibilities. And both shared a dismal view of Spanish rule. For these nineteenth-century creole writers, the colonial experience and Spanish rule were precisely what republics had to transcend. What is remarkable is how the very same formulation—down to the Black Legend tropes—could yield such different stories, different heroes, and different outcomes. One conclusion of this paper is that treating colonialism even through the monochrome of the Black Legend did not limit the potential stories that could be told of how colonies matured and eventually broke from their metropoles to become nations.

Was there a nation in colonial drag before 1810? Restrepo argued not; Mitre yes. For the former, it was forced into being by external events; the Spanish colonial experience did not leave room for creating alternative visions—even in reaction to its oppression. For the latter, it was endogenously, "organically" determined, and the revolution was under way before 1810. Colonialism did leave spaces for alternatives precisely because it was so oppressive. Clearly for one historian, the people could still occupy their heroic roles, and democratic federalism could be envisioned as a possible, if not probable, outcome in the face of great odds. Belgrano could be Moses because his Jews had innate capacities forged in resistance to their bondsmen to reject false gods. For the other, of course, the covenant failed, because this capacity could not, by the definition of Spain's legacy, emerge.

Despite their important differences, however, Restrepo and Mitre agreed that it was hard to fold their narratives into accepted histories of enlightened peoples who underwent revolutions of their own. For both, Spanish colonialism was something *against which* a new order had to be built, not an order to build upon—in contrast to Anglo America. And for both, revolutionary violence played a crucial role as the way Spanish colonialism had to be expunged, and for the prophets of revolution to deliver their people from centuries of bondage to the pharaohs of Madrid. The struggle for independence had to be more bloody and costly than the French or American revolutionary predecessors. The result was an epic narrative to create a myth of redemptive war forged by a militarized people bent upon destroying the clutches of a mythic oppressive past. Mitre's optimistic story suggested that here was a *real* revolution, making something out of nothing; Restrepo's pessimism suggested that the redemptive war was still going on even as he finalized his text.

Neither Restrepo nor Mitre—despite their use of Black Legend myths—straightjacketed Spanish American history into the status of perpetual "exception." Painting Spain and Spanish America as an exception to a general rule about progress was, of course, already commonplace. And such views continue to enjoy a great deal of currency. But what Mitre and Restrepo were offering were epic variations on a broader theme about the ways people historically imagined postcolonial possibilities. Even if Spain and Spanish colonialism appeared so devoted to the idea of resisting the progressive march of history, Restrepo and Mitre did not imply that this condemned their people to the same fate. Indeed, the purpose of their foundational narratives was to depict creole heroism to keep the cultural and political activity of creating republics going. Reflecting back on the origins of modern Spanish American history making, we might remember that these founders did not succumb to arguments that the past was destiny or that any form of colonialism determined the fates of postcolonial subjects.

NOTES

1. Thomas Bender, "Historians, the Nation, and the Plenitude of Narratives," 1–8 in Bender, ed., *Rethinking American History in the Global Age* (Berkeley and Los Angeles, University of California Press, 2002); Donald Kelley, *Historians and the Law in Postrevolutionary France* (Princeton: Princeton University Press, 1984), esp. chap. 10; Joyce Appleby, *Liberalism and Republicanism in the Historical Imagination* (Cambridge, Mass.: Harvard University Press, 1992), 4–28.

2. Jack P. Greene, "Introduction," in Greene, ed., *The Reinterpretation of the American Revolution, 1763–1789* (New York: Harper and Row, 1968); Edmund S. Morgan, "Interpreting the American Revolution," in Morgan, ed., *The American Revolution: Two Centuries of Interpretation* (Englewood Cliffs, N.J.: Prentice Hall, 1965); Michael Kammen, *The Mystic Chords of Memory: The Transformation of Tradition in American Culture* (New York: Knopf, 1991), esp. 34–42.

3. Lionel Gossman, *Between History and Literature* (Cambridge, Mass.: Harvard University Press, 1990), esp. 153–84.

4. Michael Walzer, "Intellectuals, Social Classes, and Revolutions," in *Democracy, Revolution, and History*, ed. Theda Skocpol (Ithaca, N.Y.: Cornell University Press, 1998), 127–42; and his *Exodus and Revolution* (New York: Basic Books, 1985).

5. Others were also exploring the ties between colonial legacies and postcolonial developments. For reflections on Andrés Bello and José Victorino Lastarria, see Iván Jaksic, *Andrés Bello: Scholarship and Nation-Building in Nineteenth-Century Latin America* (Cambridge: Cambridge University Press, 2001), 133–42. Also see Germán Colmenares, *Las convenciones contra la cultura: Ensayos sobre la historiografía hispanoamericana del siglo XIX* (Bogotá: Tercer Mundo, 1987), 49–70. Interestingly, both authors accented the continuities, but disagreed on whether the past (and present) was so bleak.

6. On the fear of passions, see Colmenares, *Las convenciones contra la cultura*, 87–90.

7. I will refer to the six-volume edition, José Manuel Restrepo, *Historia de la revolución de la República de Colombia* (Medellín: Editorial Bedout, 1969), hereafter referred to as *HRC*. Cite vol. 1:15.

8. In his recent pathbreaking book, Jorge Cañizares-Esguerra explores the efforts of eighteenth-century Spanish, and the occasional creole, writers to define the lineaments of a Spanish history free from much of the baggage that was dumped by some of their predecessors, but mainly other Europeans who preferred to relegate Spain as a laggard (at best) in the march toward modernity. So it will not suffice to argue that the Enlightenment simply ducked Spain. Jorge Cañizares-Esguerra, *How to Write the History of the New World: Historiographies, Epistemologies, and Identities in the Eighteenth-Century Atlantic World* (Stanford: Stanford University Press, 2001).

9. *HRC*, vol. 1:37.

10. *HRC*, vol. 1:45.

11. Ibid, 104.

12. Ibid, 150.

13. Ibid., 269.

14. Ibid., 199.

15. Miranda, in Restrepo's view, loved the principle of representative government, but he detested "with good reason" democracy, for it would "empower imprudently the ignorant people of Spanish America, bringing their disgrace instead of directing them towards the civilization, prosperity and wealth to which they were called by the nature and position of their fertile soils." Ibid., vol. 2:227, 335.

16. *HRC*, vol. 3:42.

17. Ibid.

18. Ibid., 47, 258–59.

19. *HRC*, vol. 3:44.

20. *HRC*, vol. 5:188.

21. Gossman, "Augustin Thierry and Liberal Historiography," in his *Between History and Literature*, esp. 86–105.

22. *HRC*, vol. 3:69.

23. Cited in *HRC*, vol. 3:365. Indeed, in subsequent acts, he resigned as Dictator once his military purpose was accomplished and his legal definition as Liberator obsolete. See *HRC*, vol. 5:193.

24. *HRC*, vol. 4:225.

25. *HRC*, vol. 5:289.

26. Ibid., 306, 314.

27. Ibid., 318.

28. David Bushnell, *The Making of Modern Colombia: A Nation in Spite of Itself* (Berkeley: University of California Press, 1993).

29. Bartolomé Mitre, *Historia de Belgrano y la independencia argentina*, 4 vols. (Buenos Aires: Ediciones Estrada, 1947), vol. 4:13–34 for an extended discussion of the type, sources, and selection of documents. Hereafter referred to as *HB*.

30. *HB*, vol. 1:69.

31. Ibid., 92, 115.

32. Colmenares, *Las convenciones contra la cultura*, 189–90.

33. *HB*, vol. 1:100.

34. Ibid., 69.

35. *HSM* (Buenos Aires: Ediciones Anaconda, 1950), 42.

36. *HB*, vol. 1:55.

37. Ibid., 110–13.

38. Ibid., 179–89.

39. Ibid., 217–50.

40. Ibid., 1:352–77.

41. The failures to keep the provinces of the viceroyalty together is the dominant theme of volume 2 of *HB*.

42. *HB*, vol. 2:3.

43. Walzer, *Exodus and Revolution*, 74–79.

44. *HB*, vol. 4:68, 174.

45. *HB*, vol. 2:293.

46. *HB*, vol. 3:42.

47. *HB*, vol. 4:74.

48. Ibid., 4:76–77.

CHAPTER SEVEN

WHEN TOURISTS CAME, THE MESTIZOS WENT AWAY

Hispanophilia and the Racial Whitening of New Mexico, 1880s–1940s

John Nieto-Phillips

When Spain's hegemony over the southern rim of North America ended in 1821, its long tenure left an enduring legacy that extended beyond the tangible transformation of people and places. More abstractly, Spain's legacy also lingered in American historical memory, where it took on a life of its own.

—*David J. Weber,* The Spanish Frontier in North America

INTRODUCTION

*T*oward the end of the nineteenth century, there emerged in the United States a literary movement that celebrated four centuries of Spanish civilization in the Western Hemisphere. Its creators painted a refreshing and romantic picture of Spain's colonial past: They glorified the memory of the *conquistador* who had "pacified" and then "civilized" the Indian; they extolled the self-less missionary who had defied all hardship to spread Christianity among *los índios bárbaros*; and they authored epic tales and wistful sketches of Spain's imperial grandeur. Enamored as they were of antiquarian detail—no peculiarity was too small to mention, no deed insignificant—Hispanophiles were possessed of a mission: to combat age-long prejudices against Spain's colonial past—those impulses behind the so-called Black Legend—and to trumpet Spain's historical deeds and virtues. Hence the origins of a new and romantic legend, a trope that can only be characterized as the White Legend. Of course there was nothing "new"

An extended version of this essay appears in the author's book, *The Language of Blood: The Making of Spanish-American Identity in New Mexico, 1890s–1930s* (Albuquerque: University of New Mexico Press, 2004).

Fig. 9. The romantic recasting of the U.S. Southwest as "Spanish" reached a feverish pitch in 1940. That year, New Mexico's "Cuarto Centennial" festivities marked four hundred years since the arrival of the conquistador Francisco Vázquez de Coronado. This billboard announced the reenactment of Coronado's *entrada* to New Mexico in 1540, an event that involved hundreds of participants and drew thousands of spectators. "Coronado Entrada," 1940. Courtesy of Coronado Cuarto Centennial Commission Records, Center for Southwest Research, University of New Mexico.

about the White Legend among Spaniards themselves. To them it embodied their national history, it was a fount of their Spanishness, or *hispanidad*; it represented Truth, History, the authentic past, and it was so sanctioned by the Crown and Church, and their emissary-scholars. But to New Englanders schooled in textbook renderings of Spanish treachery, greed, heathenism and barbarity, the White Legend posed an invigorating challenge to their imaginations.

The making and marketing of the White Legend in the United States, from the 1880s through the 1910s, helped to transform (though haltingly and perhaps only superficially) popular knowledge about Spain's colonial past. It was an unofficial campaign begun by an unaffiliated number of writers, including recognized figures like Helen Hunt Jackson, Hubert Howe Bancroft, and Charles Fletcher Lummis, as well as neophyte historians, such as the jurist and would-be governor of New Mexico, Lebaron Bradford Prince. Though they labored autonomously, these individuals laid the foundation for a wider appreciation of all things Spanish. Indeed, as I will argue, they were precursors to the Hispanist movement that swept the United States in the 1920s and 1930s. Writing in the spirit of a new age—of strident expansionism and progress—each rendered a vivid and dynamic vision of "Spanish America." And together, they breathed new life into a subject that, like the moldering empire itself, merely reminded the world of Spain's decadence. Notwithstanding Hispanophiles' efforts, however, the Black Legend endured and is very much in evidence today.

From the founding of the United States, Hispanophobia—the disdain for Spanish history and culture that was bequeathed to North Americans by Mother England—has been carefully tended to. In their initial dealings with Spaniards, from the Floridas to the Californias, Americans—and by this I mean white English-speaking citizens of the United States, also known as Anglo Americans—seldom questioned their own predispositions or preconceptions. As the historian David Weber reminds us, Americans often viewed Spaniards as "unusually cruel, avaricious, treacherous, fanatical, superstitious, cowardly, corrupt, decadent, indolent, and authoritarian."[1] These pejoratives, though not universally invoked, constituted the essential features of the Black Legend, and they captured the moral deficiencies that presumably brought about the collapse of Spain's once-enviable empire. One need not recite the entire evolution of the Black Legend to point out its crowning irony, that the individual who is credited with its origins was none other than Fray Bartolomé de Las Casas, Spain's first Protector de Indios (appointed in 1516) whose treatises on Spain's abuses of the Indians spawned centuries of global condemnation. If Hispanophobia endured well into the nineteenth century, it was because Americans wished to shift attention away from its own cruel treatment toward Native peoples.

What explains the emergence of the White Legend in the 1880s, when Spain was left with mere remnants of its colonial glory? Why, at this particular time, did some Americans begin to agitate directly against the Black Legend? To what end? Who stood to benefit what from such a campaign?

Before exploring the subject further, one must bear in mind that the Black Legend, though prevalent in the United States, was not uniformly subscribed to. There were those individuals who looked fondly on Spain's colonial past, or at least its people, such as Governor William P. DuVal of Florida, who in 1822 informed President James Monroe that "the Spanish inhabitants of this country are the *best* even among the most quiet and orderly of our own citizens."[2] Other such pronouncements were not common in the literature of the period, but neither were they absent, suggesting that the rhetorical fervor behind Hispanophobia had not infected the hearts and minds of all Americans. Indeed, to critics of U.S. Indian removal policies, Spain's past treatment of Native peoples was beginning to seem relatively civilized; for in its zeal to expand westward, the United States had begun to establish its own legacy of atrocities, in the name of Manifest Destiny. The White Legend, then, afforded not only a counterargument to the Black Legend, but also a prescription for how the U.S. government might better deal with its "Indian problem." It was in the context of U.S. expansion and industrialization that critics seized upon the

Spanish colonial pastoral—the beneficent White Legend—to wax nostalgic about preindustrial social relations.

THE SPANISH SOUTHWEST

By the 1880s, popular novels, history texts, travel journals, and tourist brochures began to make known the Spanish history of Florida and Louisiana. But nowhere was the White Legend more pronounced than in texts that focused on "the Spanish Southwest." That vast frontier that once was called "New Spain" today encompasses California, Arizona, New Mexico, and Texas, as well as parts of Nevada, Utah, and Colorado. Southwestern authors and historians saw commercial and political value in celebrating all that was Spanish in the region. Tales of the Spanish conquest captured a spirit of adventure, virtue, and, as was often noted in tourist literature, virility that many easterners admired. The Spanish past possessed an aura of European tradition blended with Indian antiquity that so contrasted with the United States' Anglo-Saxon modernity. Moreover, this White Legend helped to clarify—in the minds of readers, tourists, and westward migrants—the racial boundaries and historical landscape of relatively unknown lands, such as California and New Mexico. Most important, it helped Anglo Americans come to grips with the presence of more than 100,000 Spanish-speaking residents in their midst—residents who, by the 1848 Treaty of Guadalupe-Hidalgo, were deemed citizens of the United States and were, by law if not in practice, equal to Anglo Americans.

Most important, perhaps, the textual mapping of the U.S. Southwest as "Spanish" in the latter decades of the nineteenth century transformed the way many Anglo Americans looked on Mexican peoples living there. It made possible, for example, the partial admission to the nation's body politic the 60,000 Mexican citizens of New Mexico (whom I will refer to as *nuevomexicanos*). In a word, the Hispanophilic writings of the period racially "whitened" erstwhile "half-breeds" and *mestizos*, transforming them—in the American mind—into "Spanish Americans."

By celebrating the memory of Spain's conquest of the Southwest—its courage in the face of environmental obstacles, its pacification and Christianization of the Indians, its introduction of "white blood" to the land— the White Legend relieved whole communities (not just a particular echelon of Spanish-speaking society) of the stigma associated with being racially mixed "Mexicans." Figuratively speaking, it banished mestizos from the Southwest, erasing most traces of them from the historical imagination. In their publications, Hispanophiles refashioned memories of the conquest by downplaying the degree to which mestizaje took place, and by venerating those institutions that kept the races separate and maintained social order, such as the Church, the *presidio*, and the *rancho*. Readers of White Legend propaganda would come to know the colonial frontier as a kind of biracial paradise wherein enterprising Spaniards carved out European communities among the savages, then undertook to show them the blessings of Christianity. This imagined pastoral replicated all the virtues of plantation society whose demise even some Yankees had come to lament—chivalry, racial segregation, social order, tradition— without the politics of slavery that once had divided the nation.

The White Legend was the narrative template for such popular writings as Helen Hunt Jackson's 1884 novel *Ramona*, which rivaled Harriet Beecher Stowe's *Uncle Tom's Cabin* as one of the best-selling books of the nineteenth century.[3] *Ramona* mourned the passing of California's Spanish colonial era, which, in Jackson's view, represented the Golden Age of the Southwest. It was an era during which two discrete races—one Spanish, the other Indian—had thrived in relative harmony following a harrowing yet brief conflagration between the two, known as the conquest. The inevitable demise of the two symbols of that period, the mission and the rancho, at the hands of land-hungry Anglo Saxons, signaled the beginning of the end for the California Indians, according to Jackson. A renowned political activist who two years earlier had penned *A Century of Dishonor* to publicize the plight of Native Americans nationwide, Jackson wrote *Ramona* to illustrate one main point: Native Americans were better off under the Spanish mission system than under the Anglo-American regime.[4] When not campaigning to exterminate or dispossess Indians, insisted Jackson, the American government simply neglected their educational, health, and spiritual needs and allowed them to sink into squalor. Although today we might label Jackson's work "Hispanophilic," in Jackson's day, her writings were understood as pro-Indian. Ironically, three decades after its publication, *Ramona*'s pastoral narrative helped spawn a California Mission Revival in architecture and city planning. That movement's imprint is still very much in evidence in California's place names, in names of streets, communities, and shopping centers. (Today it is not uncommon to enter gated communities with incongruous names, like "Estados Encantados," which I think was meant to capture both a California state-of-mind and a middle-class ambition to live on a Spanish "estate.")

In New Mexico, as well as California, Hispanophilia was born in nostalgia and in a desire to restore in text that which never was. It was a sentiment—a yearning—to reconstruct, in an author's own imagination and in the imagination of his or her readers, a pristine, chivalric, adventurous past, a past far removed from the ills of industrial society. But it was much more than just a sentiment.

Hispanophilia was an active ideology, embodying presumably "Spanish" values and ideals that spoke to contemporary "American" political and social concerns. For Hispanophiles in the United States, Spain's colonial past was a reminder of societal virtues that were doomed to disappear with the imperial advance of the United States into the Southwest and beyond—virtues such as idealism, sacrifice for the greater good, generosity, piety, gentility, and benevolence toward "inferior" (i.e., Native American) peoples. For Jackson and others, these virtues were soon to be ploughed under by Manifest Destiny and supplanted by Anglo-American pragmatism, individualism, materialism, technology, and the systematic decimation of Indian peoples. An advocate of U.S. Indian policy reforms, Jackson mobilized others in calling for the "protection" of Native Americans by making inviolable reservations of their traditional lands, and then their gradual "assimilation" into white society by way of paternalistic "Americanization" programs in reservation and boarding schools—schools she envisioned as modern-day missions. Her agenda, it must be said, was not shared by many of the Hispanophiles who came in her wake. Others were more content to keep Indians and descendants of the *conquistadores* locked in their traditions; natural extinction or assimilation seemed merely a matter of time. Still others thought the last remnants of Spain's conquest should be preserved for the enjoyment of westward migrants and tourists, and not simply allowed to disappear. Hispanophilia, and the White Legend, specifically, was therefore a discursive tool for the promotion of ethnic preservation, boosterism, and ethnic tourism. It was, in effect, a kind of eye-catching and reassuring billboard that welcomed Anglo Americans to—as New Mexico's license plates remind us—"The Land of Enchantment."

The two individuals whose Hispanophilic writings were perhaps the most instrumental in the promotion of both tourism in and immigration to New Mexico during the late nineteenth century were Charles Fletcher Lummis and Lebaron Bradford Prince. From the 1880s through the 1910s, their popular books on Spanish colonial history delighted both Anglo Americans and, increasingly, Mexican Americans (who by the early twentieth century had adopted the ethnic designation, in English, "Spanish Americans"). They functioned as a textual lens through which the audience visualized the Spanish conquest. Much like Jackson's *Ramona*, their writings depicted two essential and clearly defined races—one Native American, the other European—and like *Ramona*, they held important political implications. First, their biracial (Spanish and Indian) depictions of the territory countered persistent accusations in Congress that nuevomexicanos descended from mixed-blood Mexicans; that, as mestizos, they secretly maintained a loyalty to Mexico and were unfit for self-government or full admission to the body politic. Second, their White Legend renditions suggested that Spain's colonial legacy easily rivaled that of England in North America and that, as a consequence, the descendants of the conquistadores were equal in virility, stamina, and racial fitness to the Anglo Saxons; by extension, the "Spanish Americans" of New Mexico were entitled to full participation in U.S. social and political life, and deserved a state government, which they repeatedly had been denied between 1850 and 1912. Third, their writings presaged a nationwide appreciation of Spanish colonial history, culture, and even the Spanish language, prompting not only greater interest in traveling or moving to New Mexico, but also greater interest, generally, in studying Spanish history and language. It may be said that Prince and Lummis were precursors to the renowned Hispanists of the 1910s and 1920s, such as Charles E. Chapman and John D. Fitzgerald, not to mention the founder of borderland studies, Herbert Eugene Bolton.

Of the two, Prince was far less flamboyant than Lummis, and far more obscure outside of New Mexico. Prince was foremost a jurist and one-time governor of New Mexico who championed the territory's fight for statehood until it was achieved in 1912. He served, during four decades, as the president of the Historical Society of New Mexico. From 1883 until his death in 1922, Prince spearheaded a membership drive that attracted leading figures in territorial society.[5] Charles Lummis, on the other hand, was but an occasional resident of New Mexico who, nevertheless, became an internationally acclaimed Hispanophile.

Charles Fletcher Lummis

In the fall of 1884, having recently graduated from Harvard University, Charles Fletcher Lummis set out on foot from Chillicothe, Ohio, to discover the U.S. West. During his five-month adventure, which took him through Santa Fe and its outlying villages, he recorded observations about the landscape and people he encountered, and published them as travel letters in the *Los Angeles Times* and the *Chillicothe Leader*. Seven years later, in 1892, those letters reappeared (though thoroughly recast) in a memoir entitled *Tramp across the Continent*. This work inaugurated a decade and a half of intense production, during which Lummis wrote more than ten books and dozens of articles on everything from Pueblo Indian pottery to contemporary Mexican politics. His most popular work was one of his earliest, *The Spanish Pioneers*. Originally published in 1893 and reissued a half-dozen times during his career, *Spanish Pioneers* established him as the Southwest's—if not the nation's—most popular authority on "Spanish" and "Indian" cultures.[6] The book also earned Lummis international recognition, for, when it was translated into Spanish and published in Madrid in 1916, Spain's Alfonso XIII knighted Lummis in the Order of Isabella the Catholic.

Lummis's letters to the *Chillicothe Leader*—numbering some two dozen, of which seven pertained specifically to New Mexico—captivated his audience with tales of danger and images of savagery, but they also exposed his readers to romantic and lasting impressions of genteel nuevomexicanos and docile Pueblo Indians. He studied the territory's inhabitants with awe and curiosity, and took copious notes about their culture and manners, which he mailed to the *Times* and the *Leader*.

On arriving in Santa Fe in November 1884, Lummis marveled at its quaint architecture, which he deemed "as handsome to me as the New Jerusalem."[7] An "ancient metropolis," Santa Fe was "one of the most interesting places on the continent, and certainly the most unique."[8] Its rustic mud houses belied a 300-year history that deserved to be told. Lummis seemed particularly impressed with the people he encountered who seemed kind and generous, and possessed what Lummis believed were the features of a virile race. On arriving at San Ildefonso Pueblo, he proclaimed its inhabitants "the best looking Indians I ever saw. They are tall, but well built and sturdy. They have light, copper complexions, and good features."[9] Lummis's letters disseminated an image of Pueblo Indians not only as robust laborers, but also as morally superior people. "I do not believe there is a christian [*sic*] American community in the world," he remarked, "which can approach in morality one of these little towns of adobe." Although the Indians had retained many of their religious traditions, they had also managed to grasp the fundamental tenets of Christianity, especially generosity, honesty, and respect for their neighbors. "The Pueblos are sharp but honest traders," Lummis noted, and they are "hospitable far beyond the average white man."[10]

Lummis also praised the nuevomexicanos whom he met on his New Mexico travels, finding them to possess similar traits of kindness and hospitality: "[W]hite folks . . . are in the minority," he noted in a letter to the *Leader* dated 25 November 1884. "But I find the 'Greasers' not half bad people."[11] The term "greaser" appeared only once in Lummis's 1884 letters and just one more time in his later writings as an admonition to his readers that the word was "a nomenclature which it is not wise to practise as one proceeds south . . . and which anyway is born of an unbred boorishness of which no Mexican could ever be guilty."[12] In contrast to Anglo Americans, Lummis explained, "Mexicans" exhibited good manners and generosity toward strangers: "There is only one sociable thing about the white folks, they will share your last dollar with you. A Mexican, on the other hand, will 'divvy' his only tortilla and his one blanket with any stranger, and never take a cent."¹³ One such exemplary nuevomexicano, observed Lummis, was U.S. Indian agent Pedro Sánchez, "a very refined and courteous Mexican. Unlike the average Indian Agent, whose highest use for the red man is to skin him alive, the Don is very plainly putting his whole energy and attention to such honest endeavor as is doing vast good." "Don Pedro" had undertaken the noble task of trying to bring education to the Pueblo Indians, despite resistance from within his own agency.¹⁴

While expressing admiration for New Mexico's "Mexicans," Lummis at first had only contempt for their ancestors. In a letter dated 1 December 1884, he described the early settlers as "old Spaniards" who had "kept the Pueblos down in regular slave fashion."¹⁵ His contempt did not last long. One month later, while visiting the San Mateo ranch of sixty-five-year-old Manuel Chaves, with whom Lummis had "many interesting talks," he described the elderly man as "one of the pioneers" of New Mexico who had survived "countless bloody encounters with the savage Apaches, Navajos, and Utes." A biography of Chaves, he observed, would "read like a romance [novel]."¹⁶ One can only speculate about the stories Chaves might have related to him, but Lummis's later writings hint that Chaves and his son Amado conveyed tales of the colonial period that may well have prompted Lummis to rethink his view of the Spanish conquest. Whatever negative impressions he might have held about the conquistadores never resurfaced following his 1885 visit to San Mateo. In mid-January of that year, he left New Mexico for California.

Lummis's first impressions of New Mexico would not be his last. Three years after arriving in Los Angeles, where he worked as city editor for the *Los Angeles Times*, he suffered a stroke and returned to New Mexico to convalesce. From 1888 until his departure in 1892, Lummis forged relationships that would endure for decades. Foremost among them were those with the Chaves family of San Mateo and the Abeita family of Isleta Pueblo. Through contact with them, he became fluent in Spanish and familiar with nuevomexicano and Indian folklore and history.

For several months in 1888, Lummis stayed at the home of Amado Chaves, who, four years earlier, had been elected speaker of New Mexico's House of Representatives, and in 1891 would be named by Governor Prince as New Mexico's first superintendent of public education.¹⁷ Lummis's return to San Mateo marked the beginning of his deep interest in Spanish colonial history. There, he likely heard "Don Amado" tell stories of his "Spanish" ancestors, for Chaves was descended from a long line of illustrious *españoles*. His lineage could be traced to the seventeenth-century Spaniard Fernando Durán de Chaves, who, as historian Ralph Emerson Twitchell noted in 1917, "was a colonel in the Spanish army and was a knight of the Order of Santiago. The Chaves family is one of the oldest in this country and for centuries has figured prominently in the history of Spain."[18] Little is known of what transpired between Lummis and Chaves, except that by the end of his convalescence, the two had cultivated what would be a lifelong friendship.

With the exception of Lummis's relationship with Chaves, his correspondence and papers leave almost no indication of intimate or lasting friendships with nuevomexicanos. Lummis's most notable (and very public) exchange with them occurred shortly after he arrived to convalesce, when he set out to photograph the Holy Week Penitentes procession at San Mateo. Accompanied by Chaves, he captured the brotherhood performing sacred rituals involving self-flagellation and crucifixion. When the brotherhood learned that Lummis had published those photos in *Scribner's Magazine*, they charged him with violating their code of secrecy and ran him out of town, promising to seek revenge. Among these particular nuevomexicanos Lummis had the reputation of being an opportunist who had abused their trust and was exploiting their culture to promote his writing career. Lummis retreated to Isleta Pueblo in the summer of 1888 where, the following February, he was shot and wounded outside his rented adobe home. Chaves rushed to his friend's bedside and tried to console him. Although the perpetrators escaped, it was widely believed that they had acted on behalf of the San Mateo Penitentes.[19]

Despite the incident, Lummis remained for three and a half years at Isleta Pueblo where he befriended individuals who provided him with enough folklore material to publish in 1894 a 257-page collection entitled *The Man Who Married the Moon and Other Pueblo Indian Folk-Stories*. In this work Lummis, like many of his "progressive" contemporaries, exhibited an attitude of paternalistic benevolence. The Indians of Isleta, he noted, possessed many admirable qualities, such as respect for their elders and a strong work ethic, yet "with all this progress and civilization, despite their mental and physical acuteness and their excellent moral qualities, the Tée-wahn [Isleta Indians] are in some things but overgrown children."[20] If Isleta Indians were but children in Lummis's mind, he was their Anglo-American father. As an interpreter and promoter of their folklore, he positioned himself between them and his English-reading audience, and used their cultural or religious traditions— often shared in confidence—for his professional gain, much as he had done at San Mateo. Some three decades after Lummis published *The Man Who Married*

the Moon, Isleta tribal officers declared his "folk-stories" fraudulent and repri-
manded his alleged informant, Pablo Abeita.[21]

Following his return to Los Angeles in 1892, Lummis continued to write
about New Mexico's residents, drawing largely on the vast array of ethnographic and historical notes he had amassed during his four-year residency.
From 1892 to 1905, he produced ten books on the Southwest, of which *Tramp
across the Continent* (1892) and *The Spanish Pioneers* (1893) became the most
popular, especially on the East Coast, and attracted glowing reviews in the *New
York Evening Post Literary Review*, *New York World*, *Boston Transcript*,
Pittsburgh Monthly Bulletin, and *New York Times*, among others.

Tramp across the Continent recounted Lummis's trek from Ohio to
California. Based on his 1884–1885 travel letters, this memoir elaborated on his
first impressions of the Southwest and helped to shape his readers' views of the
region and its peoples. The book described New Mexico as safe, enchanting,
and hospitable to Anglo-American tourists, whom he urged to reconsider their
longstanding racial prejudices against "Mexicans" and "Pueblos." For too long,
he stated, the people of New Mexico and their history had been ignored or
unreasonably judged by unknowing and prejudiced Americans. Historians had
done New Mexico and its inhabitants a disservice by perpetuating a false
impression of Spanish-speaking peoples and their past.

> There is . . . [a] dense popular ignorance as to the Spanish doings in
> the beginning of the New World, particularly in the beginning of the
> United States. Our partisan histories . . . do not seem to realize the
> precedence of Spain, nor the fact that she made in America a record
> of heroism, of unparalleled exploration and colonization never
> approached by any other nation anywhere. Long before the Saxon had
> raised so much as a hut in the New World . . . the Spanish pioneers
> had explored America from Kansas to Cape Horn.[22]

New Mexico's history, Lummis continued, was not marked by Spanish atrocities against Indians, as many Americans had been led to believe, but by the
noble deeds of "hero-missionaries" who braved great obstacles to bring
Christianity and civilization to the Indians of the Southwest. This view contrasted sharply with a Lummis letter in 1884 in which he stated that the
Spaniards had "bull-dozed the [Pueblo Indian] majority" and "kept them in
regular slave fashion."[23] Now Lummis held that "the Spanish never enslaved the
Pueblos, and were, on the contrary, the most humane neighbors the American

Indian ever had."[24] He acknowledged and apologized for his earlier views. "I had very ignorant and silly notions in those days about Mexicans, as most of us are taught by superficial travellers who do not know one of the kindliest races in the world."[25] Lummis directly challenged the popular assumption that English and Anglo-American settlers were somehow less cruel to Native Americans than were Spanish conquerors. "We talk of the cruelty of the Spanish conquests; but they were far less cruel than the Saxon ones. The Spanish never exterminated. He conquered the aborigine and then converted and educated him, and preserved him with scholarship, humanity, and zeal."[26]

Here Lummis reflected the views of such other popular writers of the day as Hubert Howe Bancroft and Helen Hunt Jackson. Unlike Lummis, they focused primarily on colonial California, but their glowing assessments of the Spanish conquest resonated with those of Lummis. Wrote Bancroft in his 1888 *California Pastoral*: "Never before or since was there a spot in America where life was a long happy holiday, where there was less labor, less care or trouble."[27] As already mentioned, Jackson captivated East Coast readers with romantic depictions of California's biracial (Spanish and Indian) mission society.[28]

Historian John R. Chávez observes that Bancroft and Jackson romanticized Spanish California just as it was being destroyed. "As Anglo settlement of California increased," writes Chávez in *The Lost Land*, "the earlier Anglo conception of the state changed; by the 1880s California was no longer the wilderness frontier of the Gold Rush, but a booming agricultural wonderland."[29] Historian David Weber has made a similar observation about the East and finds in its despoliation the causes for the romanticization of the West. East Coast Americans, repulsed by "excessive commercialism, materialism, vulgarity, and rootlessness," looked to places like New Mexico and California "for pastoral values that they imagined had existed in a simpler agrarian America."[30]

Perhaps more illustrative of Lummis's Hispanophilia and considerably more popular than *Tramp across the Continent* was his *The Spanish Pioneers*. Published in 1893, this work went through eight English and three Spanish editions during the author's lifetime. Its importance lies not in its impact on Mexican Americans' self-perception or identification—for there is scant evidence of that—but, rather, in its widespread circulation and its popularization of the White Legend.

The book began by reiterating Lummis's insistence that certain unnamed history texts had misled Anglo Americans into believing that Spaniards were villainous, treacherous, and inept conquerors. His purpose, he explained, was "to help young Americans to a general grasp of the truths upon which coming histories will be based."[31] Among those truths, he declared, was that "the Spanish pioneering of the Americas was the largest and longest and most marvelous feat of manhood in all history."[32]

> The Spanish were not only the first conquerors of the New World, and its first colonizers, but also its first civilizers. They built the first cities, opened the first churches, schools, and universities; brought the first printing-presses, made the first books; wrote the first dictionaries, histories, and geographies, and brought the first missionaries.[33]

These deeds exemplified the "humane and progressive spirit" of Spain's pioneers who "never robbed the brown first Americans of their homes," as Anglo Americans had done in their westward conquests, but instead "protected and secured" their lands for them by "special laws."[34] New Mexico's missionaries, in particular, exemplified Spain's kindhearted paternalism and warranted an entire chapter devoted to their achievements. Emerging throughout the narrative are two distinct racial and cultural archetypes: the benevolent, gallant Spaniard and the loyal, obedient Indian convert. Lummis's preeminent achievement was to establish an acceptable master narrative for other Hispanophiles, for tourists, and for nuevomexicanos who, themselves, would elaborate on it. As literary scholar Genaro M. Padilla has noted, "Lummis authorized and instituted a language that has reverberated in other travel narratives, magazine articles, scholarly studies, poetry, novels, and theater of the region."[35] In fact, Lummis himself over the next twelve years authored dozens of books and hundreds of articles reinforcing the message of his *Spanish Pioneers*. Despite becoming perhaps the foremost booster of the Southwest, Lummis had little to do with the promotion of history within New Mexico itself. That task fell to a local resident, Lebaron Bradford Prince.

LEBARON BRADFORD PRINCE

In 1883, Lebaron Bradford Prince published *Historical Sketches of New Mexico*, a book that established him as one of the territory's leading historians and proponents of the White Legend, and Hispanophilia, more broadly. Over his lifetime, Prince reinforced this reputation by writing several more books and lecturing widely. In contrast to Lummis, Prince's impact on historical and racial perceptions in New Mexico can be measured by the local reception of his writings and other activities.

From his election as president of the Historical Society of New Mexico in 1883 to his death in 1922, Prince carried out a wide range of activities that increased popular interest among Anglos and nuevomexicanos alike in New Mexico's past. The historical society that he led dated to December 26, 1859, when twenty-five men convened in Santa Fe to found an organization dedicated to collecting and preserving "all historical facts, manuscripts, documents, records and memoirs, relating to this Territory," including "[I]ndian antiquities and curiosities, geological and mineralogical specimens, geographical maps and information, and objects of natural History."[36] Within months of its founding, the members had established and displayed in Santa Fe "a well arranged collection of curiosities, specimens and documents, and a considerable number of books, pamphlets and written contributions."[37] The society disbanded in September 1863 at the height of the Civil War. Some of its relics and minerals were crated and stored, while others were sold to pay outstanding debts. For the next seventeen years, no comparable institution took its place until the advent of the railroad changed that situation.[38]

In December 1880, ten months after the railway reached Santa Fe, several citizens met in the capital and proposed a "reorganization" of the historical society.[39] Concerned about the large number of Indian "relics" and "curiosities" making their way into the hands of private collectors and institutions in New York and Washington, D.C., territorial officials looked to the society to stop what they saw as the pilfering of New Mexico's cultural patrimony. On taking office in February 1881, the reinvigorated society's new president, William Gillette Ritch, took steps to do just that. "Our abiding hope should be," he declared, "as our manifest duty is, to snatch from oblivion the wonderful evidences of the prehistoric people of the Southwest."[40] Ritch launched a drive to publicize the problem and solicit donations and memberships.[41] To many officials the crisis was the result of the railway, which had brought not only "progress" and "industry," but cultural predation as well.[42] Both Ritch and his successor, Prince, viewed the advent of the "iron steed" as a sign that a new, industrial era had begun and a preindustrial one had ended.[43]

Appreciation for New Mexico's colonial past spawned a desire to preserve the objects from that period, and Prince became a preeminent figure in the effort. During his thirty-nine years as president of the society, he pursued a twofold agenda that aided the growing commercial and symbolic value of Spanish and Indian objects. First, he sought to increase the society's collection of relics by soliciting donations of them and, second, he displayed the relics in order to encourage popular interest in New Mexico's Spanish colonial history.

Soon after taking office, Prince began accumulating Indian and Spanish "antiquities." The process of gathering such objects reveals much about perceived ethnic identities, says scholar James Clifford. By collecting the objects of "other" cultures, he writes, tourists and institutions define themselves by opposition; that is, the accumulation of such articles represents an act of self-demarcation because it divulges the collector's own values. Collections "embody hierarchies of value, exclusions, rule-governed territories of the self," notes Clifford. "[G]athering involves the accumulation of possessions" and reaffirms the notion that identities are defined by material cultures (i.e., objects, knowledge, memories, experience).[44] But in addition to possessing symbolic value, relics also accrued commercial value.

Between 1880 and the 1920s, speculation in Indian and Spanish colonial relics led to a lucrative "curio" market that Prince, by virtue of his purchases, directly supported.[45] In his collection efforts, Prince relied on Santa Fe traders who specialized in the desired objects. In 1894, for example, he purchased from Santa Fe merchant Jake Gold sixty-five dollars' worth of Spanish colonial and Mexican items, including "One old Shield; Two Matachino [sic] Frames; Four Matachino [sic] Crowns; One framed pipe; One Franciscan and Child," and several paintings.[46] That same year, Prince bought from Santa Fe curio merchant A. F. Spiegelberg fifty-nine dollars' worth of relics, including six pieces of "Pajarito" pottery, two "Old Spanish" silver forks, and several "Southern Apache" and "Mexican" items.[47]

To finance these and other purchases, Prince initiated several fund drives involving mail solicitations. In 1890, for example, he wrote to nearly fifty individuals seeking donations for the purchase of a collection of "New Mexican antiquities" valued at a thousand dollars. Of those approached, sixteen (including both Anglos and nuevomexicanos) responded with twenty-five-dollar checks, an amount that entitled them to lifetime membership in the society. Six of those contributors bore well-known Spanish surnames, such as Armijo, Otero, Montoya, and Chávez, while ten bore non-Spanish surnames, such as Hazeldine, Johnson, Browne, and Reynolds.[48] That nuevomexicanos donated to the organization and became members suggests the extent to which they valued both the society and its drive to collect historical items. It also speaks to their ability to donate, and thus, their class status, since few nuevomexicanos could afford the membership fee. By the early 1900s, the society had procured a number of large collections, thanks both to private donations and to meager appropriations from New Mexico's legislature.[49]

Another example of nuevomexicano and Anglo fascination with the Spanish past that also dated to the years just after the railway's arrival was the

"Tertio-Millennial Anniversary Celebration" in Santa Fe. Organized by Prince, it featured a series of festivities and exhibits commemorating Santa Fe's presumed 333rd anniversary.[50] Though Prince miscalculated Santa Fe's founding by some fifty-odd years, his celebration drew thousands of visitors and participants to the plaza between 2 July and 3 August 1883.[51] Skeptics—including Lummis, who later berated Prince for his brash disregard for historical accuracy—argued that the celebration was little more than Prince's scheme to promote tourism and immigration to New Mexico.[52] One pamphlet hints that this may well have been the case:

> The Tertio-Millennial exhibit is a collection illustrative of the growth of New Mexico from its earliest day, showing this historic land as it is today and as it was when Cabeza de Baca crossed its borders. This is the characteristic of our celebration which makes it such a novel and interesting sight and one which will be unusually attractive to eastern visitors.[53]

The 1883 celebration blended historical appreciation with tourism, and proved to be an ideal tool to market the region's cultural and natural wealth to prospective immigrants.[54] Prince believed that arousing popular interest in New Mexico and its history would lead to increased tourism, immigration, and industry.[55] A local newspaper concurred: "The celebration will excite great interest in New Mexican affairs throughout the country, and it will be of benefit not only to Santa Fe, but to the interests of the whole territory."[56]

Not by happenstance did Prince issue his *Historical Sketches of New Mexico* on the eve of the Tertio Millennial in 1883. The book offered a narrative of human "progress" in New Mexico in which the past was "divided into three epochs—the Aboriginal or Pueblo, the Spanish, and the American"—all corresponding to three distinct racial and cultural archetypes to whom he dedicated the book:

> To the Pueblos, still representing in unchanged form the aboriginal civilization which built the cities and established the systems of government and social life which astonished the European discoverers nearly four centuries ago;
>
> To the Mexicans, who, in generosity, hospitality, and chivalric feeling, are worthy sons of the *Conquistadores*, who, with undaunted courage and matchless gallantry, carried the cross of Christianity and the flag of Spain to the end of the earth;

To the Americans, whose energy and enterprise are bringing the appliances of modern science and invention to develop the almost limitless resources which nature has bestowed upon us;

To All, as New Mexicans, now unitedly engaged in advancing the prosperity, and working for the magnificent future of the Territory, of which the author is proud to be a citizen, these sketches of part of its earlier history are respectfully dedicated.[57]

To Prince, ethnic nomenclature did not correspond to national identities, but, rather, to cultural and racial ones. In invoking the term "Mexican" he referred not to Mexican citizens, but to Spanish-speaking New Mexicans, whom he viewed as culturally indistinguishable from *californios, tejanos, tucsonenses*, and other Spanish-speaking peoples of the Southwest. Prince deemed New Mexico's nuevomexicanos as "sons of the *conquistadores*," a characterization that seems to suggest that they traced their lineage to a romantic colonial past and were not recent Mexican migrants to the region. As if to underscore this distinction, he devoted only eight pages of three hundred to the Mexican national period (1821–1846).[58] By contrast, more than two-thirds of *Sketches* deals with the "Spanish conquest," and does so in glowing, heroic terms: "The explorer of those days was traveling entirely in the dark. Nothing in more modern times has been similar to, or can again resemble, the uncertainty and romance of those early expeditions."[59] As for the Pueblo Indians, Prince portrayed them in a positive light as heirs to "the aboriginal civilization which built the cities and established the systems of government." They represented peaceful "Aztec" antecedents to Christianity and were clearly not savages but a sedentary and civilized people with "cities . . . government and social life."[60]

Prince's reference to "Americans" sheds light on his own identity. "Americans," he wrote, personified modernity, industriousness, and capitalist values. As a people, they possessed "energy and enterprise," and had brought to New Mexico "the appliances of modern science . . . to develop the almost limitless resources [of] nature."[61] Prince celebrated the arrival of the railway and Anglo American immigrants but his concept of progress embraced more than "Americans." "Pueblos, Americans, and Mexicans," he declared, constituted "the people of New Mexico," who one day would be "one in nationality, in purpose and in destiny."[62] That day, he added, would come when New Mexico achieved statehood.

Prince's historical writings cannot be separated from his political views and, especially, his agitation for statehood that required cooperation among all

New Mexicans. Nor can his racial attitudes be divorced from his desire for tourism. His *Historical Sketches* encouraged both statehood and tourism by romanticizing and pacifying "Indians" and "Spaniards" in the imagination of his English-reading audience.

Following *Historical Sketches* Prince went into a twenty-seven-year hiatus from serious writing about the past and focused his energies on statehood, his political career, and the management of the historical society. From 1883 until the eve of statehood in 1910, the society gained visibility by emphasizing its growing collection of Spanish and Indian objects. Particularly important were its exhibits in the Governor's Palace in Santa Fe, where rooms were filled with "ancient pottery, . . . stone implements and other articles illustrating the aboriginal civilization" as well as "a multitude" of newly acquired items from the "Indigenist, Spanish, Mexican and American eras."[63] The exhibitions attracted considerable tourist traffic, which, in turn, justified Prince's preservation efforts. "The tourist travel is a source of large income to the Territory in various ways," he observed in the society's 1887 annual report, "and as the passing years destroy many of the antiquities which give New Mexico special interest to the traveler, it is very important to preserve whatever is possible, to attract and satisfy the antiquarian taste."[64] The society's role in advancing tourism became eminently clear in 1893, when thousands of visitors "from all parts of the world" came to its exhibits.[65] Within nine years, this number grew to "more than five thousand per year," and by 1910, that figure had doubled to nearly ten thousand.[66]

Not all these visitors came from outside New Mexico. Many local residents, both Anglo and nuevomexicano, viewed the society's exhibits.[67] News of the society's collection efforts regularly appeared in the *Santa Fe New Mexican* as well as in the Spanish-language newspapers.[68] In 1905, for example, an editorial in a Las Vegas, New Mexico, Spanish-language newspaper urged nuevomexicanos to lobby the historical society for monuments to "the great men who have figured in the history of this territory since its initial colonization, . . . including the *conquistador* Don Juan de Oñate and the *reconquistador* Don Diego de Vargas."[69] This effort, declared the editorial, required contributions from "patriotic citizens of New Mexico who wish to honor and perpetuate the memory of . . . their most illustrious . . . forebears."[70] Such campaigns indicated that, by the early twentieth century, at least some nuevomexicanos were voicing appreciation for their Spanish past.

Letters to the society also revealed the growing interest in Spanish colonial history among both Anglo Americans and nuevomexicanos. In 1909, H. R. Hendon of Vaughn, New Mexico, became so intrigued by the "most valuable relics" and "small library of books dealing with New Mexico in history" in the Governor's Palace that he asked Prince for "a catalogue of the books, and if Coronado's account of his expedition is among them[?] . . . What I want to do is to get a general view of Spanish exploration here in those times, and also of the Indian manners and customs."[71] In the same year Nestor Montoya, editor of Albuquerque's *Bandera Americana*, the society's vice-president in Bernalillo County, launched into a sermon to Prince on the importance of the society's mission:

> The time has come, I think, when every true son of our Nuevo Mexico should take an interest in preserving its incomparable history, tradi tions and lore, of one of the most brilliant epochs in the history of mankind, the discovery and settlement of the New World. Our ances- tors of Spanish, English and French stock made it possible for human- ity to people this continent today with a phalanx of free Republics, and then why should we not be proud to keep our history, our names and land marks which remind us of that glorious epoch? More united should we be in this, in view of the fact, that vandals would even try to despoil us of our historic name.[72]

Montoya's letter suggests that nuevomexicanos had not only become more appreciative of their "own history," but also more visible within the historical society. Surviving records do not include the society's membership lists, but they identify "life members."[73] Between 1881 and 1908, some forty-six individuals became life members by contributing twenty-five dollars or more to the society. Of these, fourteen possessed Spanish first names and/or surnames, and included such prominent individuals as three former delegates to Congress, Antonio Joseph, Mariano Otero, and José Pablo Gallegos.[74] The remaining thirty-two sur- names were non-Spanish, and included William Gillette Ritch (president of New Mexico's Bureau of Immigration) and Judge William Hazeldine.[75]

Nuevomexicano participation in the society was not limited to member- ship alone, but included some who, like Montoya, became officers or otherwise worked actively to promote the organization's goals. Public lectures were one way of doing so as illustrated by Colonel J. Francisco Chaves's talk in 1904 on his "Personal Reminiscences of the Primitive Days."[76] Other speakers over the years included Amado Chaves, Benjamín M. Read, Nestor Montoya, and Jocobo Chaves.[77] Each of these individuals also held prominent positions in northern New Mexico. Amado Chaves, for example, was Superintendent of Public Instruction (1891–1897 and 1904–1905), mayor of Santa Fe (1901–1903), and Santa Fe County's representative to the territorial senate (1903–1904); Benjamín Read was a notable nuevomexicano attorney and speaker of the New Mexico House of Representatives (1901–1902).[78] In 1907, Prince invited a young professor of "Romance Languages" to speak to the society on "New Mexican Spanish." Aurelio Macedonio Espinosa eagerly accepted and delivered a "talk . . . of a popular nature" that helped instill among nuevomexicanos a sense of ethnic pride.[79]

By 1913, nuevomexicanos were giving society lectures nearly as often as non-nuevomexicanos. That year's public meeting, held on successive evenings in the state's Hall of Representatives, featured six guest speakers, of whom three were nuevomexicanos. One of them, Antonio Lucero—a former legislator, New Mexico's first Secretary of State, and former editor of the Las Vegas, New Mexico, *La Voz del Pueblo*—addressed the meeting in Spanish, though the title and topic of his speech went unrecorded. Another, Benjamín Read, lectured in English on "Inconsistencies of History," while Antonio DeVargas recounted "The Glories of the Spanish Era."[80]

While male nuevomexicanos rose to prominence within the society, extant records give little indication of how women (nuevomexicana or not) fared in the organization. Indeed, there is no mention of a woman until 1906, when "Miss Bertha Staab" is listed as the society's "corresponding secretary." Two years later "Mrs. Ella May Chaves" was identified as a life member, but nothing else was said about her participation.[81] In 1911, Prince established a "Ladies' Advisory Committee," but if the women ever offered any advice, no one took note of it.[82] Occasionally a woman was recognized for meritorious achievement. In 1912, Matilda Coxe Stevenson, "the distinguished ethnologist," received an "honorary membership" for "making New Mexico the scene of her remarkable researches."[83] Though women barely surfaced in the society's records, they increasingly were playing major roles, especially in the twentieth century with the influx of artists, the demand for suffrage, and the movement for cultural preservation. Historians Barbara Babcock and Marta Weigle have demonstrated that women achieved prominence as anthropologists, writers, tourists, boosters, and producers and distributors of "traditional" Pueblo Indian and Spanish tourist items.[84]

As statehood approached, Prince resumed his historical research and writing. Following passage of the statehood enabling act in 1910, he authored a 128-page work entitled *New Mexico's Struggle for Statehood: Sixty Years of Effort to Obtain Self Government*, which narrated the congressional battles over the statehood question. Two years later, he issued *A Concise History of New Mexico*, which he modeled after his earlier *Historical Sketches*. His conceptual and organizational framework mirrored that in his first book.[85] Though shorter, the newer publication projected a more romantic image of Pueblo Indian and nuevomexicano communities, past and present.[86]

> [T]he observer may in a single day visit an Indian pueblo exhibiting in unchanged form the customs of the intelligent natives of three and a half centuries ago; a Mexican town, where the architecture, the language and the habits of the people differ in no material respect from those which were brought from Spain in the days of Columbus, Cortez, and Coronado; and an American city or village, full of the nervous energy and the well-known characteristics of modern western life.[87]

While Pueblo Indians and nuevomexicanos remained static, locked in time, "Americans," as in the earlier account, were the agents of change and purveyors of progress. This was true as well of Prince's *The Student's History of New Mexico*, a condensed, textbook version designed for high school instruction and published in 1913. Though written in a simpler and more vivid style, it resembled the earlier works in content and organization. Prince actively promoted *Student's History* for high school classroom use through advertisements in the *New Mexico Journal of Education*, but it remains unknown whether the text was adopted anywhere.[88]

In 1915, Prince issued his last major monograph, *Spanish Mission Churches of New Mexico*. Written at the height of the California Mission Revival, this work argued that New Mexico, like California, possessed Spanish missions worthy of historical attention and touristic appreciation: "Outside of the boundaries of New Mexico, practically nothing is known of the far more interesting structures that render the Sunshine State [New Mexico] the paradise of the tourist, the antiquarian, and the religious enthusiast."[89]

Prince's later publications and activities until his death in 1922 were overshadowed by other developments: the establishment in 1907 of the School of American Archaeology (renamed the School of American Research in 1917), the appearance of the Spanish Colonial Arts Association in 1912, and the "revival" of the Santa Fe Fiesta in 1919.[90] These events rivaled the historical society's visibility and cultural influence. This is not to say that the society diminished in size or touristic appeal. By 1921, membership was said to have grown considerably, and the annual visitors to the Governor's Palace exhibit surpassed 40,000, double the volume of 1910.[91] Nonetheless, other organizations devoted to cultural commodification proliferated between 1909 and the 1920s, and competed with the historical society for resources, attention, and influence.

CONCLUSION

The 1925 Talleres Calpe *Diccionario de la Lengua Española* defines a Hispanophile as "a foreign devotee[s] of Spanish culture, history and customs of Spain" and Spanish America.[92] Lummis and Prince clearly fit this definition. But they were much more than devotees; they were propagandists on a mission to encourage popular interest in New Mexico's Spanish past. They lamented the seemingly inevitable decline of New Mexico's "traditional" cultures, which both viewed as casualties of the march of Anglo-American "progress."[93] Anthropologist Renato Rosaldo explains this wistful sentiment as "imperialist nostalgia," noting that the agents of imperialism celebrated "the very forms of life they intentionally altered or destroyed."[94] Premised on the certain demise of Pueblo and nuevomexicano cultures, Anglo-American nostalgia contrasted sharply with nuevomexicanos' growing determination to prevent encroachments on their land, Spanish language and traditions, and political rights. By the 1910s, Hispanophiles had succeeded in shaping many Anglo Americans' perceptions of the Southwest as "Spanish" and of nuevomexicanos as "Spanish Americans." In 1914, a columnist for *Harper's Weekly* registered this fact, explaining: "These Spanish people of New Mexico . . . are not of the mixed breed one finds south of the Rio Grande, or even [in] Arizona. . . . Indeed, it is probable that there is no purer Spanish stock in Old Spain itself."[95]

NOTES

1. David J. Weber, *The Spanish Frontier in North America* (New Haven: Yale University Press, 1992), 336.

2. William P. DuVal to President James Monroe, Pensacola, Sept. 10, 1822, in Carter, comp. and ed., *Territorial Papers of the United States* (Washington, D.C.: U.S. Government Printing Office, 1934–), 22:532. As cited in Weber, *The Spanish Frontier*, 338.

3. Helen Hunt Jackson, *Ramona* (New York, 1884); Harriet Beecher Stowe, *Uncle Tom's Cabin* (1852; reprint, Cambridge, Mass.: Harvard University Press, 1962).

4. Helen Hunt Jackson, *A Century of Dishonor* (New York: Harper, 1881).

5. Frank W. Clancy, "In Memory of L. Bradford Prince, President of the Society," Historical Society of New Mexico Publications No. 25 (Santa Fe, 1923), 7–11; Lebaron Bradford Prince, *Historical Sketches of New Mexico from the Earliest Records to the American Occupation* (New York: Leggat Brothers, 1883); *New Mexico's Struggle for Statehood: Sixty Years of Effort to Obtain Self Government* (Santa Fe: The New Mexican Printing Company, 1910); *A Concise History of New Mexico* (Cedar Rapids, Iowa: The Torch Press, 1912); *The Student's History of New Mexico* (Denver: The Publishers Press,

1913); and *The Spanish Mission Churches of New Mexico* (Grand Rapids, Iowa: The Torch Press, 1915). For a brief biography of Prince, see Marc Simmons, "Introduction," in Lebaron Bradford Prince, *Spanish Mission Churches of New Mexico* (Grand Rapids, Ia.; reprint, Glorieta, N.M.: Rio Grande Press, 1977), 9–14.

6. James W. Byrkit, *Charles Lummis: Letters from the Southwest, September 20, 1884 to March 14, 1885* (Tucson: University of Arizona Press, 1989), xi–xii, xlvi.

7. Lummis to *Leader*, 25 November 1884. Quoted in Ibid., 108.

8. Lummis to *Leader*, El Rito, 1 December 1884. Quoted in Ibid., 123.

9. Lummis to *Leader*, Santa Fe, 25 November 1884. Quoted in Ibid., 120.

10. Lummis to *Leader*, Santa Fe, 25 December 1884. Quoted in Ibid., 192.

11. Lummis to *Leader*, Santa Fe, 25 November 1884. Quoted in Ibid., 112.

12. Charles F. Lummis, *A Tramp across the Continent* (New York: Scribner, 1920; reprint, with an introduction by Robert E. Fleming, Lincoln: University of Nebraska Press, 1982), 75.

13. Lummis to *Leader*, Santa Fe, 25 November 1884. Quoted in Byrkit, *Letters from the Southwest*, 112–13.

14. Lummis to *Leader*, El Rito, 1 December 1884. Quoted in Ibid., 131–32.

15. Ibid., 124.

16. Lummis to *Leader*, San Mateo, 1 January 1885. Quoted in Byrkit, *Letters from the Southwest*, 217.

17. Marc Simmons, *Two Southwesterners: Charles Lummis and Amado Chaves* ([Cerrillos, N. Mex.]: San Marcos Press, 1968), 14.

18. Ralph Emerson Twitchell, *The Leading Facts of New Mexican History* (Cedar Rapids, Iowa: The Torch Press, 1917), vol. 5:124, n. 891.

19. Simmons, *Two Southwesterners*, 18.

20. Charles F. Lummis, *Pueblo Indian Folk-Stories* (New York: Century Co., 1910; reprint, with an introduction by Robert F. Gish, and titled *Pueblo Indian Folk-Tales*, Lincoln: University of Nebraska Press, 1992), 5.

21. Ibid., xxv–xxvi.

22. Ibid., 95.

23. Lummis to the *Chillicothe Leader*, El Rito, 1 December 1884. Quoted in Byrkit, *Letters from the Southwest*, 124.

24. Lummis, *Tramp across the Continent*, 113.

25. Ibid., 137.

26. Ibid., 195.

27. Hubert Howe Bancroft, *California Pastoral, 1769–1848* (San Francisco: The History Company, 1888), 179. Quoted in David J. Langum, "From Condemnation to Praise: Shifting Perspectives on Hispanic California," *California History* 61 (winter 1983): 284.

28. Jackson, *Ramona*.

29. John R. Chávez, *The Lost Land: The Chicano Image of the Southwest* (Albuquerque: University of New Mexico Press, 1984), 87.

30. David J. Weber, "The Spanish Legacy in North America and the Historical Imagination," *Western Historical Quarterly* 61 (1992): 11–12.

31. Charles F. Lummis, *The Spanish Pioneers*, 8th ed. (Chicago: A. C. Motley and Co., 1920), 18.

32. Ibid., 11–12.

33. Ibid., 23.

34. Ibid., 149.

35. Genaro M. Padilla, *My History, Not Yours: The Formation of Mexican American Autobiography* (Madison: University of Wisconsin Press, 1993), 208.

36. Records of the Historical Society of New Mexico, microform roll 1, frames 6–8. Hereafter cited as RNMHS.

37. Historical Society of New Mexico, *Inaugural Address Delivered by Hon. W. G. Ritch at the Adobe Palace, February 21, 1881* (Santa Fe: New Mexican Book and Job Printing Department, 1881), 10.

38. *Constitution*, RNMHS, 1f1–9.

39. Historical Society, *Inaugural Address*, 17–20.

40. Ibid., 11–13.

41. Pamphlet, 1882, RNMHS, 2f3.

42. Historical Society, *Inaugural Address*, 13–14.

43. Ibid., 12–13.

44. James Clifford, "On Collecting Art and Culture," in *Out There: Marginalization and Contemporary Cultures*, ed. Russell Ferguson et al. (New York: The New Museum of Contemporary Art, 1990), 143.

45. Merchants often approached Prince offering to sell him relics. In a letter dated December 31, 1890, J. J. Leeson of Socorro, New Mexico, urged Prince to purchase a "lot of pottery, beads, hammers . . . skeletons and other curiosities" for $100 saying, "I consider this cheap. If they were mine, three-hundred dollars could not purchase them." Leeson to Prince, 31 December 1890, RNMHS, 2f7.

46. Miscellaneous receipt, RNMHS, 2f540. In 1862, Jake Gold established a business dealing in Indian and Spanish antiquities. His letterhead proclaimed him a "Dealer in Ancient and Modern Aztec and Pueblo Pottery, Navajo Blankets, Turquois [*sic*], Old Spanish Relics, Mexican Hair Bridles, Chains and Whips, Indian Views, Cactus Cane, and All Sorts of Indian Curiosities." RNMHS, 2f576.

47. Miscellaneous receipt, RNMHS, 2f538.

48. RNMHS, 2f228. Another circular, dated July 21, 1913, and signed by Prince, was sent to "just a few individuals that I think will be interested," appealing for additional support to purchase display cases for the Palace of the Governors. RNMHS, 2f256.

49. RNMHS, 2f47. That both *hispanos* and Anglos viewed such items as historically symbolic and contributed to the commodification of things "Spanish" and "Indian" runs counter to the assertions of some Chicana and Chicano scholars—John Chávez foremost among them—who argue that such commodification represented a predominantly Anglo-American endeavor. Rather, it was a joint endeavor that speaks to a mutual fascination with the Spanish past. Chávez, *The Lost Land*, 87. Also see Erlinda Gonzales-Berry, ed., *Paso por Aqui: Critical Essays on the New Mexican Literary Tradition, 1542–1988* (Albuquerque: University of New Mexico Press, 1989), and Padilla, *My History, Not Yours*, esp. 202–13.

50. Folder 2, Lebaron B. Prince Collection, New Mexico State Records Center and Archives. Hereafter referred to as Prince Collection.

51. RNMHS, 2f488. Also see "Official Invitation" in Folder 2, Prince Collection.

52. Oliver La Farge, *Santa Fe: The Autobiography of a Southwestern Town* (Norman and London: University of Oklahoma Press, 1959), 120.

53. *Santa Fe New Mexican*, 3 July 1883. As quoted in La Farge, *Santa Fe*, 120–21.

54. RNMHS, 2f488.

55. Pamphlet, RNMHS, 2f3.

56. *Santa Fe New Mexican*, 3 July 1883. Quoted in La Farge, *Santa Fe*, 121.

57. Prince, *Historical Sketches*, 11, 3.

58. Russell S. Saxton, "Ethnocentrism in the Historical Literature of Territorial New Mexico" (Ph.D. dissertation, University of New Mexico, 1980), 105–6.

59. Prince, *Historical Sketches*, 16–17.

60. Ibid., 11.

61. Ibid., 3.

62. Ibid.

63. Historical Society, *Official Report of the Historical Society of New Mexico* (Santa Fe: New Mexican Printing Co., 1887), 1–4.

64. Ibid., 3.

65. Historical Society, *Official Report of the Historical Society of New Mexico* (Santa Fe: New Mexican Printing Co., 2 January 1893).

66. Historical Society, *Informe Bienal de la Sociedad Historica de Nuevo Mexico. Diciembre 1, 1904* (Santa Fe: Compañia Impresora del Nuevo Mexicano, 1905), 5; Historical Society, *Official Report*, 1898, 1904, and 1912.

67. Historical Society, *Official Report*, 1912. Unfortunately, the record does not indicate whether or how many Native Americans visited the museum or participated in the historical society.

68. Miscellaneous newspaper clippings, RNMHS, 2f746–54.

69. Undated newspaper clipping, RNMHS, 2f754. Also see a similar editorial dated 13 August 1905, which appeared in an unnamed Las Vegas newspaper. Miscellaneous newspaper clipping, RNMHS, 2f747.

70. Unidentified newspaper clipping, RNMHS, 2f754.

71. H. R. Hendon to Prince, 27 January 1909, RNMHS, 2f128.

72. Nestor Montoya to Prince, 30 January 1909, RNMHS, 2f132.

73. Historical Society, *Constitution*, RNMHS, 1f1–9.

74. Also included in that list was Félix Martínez. C. E. Hodgin, "The Early School Laws of New Mexico," *Bulletin*, University of New Mexico Educational Series (Albuquerque: University of New Mexico, 1906), vol. 1:36.

75. Historical Society, *Official Report*, 1912, 3.

76. Historical Society, *Official Report*, 1904, 6.

77. Titles of their lectures are not given. Historical Society, *Official Report*, 1906 (Santa Fe: New Mexican Printing Co., 1906), 8.

78. C. E. Hodgin, "The Early School Laws of New Mexico," *Bulletin*, University of New Mexico Educational Series (Albuquerque: University of New Mexico, 1906), vol. 1:35.

79. Aurelio Macedonio Espinosa to Prince, 15 January 1907, RNMHS.

80. Twitchell, *The Leading Facts*, 156 n. 914; Historical Society, *Official Reports of the Society, 1912 and 1913*, Historical Society of New Mexico Publications No. 19 (Santa Fe: New Mexican Printing Co., 1914), 9.

81. Ibid., 4; Historical Society, *Official Report*, 1906.

82. Prince to "Madame," 26 January 1911, RNMHS, 2f185.

83. Historical Society, *Official Report of the Society, 1912*, Historical Society of New Mexico Publications No. 18 (Santa Fe: New Mexican Printing Company, 1913), 5.

84. Barbara A. Babcock, "Mudwomen and Whitemen: A Meditation on Pueblo Potteries and the Politics of Representation," in *Discovered Country: Tourism and Survival in the American West*, ed. Scott Norris (Albuquerque: Stone Ladder Press, 1994), 180–95; Babcock, "'A New Mexican Rebecca': Imaging Pueblo Women," *Journal of the Southwest* 32 (1990): 400–437; Marta Weigle, "Selling the Southwest: Santa Fe InSites," in *Discovered Country*, 210–24.

85. Prince, *Concise History*, 20.

86. Ibid., 10–11.

87. Ibid., 20.

88. Ibid. Also, L. Bradford Prince, *The Student's History of New Mexico* (Denver: Publishers Press, 1913).

89. Prince, *Spanish Mission Churches*, 7.

90. Marta Weigle and Peter White, *The Lore of New Mexico* (Albuquerque: University of New Mexico Press, 1988), 437.

91. Miscellaneous newspaper clipping, 19 February 1921, RNMHS, 1f753.

92. *Diccionario de la Lengua Española*, 15th ed. (Madrid: Talleres Calpe, 1925).

93. For a discussion of declining Native American populations see Albert Hurtado, *Indian Survival on the California Frontier* (New Haven: Yale University Press); and Russell Thornton, *American Indian Holocaust and Survival: A Population History Since 1492* (Norman: University of Oklahoma Press, 1987).

94. Renato Rosaldo, *Culture and Truth: The Remaking of Social Analysis* (Boston: Beacon Press, 1989), 69, 81.

95. McGregor [pseud.?], "Our Spanish-American Fellow Citizens," *Harper's Weekly*, 20 June 1914. Quoted in Chávez, *Lost Land*, 92.

CHAPTER EIGHT

EPICS OF GREATER AMERICA
Herbert Eugene Bolton's Quest for a Transnational American History

Samuel Truett

"Although we might want to ignore it," writes Anthony DePalma in his recent bestseller, *Here: A Biography of the New American Continent*, "our history is thoroughly entangled with the history of our neighbors." The U.S., Mexico, and Canada, he observes, not only claim common historical strands of discovery, colonization, and eventual independence from Europe, but they also emerged together as nations. A growing body of scholars shares DePalma's continental perspective; with globalization and economic integration, they propose, Americans will require new histories. The North American Free Trade Agreement, argued Latin Americanist John Wirth in 1998, has given rise to "nothing less than a paradigm shift—a new way of looking at things from a continental, or regional, perspective." By hitching their work to the "paradigm shifts" of free trade, historians such as DePalma and Wirth see themselves as pioneers on a brave new conceptual frontier. "Christopher Columbus would turn green with envy," proposes television journalist Bill Moyers of this "new New World that old-timers once called Mexico, Canada, and the United States."[1]

Yet, like Columbus, these visionaries of a greater American past have planted their flags on a virgin land that is more imagined than real. This same terrain was explored almost a century ago by a generation that began to envision a transnational American history in the light of U.S. commercial and military expansion, the creation of the Panama Canal, and World War I. By the 1920s, scholars had begun to systematically rethink the international dimensions of U.S. history, and by the 1930s, continental and hemispheric approaches

I would like to thank Claire Fox, Carmen Nocentelli-Truett, David Weber, David Igler, Donald Worster, Jonathan Porter, and the late John Wirth for their suggestions on drafts of this essay.

to the American past had penetrated the profession's core. Yet their story is rarely remembered, in part due to the nature of scholarly discovery: "new" worlds quickly fade into old worlds, and pioneers become "old-timers." What some today view as an older, divided American history is, in fact, partly the result of newer histories between the 1940s and 1960s that sought to transcend the transnational "dogma" of this earlier generation.

What can the story of earlier transnational visionaries tell us about our own "new worlds" of American history in the twenty-first century? To answer this question, one might begin by looking at the pedagogical and scholarly career of one of the earliest proponents of a transnational American history, Herbert Eugene Bolton. Bolton's vision was most boldly articulated in his 1932 presidential address to the American Historical Association, "Epic of Greater America," in which he urged other historians to seek common ground between the United States and the western hemisphere at large. His ideas were controversial in 1932, and remain so today. Many dismissed Bolton's hemispheric vision as an artifact of the "romantic Pan-Americanism" of Franklin D. Roosevelt's "Good Neighbor" era—and in the 1960s, they negatively judged its "hemispheric unities" according to a new standard of cultural difference, shaped in part by the rise of Latin American studies.[2] So completely did historians sweep Bolton to the margins, in fact, that his absence from ongoing discussions about transnational history in the Americas hardly raises an eyebrow.

Yet if one revisits Bolton's intellectual boneyard, one finds more than weathered monuments to a forgotten age. One finds on all sides the signs of a hasty burial. Bolton's greater America was a victim of its time, its gravestone reads: It shone briefly in the 1930s as "pan-American doctrine," but failed to reach maturity as a respectable paradigm. Yet as one digs deeper among the ruins one finds that Bolton began to develop his transnational vision three decades earlier. His "Epic of the Greater America" engaged the pan-Americanism of its time, but it was also a culmination of work associated with earlier times and places. By failing to put Bolton in context, critics reduced his perspective to a fad, erasing a longer, mainstream discussion about U.S. history in an international world. One also learns that Bolton helped to establish Latin American history—another field that engaged with pan-Americanism, but whose reputation remained relatively untarnished. Why one transnational history endured and another declined is a riddle worth contemplating.

It is also worth considering what we do remember. Most scholars know Bolton as the father of Spanish Borderlands history, a field that emerged in the 1920s after Bolton published *The Spanish Borderlands: A Chronicle of Old*

Florida and the Southwest (1921). Although this field focused primarily on Spain's colonial past in what became the United States, Bolton saw this history within a hemispheric framework. The Spanish Borderlands, he observed, were "the meeting place and fusing place of two streams of European civilization"— Saxon and Latin he called them—that had flowed through lands as far-flung as Labrador, Alaska, and Patagonia. Yet later scholars usually saw Bolton as two distinct people, Bolton of the Borderlands, and Bolton of the Americas. Bolton's own student, John Francis Bannon, endorsed this divide. In a 1964 collection of his mentor's essays, he downplayed Bolton's hemispheric approach, which had recently come under fire. "Bolton's correct place in the history of American historical writing may be obscured to the point of being overlooked," Bannon wrote. He made only passing reference to "the other Bolton" of the Americas—urging readers to embrace "the more fundamental, the more enduring, the unimpeachable Bolton of the Borderlands."[3]

If Bolton's dual persona reflected political shifts, it also underscored fundamental differences in what his histories were about. Spanish Borderlands history was essentially a subset of U.S. history, not least because it told about regions that eventually became part of the United States. Bolton tried to make this history palatable by replacing negative stereotypes of Hispanic America, codified by the so-called "Black Legend," with a romantic "White Legend" that depicted the Spanish as benevolent, effective colonizers. To be sure, Bolton argued that the Borderlands extended into Mexico, and that its heroes might also be Mexico's heroes, but his efforts to "whitewash" the Spanish pioneer process made it particularly useable for U.S. national histories.[4] Bolton's hemispheric history was completely different. Unlike the Spanish Borderlands, which could be incorporated as a regional subset of U.S. history, the hemisphere could not be so easily domesticated. The history of the greater America was primarily a story about international relations between the United States and the wider world, and as such could not be put easily to the same historical uses.

To envision this relationship between national and international history, it may also be useful to think about the literary form of epic, since it was a term that Bolton embraced. The title "Epic of Greater America" is unintentionally ironic, for the international history it encapsulated was anything but epic. "The world of the epic is the national heroic past," Mikhail Bakhtin notes; "it is a world of 'beginnings' and 'peak times' in the national history, a world of fathers and of founders of families, a world of 'firsts' and 'bests.'" If Bolton told epic tales, it was in the Spanish Borderlands, where one could find new "American" pioneers. The borderlands were also attractive in this regard because of their temporal distance. The epic poet and audience, observes Bakhtin, "are located in the same time and on the same evaluative (hierarchical) plane, but the . . . world of the heroes stands on an utterly different and inaccessible time-and-value plane, separated by epic distance." This gap between epic poet and subject, he adds, is the terrain of national history. In other words, epic serves as preface to national history; it both precedes and prepares the space for this history. Borderlands history served this role nicely because it ended before the U.S. Southwest began and played foil to the later national story of America. Greater American history, by contrast, lacked both a nation-centered telos and epic distance; as a tale that trailed off into a transnational present, it lacked epic power.[5]

The gap between epic and history also had another function in the Borderlands: it policed a cultural and racial divide. The epic "is walled off absolutely from all subsequent times, and above all from those times in which the singer and his listeners are located," Bahktin writes. It was precisely this narrative form and its segregation of story and storyteller that allowed Anglo-American histories to assimilate the Spanish "other" as an "American" pioneer hero without entering suspect terrain.[6] Because no such barrier neatly divided Spanish past from Anglo present in Bolton's greater America, it was more problematic as foundational fiction. It is telling that when American historians debated Bolton's "Epic of Greater America" in the 1960s, they were concerned about its failure to preserve cultural and racial distinctions. How could the United States, South America, and Caribbean America share a common history, the argument ran, when the citizens of these nations were so culturally and racially different? Spanish Borderlands history, meanwhile, generated no such problem because its narrative form preserved—through the alchemy of time—an accepted cultural (cum racial) order.

In short, when historians mapped distinctions between Bolton's Borderlands and his greater America, they were speaking to an ambivalent relationship between two different histories. The first history—that which most closely echoed the literary epic form—was a story of origins, which in the twentieth century was generally a story of national origins. The second history, reflected in Bolton's "Epic of Greater America," was a more open-ended narrative of national relations. Both were, from Bolton's perspective, stories about our cultural and national selves. "We learn from the world," he would write of international history later in his career, "in order to be modest about ourselves." But the historical relationship between origins and relations, between "ourselves" and the world, was an unstable and tenuous one in the early twentieth-century United States, perhaps because the idea of a standard national history—supported by universities, textbooks, and state-monitored curriculums—was still a work in progress.

This ambivalent relationship between the self, nation, and wider world is still with us today, and is reflected in part by the awkward "unnaturalness" of transnational histories for a post-NAFTA America. It is my hope that by revisiting Herbert Eugene Bolton's early twentieth-century quest for a transnational American history, we might extract modest lessons for our own efforts to write new American tales for a global age. I start with Bolton's early attempts to widen his historical horizons, first as a researcher and then as a teacher, between 1902 and 1932. It was at this time, years before the "Good Neighbor" era, that Bolton laid the foundations for his transnational perspective. I then discuss his scholarly presentation of these ideas in his "Epic of Greater America" address, touching on subsequent critiques and revisions. I then move to tensions between Bolton's transnational and national stories, with special attention to the relationship between his "History of the Americas" and Latin American history. In the end, the American past was split between U.S. history and its Latin American counter-histories, but historians—many of them Bolton's own students—would continue to make transnational journeys through this divided land as they tried to make sense of their shifting relationship to a wider American world.

Bolton's Wider Horizons

Herbert Eugene Bolton started his scholarly career at the University of Wisconsin, where he studied under U.S. historian Frederick Jackson Turner and medievalist Charles Homer Haskins. He arrived shortly after Turner delivered his famous frontier thesis. To understand U.S. history, Turner had argued in 1893, scholars needed to turn away from Europe, where they traditionally searched for the "seeds" of American development, and look instead to the American frontier, where Europeans had become Americans. Turner's ideas, along with the popular romance of the frontier, captivated Bolton. Although he later transferred to the University of Pennsylvania, where he finished his Ph.D. with U.S. historian John Bach McMaster, Bolton remained motivated by Turner's work in frontier history. Turner, for his part, would continue to consider Bolton one of his "boys." After graduating in 1899, Bolton began to look for a job in U.S. history, where he could—in the later words of one of his students—"put some of the Turner ideas and insights to work."[7]

The journey toward his goal was anything but straightforward. In 1901, he found a position as a medieval and early modern Europeanist at the University of Texas. He initially hoped to be able to teach classes in U.S. history, but learned that his department chair, George P. Garrison, jealously claimed this field as his own. Initially frustrating, Bolton's exile from U.S. history proved propitious, for it forced him at an early stage to approach America in a new way. In 1902, he offered a class on European expansion, which carried him to American shores within a broader imperial context—and it was around this same time that he found another way into U.S. history through Texas. Garrison taught Texas history as part of U.S. history, and another colleague, Eugene Barker, covered Mexican and early Anglo-American Texas, but nobody taught classes on the Spanish in Texas. Realizing that he might be able to claim an American field of his own, Bolton invested part of his modest salary in Spanish lessons. Spanish, he wrote his brother, "is the key to Southwestern history, in which I must work as long as I am here."[8]

When his first summer vacation arrived, Bolton boarded a train to Mexico City, and returned with a suitcase of documents on Spanish Texas. This was the first of several summers "grubbing" in Mexican archives to fuel a newfound passion for Spanish North America. He published his findings in the Quarterly of the Texas State Historical Association, soon developing a reputation as a state historian. "Texans were appreciative of being told about their 'ancient' history," explained Bolton student and biographer John Francis Bannon: "[I]t was a source of pride to them to be able to proclaim that their history went back farther than that of some of the Atlantic seaboard and all the rest of the American states."[9] Anglo Texans did not link their identities to this history in the same way they did with the Alamo and Texas Republic, yet the story of the rise and fall of the Spanish empire—associated with romantic ruins of missions and other Spanish architecture—contained all the traditional elements of the imperial epic. If the story was told so Anglo victory followed on the heels of Spanish romance, Anglo Texans might embrace this greater imperial narrative without unsettling the cultural, racial, or religious status quo.[10]

In 1902, Bolton went to the Archivo General de México (AGN) in Mexico City for materials on Southwestern history, and the following summer he revisited the AGN, this time for documents on Texas.[11] In 1906, his work caught the eye of J. Franklin Jameson of the Department of Historical Research of the Carnegie Institution of Washington, who was creating a set of guides to U.S. history documents in foreign archives. Jameson wrote Bolton, asking if he would be interested in writing a guide to documents in Mexico, with an eye not only to Texas, but also to New Mexico, Arizona, and California. Bolton agreed, and in 1907, on the payroll of the Carnegie Institution, he took a leave of absence from Texas. He spent a year in both Mexico City and state archives, and with the assistance of students and research assistants on both sides of the border, created a 550-page volume that more than doubled the known documentary base for Southwestern and northern Mexican history. When the *Guide to Materials for the History of the United States in the Principal Archives of Mexico* appeared in 1913, it helped establish Bolton as the leader of a new field of colonial and international history.[12]

In Bolton's *Guide to Materials*, one sees a maturing scholar who gained much from his time in Mexico. In 1902, Bolton looked to Mexico for a way out of Europe and into America. Concealed by the uncharted thickets of Texas history, he smuggled himself north across the border. He wrote about the Spanish past with the United States in mind, publishing for readers who cared about U.S., not Mexican, identities. By 1907, however, Bolton had stumbled onto something larger. This was partly due to the Carnegie Institution; to open doors for Bolton, Carnegie officials assured Mexicans that Bolton's research would be used to promote "mutual understanding" between the United States and Mexico. They also relied on U.S. Secretary of State Elihu Root and U.S. Ambassador David E. Thompson to endorse their project. According to Bolton, such connections were crucial. For their letters of introduction and various local courtesies, he acknowledged ambassadors, foreign ministers, cardinals, and even President Porfirio Díaz.[13]

The men who sponsored Bolton in Mexico most likely saw "mutual understanding" through a larger lens of U.S. commercial expansion and resource extraction in Mexico under Díaz, and it was not hard to see the Carnegie effort as a similarly extractive endeavor.[14] Bolton hoped to incorporate Mexican documents into the "American" epic, as he had previously done for the smaller-scale epic of Texas. Yet along the way, he grew ambivalent about, even resistant to, the vampire-like nature of his task. He had written the *Guide to Materials* for U.S. historians, he admitted in 1913, but it also had many references to "characters and events of Mexican history proper," and thus should be of "equal utility to the history of either country." In a sense, Bolton took this idea of "mutual understanding" more seriously than his sponsors may have intended. His earlier devotion to a national paradigm, in which Mexico was mined for colonial precursors to U.S. history, was yielding to a more open-ended transnational perspective, based in part on the simple act of crossing the border and opening up new scholarly dialogues. "I hope that the *Guide* may prove useful," he wrote in the introduction, "to my numerous friends in Mexico who are students of their national history."[15]

By the time his *Guide to Materials* appeared in 1913, Bolton's world was swiftly changing. Not only had the Mexican Revolution transformed U.S.-Mexico

Fig. 10. "The Americas at the end of the eighteenth century. Nearly all the Western Hemisphere was still in the colonial status." From Herbert Eugene Bolton, *History of the Americas: A Syllabus with Maps* (Boston: Ginn and Company, 1928), 140.

relations, but Bolton himself was on the move. In 1909 he departed Texas for Stanford, where he was allowed to fully embrace his growing interest in Spanish America and the American West. In 1911 he moved again, to the University of California at Berkeley. Even more than Texas or Stanford, Berkeley was an ideal place for Bolton to build on his broader vision of American history. His department chair, Henry Morse Stephens, had begun to build a program in Hispanic American history in 1902, and in 1905 he had negotiated the purchase of the enormous library of Hubert Howe Bancroft, an early aficionado of Spanish America. Due to promotional efforts by the likes of Charles Lummis, Californians were fond of their Spanish history, and Stephens milked this vogue. He helped establish the Native Sons of the Golden West, a historical society with a keen interest in things Spanish, and then turned to its members for academic funding. Many of Bolton's students would work in Mexican and Spanish archives on Native Sons of the Golden West travel fellowships that Stephens helped establish.[16]

Even if it was Stephens—not Bolton—who laid the early foundations for a greater American history at Berkeley, Bolton enthusiastically took up the reins. In a 1911 report to Berkeley President Benjamin Ide Wheeler, he laid out a plan of action for making Berkeley a center for Hispanic history in North America. This legacy had been neglected, he wrote, because U.S. history had been "written almost solely from the standpoint of the East and of the English colonies." Even Frederick Jackson Turner had overlooked the true significance of U.S. history west of the Mississippi, Bolton observed, and the reason was simple: The documents for this history were stored in foreign archives, mostly in Mexico and Spain. While in Mexico, he noted, he found over 3,000 archival references to California, including diaries and reports from such local pioneers as Junípero Serra, Gaspar de Portolá, and Juan Bautista de Anza. "Little need be said to show that in order that these historical materials may be studied and utilized, they must first be gathered and published," Bolton proposed. "The lead in the investigation of this field must be taken by us here in the West."[17]

If interest in local heroes paved the way for Spanish Borderlands history, California's unique relationship to the wider world pulled Bolton more deeply into greater American history. Soon after he came to Berkeley, the Panama Canal joined Atlantic and Pacific worlds in profoundly new ways. In 1915, the American Historical Association commemorated the event by meeting in Berkeley, San Francisco, and Palo Alto for a Panama-Pacific Historical Congress, part of the larger Panama-Pacific International Exposition. Bolton and Stephens gathered the papers into a 1917 collection, *The Pacific Ocean in*

History. California lay at the crossroads of a new global era, they insisted, and like Turner in 1893 they tried to capture a passing world: Their anthology was a "memorial" of the "chief features of the old and isolated Pacific Ocean of the era before the Canal was made." But they looked not to the nation, as Turner had, but instead to a brave new international world. "The Panama Canal must inevitably change the relations of the American, the Asiatic, and the Australasian countries bordering upon the Pacific Ocean toward one another," Bolton and Stephens proclaimed. "One era of Pacific Ocean history comes to an end; another begins."[18]

Bolton thus faced a global world that far exceeded his modest summer jaunts across the line into Mexico. A canal reoriented America—and introduced Bolton to an internationalism that would expand his historical horizons. At the Panama-Pacific Historical Congress he mingled with consular delegates from distant nations, and explored common histories of Spain, Peru, Japan, Canada, New Zealand, and the Philippines. But as he gazed west, Bolton also saw the world in more conventional ways. He would later write a biography of one of his new Pacific heroes, Juan Bautista de Anza, the founder of San Francisco. Here was a man to match Bolton's expanding horizons. "Anza was not confined within the boundaries of a single nation," he wrote, and yet his global horizons placed him in that most traditional of nation-bound epics, the tale of westward expansion. This pioneer, though northward bound, was "the forerunner of Mackenzie, Thompson, Lewis and Clark, Smith, Frémont, the forty-niners, and all the eager-eyed throng who have since yielded to the urge of Westward Ho," Bolton argued. "His monument is the Imperial City which stands beside the Golden Gate and looks out across the Western Sea."[19]

Bolton—like his Spanish hero, Anza—stood on an ambivalent threshold between the nation and the world. In the shadow of the Imperial City, he began to create new stories for a new age, but these tales did not always point in the same direction. New winds tugged at his sails, and compelled him to look abroad. In California, even the "Native Sons of the Golden West" embraced the global dimensions of local history, and with their travel fellowships, many of Bolton's students left the shores of U.S. history forever. Yet California's wider horizons could be deceiving; for nation-bound tales remained a powerful force in this land of prophecy. Bolton's story of Anza spoke to the world beyond the nation, but also pointed to the interior spaces of U.S. history and men like John Frémont and Alexander Mackenzie, whose stories had little to do with the Spanish empire of San Francisco's founding father. Anza's story was transnational history turned to national ends, among other things, to naturalize

America's empire. "The seat of empire begins to shift from the Atlantic to the Pacific," insisted John F. Davis of the Native Sons of the Golden West, at the 1915 Panama-Pacific Historical Congress. "In this very congress, whose sessions are now closing, you have been given the historical background and framework of [this] new arena."[20]

PEDAGOGICAL FRONTIERS

With such resilient nation-bound currents, and his affection for epic heroes, how did Bolton maintain his open-ended international perspective? For our answer, we must shift to the classroom, for that is where Bolton's greater America took shape. As early as 1912, he was teaching the history of the American West "from a continental and European standpoint," a perspective, Bolton wrote, which "will cause a rewriting of textbooks, much as Turner's work did." In 1915, he asked former pupil Thomas Maitland Marshall to help him make this dream a reality. Their coauthored volume, *The Colonization of North America, 1492–1783*, came out in 1920, and introduced Bolton's continental vision to undergraduates. It moved beyond the thirteen colonies to other English colonies (Florida, Canada, and the Bermudas), as well as Dutch, French, Swedish, and Spanish North America. Bolton and Marshall also included early Mexican history to counter the tendency to move immediately from the Spanish "discoveries" to "territory now within the United States." We forget "these regions [the Spanish Borderlands] were to Spain only northern outposts," they argued, and thereby overlook "the wonderful story of Spanish achievement farther south."[21]

"A new field for scholarship has definitely been opened," wrote U.S. frontier historian O. G. Libby in his 1921 review of *The Colonization of North America*. Events between the time the book was begun in 1915 and published in 1920, he added, made Bolton's vision only more compelling. "If the great war has been of service to us it is perhaps in that we have somewhat enlarged our horizon and have begun consciously to fit ourselves into the larger international scheme of things," he noted; this textbook "provided a "truer realization of our national relation to the larger community." Libby was not alone; educator Lewis Harley had also tied World War I to the need for an enlarged U.S. history in 1919. "We have just learned in the Great War, and we are now learning in the peace deliberations, that no country can exist for itself," he insisted. Just as early America had been shaped by "frontiers of empire," so had "frontiers of democracy" transformed America's place in the world. If American historians hoped to understand these changing international relationships, he proposed, they needed to transcend the "narrow provincialism" of their field.[22]

It is in this postwar context, not the emerging "Good Neighbor" era of the early 1930s, that we find the roots of Bolton's hemispheric vision. Looming large in 1920 was not only World War I, but also recent territorial and commercial expansion overseas. Now that the U.S. had gained its "full North American heritage" with the Panama Canal and "far-sundered territories like Alaska and the Philippines," Libby argued in his 1921 review, it was "fit and proper" for historians to tell new tales. Indeed, it was during this era that Latin American history was beginning to take form, and Libby had precisely these wider horizons in mind. "When we can enlarge this [continental] idea so as to present the western hemisphere in a single study," he proposed of *The Colonization of North America*, "we shall have a history which may fairly supplement the works on European history as a whole."[23]

This observation might seem prophetic, were it not for the fact that two years earlier, Bolton had already made the hemispheric leap. In 1919, as department chair, he replaced the U.S. history survey at Berkeley with a lecture class called "History of the Americas." His goal was to establish a synthetic course that would follow the transnational approach of European history, and he billed it as "a general survey of the western hemisphere from the discovery to the present time." Due to the experimental nature of the class, Bolton did not expect a large turnout. He was therefore surprised when some 800 students showed up the first semester, followed by 1,248 the next spring. He found the ambitious scope of the class daunting. Since there were no textbooks on the topic, he spent day and night reading in preparation. Even then, explained one of his former teaching assistants, Bolton had to "work hard . . . to bring the new course into sharp and manageable focus."[24]

Despite these hurdles, "History of the Americas" thrived, and soon spread to other schools. Many of Bolton's graduate students brought the class to their new teaching posts, and Bolton often underscored readiness to teach the Americas survey in letters of recommendation. He also inspired teachers elsewhere with a paper he delivered at the American Historical Association's 1923 meeting, in which he urged colleagues to approach American history "as a whole" rather than as a "history of the United States." Those who were not present at the AHA could read about Bolton's pedagogical frontiers in the January 1924 issue of *The Historical Outlook*, where he gave teachers a brief outline of classroom lectures for "History of the Americas." Another factor in the course's diffusion was the publication of its syllabus in book form by Ginn and Company in 1928. In earlier years, Bolton had simply prepared a syllabus (initially mimeographed but later printed) for students. "Originally I had no thought of publishing the Syllabus," he noted in his 1928 *History of the Americas: A Syllabus with Maps*, "but the demand for it has become so widespread that I have now consented to do so."[25]

In 1926, the Pan American Union and the American Historical Association took the pulse of Latin American history in the United States. In general, class offerings in the field were spotty—and were absent at such top programs as Princeton, Yale, and Wisconsin—with one key exception. At many institutions, "especially those on the Pacific coast," they noted, "considerable attention was paid to Latin America in courses on the History of the Americas." A number of these used Bolton's still-unpublished syllabus, perhaps reflecting the migration of his students to other schools. In her 1934 survey of academic study in Canadian American relations, Edith Ware noted that Bolton's class had, by that time, "nearly a score of imitators," and sixteen other counterparts under such names as "The History of the Western Hemisphere," "Our Neighbors, Canada and Mexico," and "The Pacific Ocean in History." Many of these were taught at smaller junior colleges in the U.S. West. "In the realm of scholarship perhaps all these junior college courses are not of very great importance," Ware admitted, "but in the realm of public opinion they may not be without real value."[26]

"History of the Americas" derived much of its content and form from Bolton's earlier forays into continental history. Though Central and South America had been added, the story was basically the same as that in *The Colonization of North America*. Students started with the Spanish conquest, and then moved sequentially through early French, British, Dutch, and Swedish colonial ventures. They then turned to imperial governance, expansion, and rivalries during the seventeenth and eighteenth centuries. The first semester ended as *The Colonization of North America* did, with the transition from empires to nations by the early nineteenth century. What made the pedagogical shift from continent to hemisphere easy was an emphasis on imperial processes and subjects; by favoring a view from the European metropole, Bolton reduced American peoples and locales to variations on a greater theme. Insofar as these American stories could be assimilated to a master narrative of European expansion overseas—a plotline that Bolton had perfected as early as 1902, as a Europeanist at the University of Texas—the larger motion of the class was anything but innovative.

The second semester of "History of the Americas" was more challenging, and ultimately less successful. As empires became nations, Bolton not only left his earlier continental history textbook behind, but he also entered a terrain—national history—that had little to do with his own research. Perhaps for this reason, Bolton became less confident about his transnational vision, and the course fell into more conventional containers. He began the semester with foundational narratives of the U.S., British Canada, and Latin American nations, and then shifted his focus to westward expansion in the United States. He attempted to finish the semester with a treatment of "American Neighbors: Developments and Interrelations." The hemisphere was now becoming home to national neighbors whose stories could no longer be easily piggybacked on a master narrative of European expansion. So Bolton seized on an event that helped shape his wider horizons in the first place: World War I. All across the hemisphere, World War I had "strengthened the national bonds, and it shocked each republic into a clearer sense of national responsibility," Bolton boldly argued: "It promoted Western Hemisphere solidarity."[27]

In this way, Bolton wove into his greater America narrative a classic epic subject: that of the rise and fall of empires. Just as Aeneas emerged from the ashes of Troy to build the new empire of Rome, so too was America—in Bolton's story—reborn from the ashes of Europe (twice: first in the wars of Independence, then in world war), stronger, more united, and with a renewed sense of moral legitimacy. It was a plotline that was familiar to many in the United States. Regeneration and rebirth were central to the American frontier narrative that had been given academic legitimacy by Frederick Jackson Turner, and political currency by the likes of Theodore Roosevelt, when Bolton was starting his career. Bolton's innovation, in essence, had been to rework this foundational fiction for a newer, more international generation.[28]

Yet it is also possible to read too much into Bolton's classroom narrative; for, as his students would later testify, he rarely made it to the end of his story. "Bolton was a colonialist at heart," and even in the second half of the History of the Americas class "was most interested in the colonial-like parts, such as the western expansion of the United States," recalled one former student: "the second semester disappeared around 1890." It is also useful to remember that despite Bolton's emphasis on parallels and convergences, he left abundant room for difference and discord. He generally saw the hemisphere less as a unified space, and more as a new setting for national stories. Finally, despite his focus on hemispheric history, Bolton felt national history still mattered. He envisioned a future with two kinds of college classes in American history: an "introductory synthetic course" on the western hemisphere, analogous to European history, complemented by national history classes, "dealing with the history of the United States or of any other individual American nation."[29]

BOLTON'S "EPIC" AND ITS DISCONTENTS

Bolton's 1932 presidential address, "Epic of Greater America," summarized his "History of the Americas" narrative for his colleagues. He was inspired by the fact that the American Historical Association was meeting in Toronto; this provided "special fitness to a presidential address dealing with some of the larger aspects of Western Hemisphere history." It also seems to have emboldened him to add a polemical edge to his ideas. He urged scholars to "supplement the purely nationalistic presentation" of American history, whereas in his syllabus, he had simply used the word national. As he often did in the classroom, he chided his audience for studying the thirteen colonies and the U.S. in isolation, since this "obscured many of the larger factors in their development." But this myopia had also, he now added, "helped raise up a nation of chauvinists." If he failed to provoke with these remarks, he would certainly do so with the twentieth-century conclusion of his story. World War I, he had told students, "promoted Western Hemisphere solidarity." Now he strengthened that claim. It was significant that "all America" was on the same side or neutral, he insisted: "The essential unity of the Western Hemisphere was revealed by the Great War."[30]

In other ways, Bolton's "Epic of Greater America" was far from provocative. It remained a modest call for hemispheric history as a supplement to national history, "a setting in which to place any one of our national histories." It certainly had "political and commercial implications," he admitted, but it also made sense "from the standpoint of correct historiography." New historical data (notably in foreign archives), he noted, simply did not make sense within older national paradigms.[31] Indeed, as engaged as Bolton was in the Pan-Americanism of the time, he wrote "Epic of Greater America" for historians, and doubted it would address the concerns of nonspecialists. He said as much when he mailed a copy of his 1932 address to Simon J. Lubin of the Pan-American Institute. "It is purely historical, and may not be what you were expecting," he explained. Bolton intended to provoke, but he seemed more interested—as least in his 1932 address—in critiquing short-sightedness among historians than fueling an emerging "Good Neighbor" ideology, or converting history into what U.S. historian John Higham would call "Pan-American doctrine."[32]

One final aspect of "Epic of Greater America" was its tentative nature. Critics later attacked what they called the "unity-of-all-the-Americas thesis" or the "Bolton theory," but as John Francis Bannon later wrote, "Bolton never claimed to have a thesis to be proved." Indeed, Bolton said he had sketched the "larger historical unities and interrelations" of America only in an "imperfect

way," intending his address "merely as an illustration" of a story that future historians might be in a better position to write. "We need [a historian] to sketch
the high lights and the significant developments of the Western hemisphere as a
whole," Bolton argued, yet "perhaps the person who undertakes the task, as a
guarantee of objectivity ought to be an inhabitant of the moon." Bolton was
therefore not only aware of the shortcomings of his hemispheric view, but he
offered it as a tentative, open-ended guide for future work, rather than a fully
formed narrative. Such a story would require new archival work, demanding not
only "special researches that have already been consummated," but also "data
which we do not possess." It suggested, in short, "a thousand new things to do."[33]

If Bolton hoped to inspire a rush to the archives, as Turner had done in
1893, he was sorely disappointed. The weeks after Toronto were unnervingly
silent. "I have heard very few echoes," he wrote a colleague: "I hope it was not
too rotten." To a friend he admitted: "the silence is somewhat ominous." In fact
it would be almost seven years, after it was reprinted in a 1939 anthology entitled *Wider Horizons of American History*, before his "Epic of Greater America"
gained critical attention. Its critics were less troubled by its political overtones
than its historical claims. Arthur Whitaker argued that "the essential unity of
the Western Hemisphere" might be a fine ideal for the future, but poorly
described the past. Mexican historian Edmundo O'Gorman criticized Bolton's
disregard of cultural and religious difference. "He sketches common roads,
leaps over political barriers, but what . . . has he done with the men, with the
history-making human material?" O'Gorman wrote. Bolton's larger "historical
unities," he explained, "appear to me as unities which may be found in any
group of men, simply because they have all been born and raised, they all eat
and work. Larger unities, no doubt, but unities of Nature and not of human
nature, which is the essence of history."[34]

It was this aspect of Bolton's address, his claim of "historical unity," that
became its Achilles heel. Yet O'Gorman was concerned less with the idea of
unity than with how Bolton saw the nature of this unity. Bolton began by
focusing on the expansion and consolidation of imperial power in the
Americas, a story that ended with hemisphere-wide movements for national
independence. He then shifted his gaze to processes of nation formation, and
the incorporation of the Americas into global markets. This narrative might
seem compelling and familiar to scholars of worlds system and state formation
in the Americas today, but in 1932 Bolton viewed these relationships within a
progressive, U.S.-centered story of economic development. He praised the positive role of railroads, plantations, nitrate works, mines, and oil wells in the

"A B C countries," while lamenting a "lack of progress" in the Caribbean. "Areas which were most developed in early colonial days are now most retarded," he claimed. "Nevertheless, backwardness is only relative, and some of these tropical regions, with their fruit and oil, have recently attracted capital and been developed at a tremendous rate."[35]

This development-centered, modernizing vision was not lost on O'Gorman. "Everything is moving smoothly, seems to be the conclusion of Professor Bolton's address," he noted:

> The two Americans progress and soon the one lagging behind (Hispanic America) will find itself on the same level as Saxon America. It was inevitable to come across the idea of progress. The entire speech is inspired with it; from all sides are presented evidence of material prosperity: railroads, plantations, oil wells, investments, foreign capital, raw materials; but—how about culture?[36]

Bolton's treatment of culture, O'Gorman wrote, was troubling. "Culture progress," Bolton claimed, "has followed material prosperity." Replied O'Gorman: "Might it not be better to say that a culture crisis has followed in the wake of a dangerous material prosperity?" In Bolton's story, development, like common roads, transcended nations, but in a way that threatened to trade in one kind of nation-centered history for another. Rather than asking how American nations and cultures made sense of these changes, Bolton turned to the language of U.S. imperialism, in which America was measured on U.S. terms. It was this framework that allowed Bolton to see "remarkable A B C powers" facing "retarded" Caribbean neighbors across the unevenly "modernizing" fabric of Hemispheric America. "The formulae of economic efficiency developed in the United States do not work in other parts of the Continent," retorted O'Gorman. This nation-centered view, he insisted, motivated Bolton "with unjustified superciliousness and short-sightedness" to divide the Americas into "progressive" spaces, which were like the United States, and "backwards" spaces, which were not.[37]

Bolton never responded to O'Gorman, but according to John Francis Bannon, he regretted "one or more sweeping statement made in his AHA presidential address." Whether in response to O'Gorman or to atone for general sins of overstatement, Bolton modified his position in 1939, in a lecture to a State Department Conference on Inter-American Relations on "Some Cultural Assets of Latin America." He began by countering the materialism of his 1932 address. With Latin America, the United States has "many things in common, because of common or analogous origins," he observed, "but in a thousand ways their culture complements our own, and offers the stimulus and enrichment that spring from contrast and variety." Throughout the lecture Bolton reiterated the importance of inter-American linkages, but he also underscored the importance of viewing culture in national terms. "A nation's culture embodies the sum total of the nation's heritage," he noted. "We may study [another culture] to find the roots of our own civilization," he went on to propose, "or we may prize it for its contrasts with our own."[38]

Curiously, it was during this time—while striving to add cultural and national complexity to his hemispheric perspective—that Bolton began to participate in Pan-American politics. In 1938, he went to Peru for the Seventh Pan American Conference in Lima, and was subsequently named "Pan American Day Speaker" at UCLA. While qualifying earlier hemispheric claims, his "Cultural Assets" lecture also reflected Bolton's new Pan-Americanism. In it, he reinforced the "common tradition of an American struggle," not in world war, but in nineteenth-century independence movements. "It is this common history and common ideology which have formed the basis for a Western-Hemisphere political doctrine," he proposed. Meanwhile, his critique of historical myopia—his initial motivation for urging scholars across borders—had become more generalized. American historians should look abroad "for breadth of outlook upon the great World of which any one of us is so infinitesimal a part, and of which any one nation's civilization is but a minor portion," he observed. "We learn from the World in order to be modest about ourselves."[39]

In his 1932 "Epic of Greater America," Bolton proposed that each nation's story was "but a thread out of a larger [hemispheric] strand." By 1938, despite his growing interest in Pan-American politics, his gaze had begun to move away from the Americas to other regions: the hemisphere had become the "great World." Had Bolton continued this line of thought, he might have found himself able to address yet another problem implicit in critiques of his work. Perhaps, as he argued, nations imposed imperfect and problematic divisions within history, but were continents or hemispheres any better? O'Gorman's critique of Bolton suggested that instead of widening our horizons, Bolton had simply located a new historical "unity" that future scholars would have to challenge and deconstruct. What might have happened had Bolton continued to shift his gaze toward world history? Might he have developed a more critical greater American perspective?

BOLTON'S AMBIVALENT LEGACY

These would ultimately become questions for future generations, for by 1939, Bolton was on the threshold of retirement. In May 1940 he delivered his last "History of the Americas" lecture and passed the course on to his successors, most of them former students. From this point on he would devote his remaining energies to scholarship on the regional scale of "Spanish Borderlands" history, with an emphasis on its founding fathers. In 1930 he had given Californians the heroic tale of Juan Bautista de Anza, and during the next two decades he would give the U.S. Southwest two more epic heroes, Arizona Jesuit "pioneer" Eusebio Francisco Kino, and his secular New Mexican counterpart, Francisco Vázquez de Coronado.

For one who had spent his career crossing national borders, Bolton's fascination with Anza, Kino, and Coronado was strangely traditional. I have already touched on his treatment of Anza, that ambivalent hero of the transnational Pacific World and the national U.S. West, who joined frontier heroes Alexander Mackenzie and John Frémont. Kino, far more than Anza, leapt from the pages of Bolton's 1936 *Rim of Christendom* as a national hero with a distinct frontier air, like a character from a Southwestern pulp novel. He was a well-assimilated American "frontiersman" with little evidence of his passage through Europe or Mexico. A blazer of trails "untrod by civilized man," he was not only a man of the cloth, Bolton suggested, but also an explorer, rancher, and "cattle king." "Southwestern cowboys stand aghast and almost skeptical at his well authenticated feats in the saddle," he added in an abridged biography, *The Padre on Horseback*. Like Zane Grey's lone, enigmatic desert heroes, Kino was a "born individualist," and was "happiest on the border."[40]

Not unlike Kino, whose dashing pioneer tale would inspire Arizonans to give him a coveted spot in Washington, D.C.'s Statuary Hall, Coronado was a local hero with national horizons. Bolton wrote his story for New Mexico's Coronado Cuatro Centennial, which commemorated the 400-year anniversary of Coronado's 1540 entrada. The Coronado Cuarto Centennial Commission organized the event not only to generate tourist dollars, but also to integrate New Mexico more fully into the national fold by promoting its "tri-cultural" heritage, an imagined tradition that satisfied a growing national desire for cultural alternatives without threatening the religious and racial order. Coronado was an ideal icon for this project due to his epic distance. Since his life prefaced and thus prepared the space for U.S. national history—by initiating a Spanish experiment whose failures (but also romantic interludes) played foil to later narratives of Anglo-American conquest—Coronado could become an

"American" pioneer in ways that later Latin Americans could not. By extension, New Mexico could celebrate a "Spanish American" heritage that might appear both temporally and racially distinct from Mexico, and therefore easier to assimilate into the American mainstream.[41]

Bolton's biography of Coronado reinforced this larger process of assimilation. He compared his Hispanic hero to Daniel Boone, and likened his path into North America to Boone's Wilderness Road. This Spaniard's chief contribution, Bolton argued, had been his discovery of lands that would be "combined by Anglo-Americans under the name of the Southwest, or the Spanish Borderlands." Coronado claimed allegiance to the Spanish crown, but teleology would transform him into a North American hero. When Bolton proposed that American history "from California to Nebraska" began with Coronado's journey, he clearly articulated these narrative boundaries: here was the physical and moral geography of U.S., not Mexican, history.[42]

Yet even when Bolton situated Kino and Coronado within national epics, he subverted these tales with references to America's wider horizons. Bolton first met Kino in 1907, when he found his memoirs in the Mexico City archives. It was at this time that Bolton had begun to imagine an open-ended, transnational North American history, and this may have shaped his subsequent view of Kino. His was "not merely the life story of a remarkable individual," he noted in his 1936 biography, but it also illuminated the "culture history of a large part of the Western Hemisphere in its pioneer stages." Among other things, it linked the Southwest to distant Jesuit frontiers of New France and Paraguay. Bolton's biography of Coronado had a similar inflection. Coronado's search for El Dorado in New Mexico, he told readers, was "not greatly different from the remarkable treasure hunts which swept over a large part of the Western Hemisphere." His role as explorer and statesman also found a place in Mexico. He provided "an immortal link between the republics of Mexico and the United States," Bolton noted, and to commemorate this "early historic bond," the two nations had decided to create a monument to their transnational hero on the borderline between Sonora and Arizona.[43]

In this way, Bolton worked until the end of his life to reconcile his national and transnational tales. Yet the days of his larger hemispheric vision were numbered. In 1945, his students published *Greater America*, a 550-page festschrift with essays embracing the Americas from Alaska to Patagonia, covering colonial and national eras. The collection was "an impressive achievement, whether judged by bulk or any other standard," insisted Latin Americanist Lewis Hanke in a 1946 review. Yet it was a series of fragments in search of a center. Its editors did not engage Bolton's larger framework, and the individual essays rarely crossed regional or national borders. This echoed a trend among Bolton students: Many were leaders in Latin American and U.S. history, but few championed their mentor's wider horizons. This seemed to be true even in the classroom. By 1949, few taught "History of the Americas," and the popularity of the class at Berkeley had plummeted. Within a decade of Bolton's retirement there, enrollments had dropped from 1,060 to 150.[44]

There were undoubtedly many reasons for this waning interest in hemispheric history. Like Bolton, many of his students published prodigiously, but they often did research that reinforced rather than crossed borders between North American and Latin American history. This reflected a growing division of labor between Latin American and U.S. historians in research university settings, where Bolton's best students got jobs. Even if these young academics wanted to cross borders, new scholarly winds in the distinct fields of Latin American and western U.S. history tugged at their sails as well. Bolton was likely pleased by the growing institutional interest for Latin American history—forty-three of his own students went on to work in the field—but it came at a cost. Ever since 1932, Bolton had been working on a textbook to replace his History of the Americas syllabus, and yet soon, recalled John W. Caughey, "the all-knowing bookmen were saying that the course was going into decline and that it was too late for such a book." It would remain unfinished. One can still find the chapters in his papers, monuments to a larger vision that had slowly yielded to separate epics: the national story of the U.S., and that of its new hemispheric alter ego, Latin America.[45]

And yet the story was never this simple. Latin American studies not only had its roots in the same world that pushed Bolton across the Texas border in 1902, but many later considered Bolton's early Mexican research as pioneering work in the field. In the years that followed, Bolton's "greater American" history and Latin American history—often recalled as radical opposites, one emphasizing unities and the other preserving distinctions—led parallel, often overlapping lives. In the 1930s and 1940s, the Pan American Union published a series of studies on classes in Latin American studies in U.S. universities and colleges, which suggested that hemispheric history and Latin American history both boomed during this era, despite claims of declining enrollments and textbook sales for "History of the Americas" (although hemispheric history did remain the smaller sibling). The 1935–1936 report counted 269 classes in Latin American history and 32 on History of the Americas or its equivalent; in 1938–1939, there were 362 in the former and 45 in the latter; and 1948–1949 saw a total of 818 Latin American history classes and 98 hemispheric history classes. Both courses therefore grew at roughly the same rate—increasing by just over 300 percent—between 1936 and 1948.[46]

The data suggest that the "History of the Americas" was hardly in decline, and was actually on the rise between the 1930s and late 1940s. Even though Latin American history had more classes and more students, it was not replacing hemispheric history.[47] The data indicate two additional trends. The first had to do with the institutional support for hemispheric history. In her 1934 report on the study of international relations, Edith Ware observed that the home for the class tended to be junior colleges, and according to Pan American Union surveys, this was even more marked between 1936 and 1949, as junior colleges (but also teachers colleges and Catholic/Jesuit colleges) went from 60 percent to 80 percent of all institutions offering History of the Americas. Hemispheric history, then, was thriving specifically in smaller institutions, where fewer teachers and economic resources no doubt increased the appeal of a class that promised—with its attention to both North and Latin America— to kill two birds with one stone.[48]

A second trend that emerged by the 1940s was that teachers were replacing Bolton's History of the Americas syllabus—the former bible of hemispheric history—with a wider range of textbooks and readings.[49] They often combined textbooks on Latin American history, U.S. history, Canadian history, and U.S.-Latin American relations, a trend that might explain why publishers were less than enthusiastic about Bolton's proposed hemispheric magnum opus. The shift away from the Bolton syllabus also reflected innovations such as team-teaching, which allowed teachers to play to regional and national strengths, and new frameworks. One innovator was Harold E. Davis, whose 1938–1939 "History of the Western Hemisphere" at Hiram College followed Bolton's syllabus "but with much more emphasis upon cultural and social development and with a radically different organization." In 1949, at a new post at American University, Davis taught "Civilization of the Americas," in which he included the "influences of land, Indians, [and] Negroes." Charles D. Kepner Jr.'s "History of the Americas" at Shauffler College selectively targeted Argentina, Brazil, Chile, Mexico, and the United States in the nineteenth century, whereas former Bolton student Mildred Gentry Williams divided her class at San José State College geographically, so the first semester dealt with Mexico and the Caribbean, and the second semester focused on South America and international relations.[50]

What emerges from the Pan American Union reports, then, is a rather different picture from what John W. Caughey and others suggested after Bolton's death. Instead of following its founder into retirement, History of the Americas thrived well into the next decade, cultivating new ties to the field of Latin American history, and often assuming new forms. The fact that the class increasingly found its place in smaller colleges suggests that its survival might have been a matter of convenience rather than choice. It also indicates a grow-ing separation from centers of scholarly production. But it forces us to rethink the common view of Bolton's hemispheric epic as a shooting star that burned out quickly after 1932. Another part of the story also demands attention. The Pan American Union reports also show that although Latin American history was articulating a space of its own, defying whatever hemispheric unities Bolton imagined, it was also becoming increasingly interested in pan-American relations. Even if instructors introduced connections to clarify con-trasts, many concluded their classes on a triumphal note of pan-American cooperation and inter-American "partnership."[51] Historians later condemned Bolton for his romantic and doctrinaire perspective, as if his vision was an exception to an otherwise rationally divided canon. Yet the borders between Latin American and greater American epics were anything but rigid. What his-torians would remember as clear discursive borders were actually porous membranes of creative scholarly exchange.

These fuzzy borders were perhaps most clearly exposed when historians tried to forge larger synthetic narratives. In 1944, Latin American historians James F. King and Samuel Everett sat down to assess the strengths and shortcom-ings of Latin American history textbooks. The typical textbook began with European tales of discovery, exploration, conquest, and settlement. After exam-ining the various aspects of colonial life, it then moved to nineteenth-century movements for independence, where the story began to fall apart. "The nature of Latin American history until the national period, as it is conventionally pre-sented, possesses somewhat artificial unities lent by the fact of domination by the mother countries," King and Everett noted. "With the removal of these unities as a result of the successful independence movement, authors are presented with the problem of telling the story of increasingly numerous sovereign entities." The typical solution, they explained, was to devote a separate chapter to each nation. So readers found a stark contrast between the colonial and national halves of Latin American history textbooks—a problem that would have seemed haunt-ingly familiar to readers of Bolton's earlier hemispheric syllabus.[52]

One thing that made Latin America's story different, of course, was its exclusion of English- and French-speaking North America. But if one brought inter-American relations into the mix, this distinction faded. King and Everett found they had to engage Bolton's hemispheric perspective, and their attempt to lay down rules for this engagement showed just how artificial and problematic the bounding of the American past could be. They urged textbook authors to "recognize the numerous basic differences" between the two Americas, and echoing Bolton's 1939 "Cultural Assets" speech, they argued that these distinctions added to "the color and richness of New World civilization." Yet even if one found no "essential similarity" between the two Americas, there were still "valid unities" that demanded emphasis: "common characteristics of early rule by European mother countries, the interrelations and common aspirations of the struggle for independence, mutual strivings towards a democratic ideal, [and] common social problems." Indeed, they argued, textbook writers might very well solicit "guidance from books on the history of the Americas, which emphasize comparisons and interrelations of all the nations of the hemisphere."[53]

What we see here is not the replacement of one paradigm with another, but rather a creative middle ground, where a new generation liberally folded insights of the previous generation into their own "useable past." The only difference between King and Everett's picture of Latin America, and Bolton's 1939 "Cultural Assets" version of the greater America, is that King and Everett started with cultural differences and then moved to common legacies and connections. This was simply the later Bolton turned upside down and placed in a new Latin American framework; little else had changed. Moreover, as Latin American history developed as a field, it would be plagued by the same problem of transnational synthesis that haunted Bolton. Since history was a child of the nation-state, national history seemed natural, but efforts to view the past on larger scales seemed artificial and constructed. If this undermined Bolton's hemispheric history, it also made the notion of Latin American history at least partially dependent on that of American history. For it was its collective distinctiveness from American history—the narrative conceit of a nation that claimed an unqualified "American" identity for itself—that helped many to imagine a greater Latin American past.[54]

BUILDING ON BOLTON

What role did Bolton's own students come to play in this bifurcated terrain? Did they try to preserve or enlarge Bolton's wider horizons, did they reject his transnational dreams for the realities of a divided academy, or did they just avoid the issue altogether? At first blush, it is hard to discern signs of enthusiasm among these students for Bolton's wider horizons. The absence of a conceptual center to the 1945 festschrift *Greater America* seems to support what John Francis

Bannon and Lewis Hanke later suggested: Bolton's own students led the way in sweeping his greater America into the dustbin of outdated notions. Yet, as with Latin American history's supposed eclipse of hemispheric history, one can profit from a closer look. The ways Bolton's students caught the shifting winds of American history reveals that their retreat to conventional shores was more apparent than real—and that Bolton's greater America survived in creative, unexpected ways in the freshly bounded historical terrain of the Americas.[55]

We can begin by revising the usual assumption that these students went on to become either Latin American historians or historians of the American West. Some worked in Canadian history, others became Mormon historians with little interest in the West as a region, some built on Bolton's early forays into the Pacific World, others became historians of comparative Atlantic frontiers, and a significant number retreated to the Spanish borderlands, with little interest in either the U.S. West or Latin America. It is also hard to pin these often-nomadic scholars down to one field. Only 36 percent (38 of 105) can be classified as doing only western U.S. or Latin American history, and if one factors in those focusing only on Canadian history, Spanish Borderlands history, Mormon history, etc., this total of single-field specialists grows to 59 percent (62 of 105). This means 41 percent (43) were "border crossers" of one sort or another—that is, scholars who worked and taught across field boundaries.[56]

Many crossed borders that few historians traverse today. Even if one teaches both U.S. and Latin American history, one is unlikely to publish in both fields, and is often discouraged from doing so unless a specialist in borderlands history or a comparative framework (the Atlantic World or U.S.–Latin American relations, for instance). By contrast, Bolton's students were strikingly cosmopolitan. Even if they eschewed Bolton's hemispheric vision, some nevertheless matched—often exceeded—their mentor's geographical range in scholarship and in the classroom. One such border crosser was Herbert I. Priestley, who received his Ph.D. in 1917 and joined Bolton at Berkeley as a Mexicanist, offering courses in Mexican, Latin American, and U.S. diplomatic history. His greatest interest was modern Mexico—notably the Mexican Revolution—but he also did significant work in the Spanish borderlands, from California to Florida, and in modern French imperialism (winning major awards in these two fields). His presence in the diverse scholarly communities of Latin America, California, and global history was reflected by service on the editorial boards of *Pacific Historical Review*, *Hispanic American Historical Review*, and *World Affairs*.[57]

Two others who embraced Bolton's wider pedagogical and research horizons were Abraham P. Nasatir and Alfred Barnaby Thomas. A child prodigy,

Nasatir received his Ph.D. in 1926, at the tender age of 21. At San Diego State University, he regularly offered courses on the History of the Americas, South America, Mexico, and the Caribbean, even though his research focused on colonial North America. He was an authority on the Mississippi River borderlands, a former meeting ground of French, British, and Spanish empires (and later the United States and Mexico). His multinational approach was unprecedented, due partly to his linguistic abilities: He read French and Spanish, and his interest in the multilingual precursors of Lewis and Clark carried him to Spanish, French, British, Canadian, and U.S. archives. His 1945 *French Activities in California* introduced materials on California history in Paris archives—a Francophone counterpart to Bolton's 1913 *Guide to Materials* that extended beyond U.S. borders to document French voyages in the Pacific, the French in Mexico and Central America, and the history of Hawaii. As if these efforts to map out all corners of imperial North America were not enough, Nasatir also made regular contributions to Latin American and Jewish history, including a history of Jews in the Mississippi borderlands.[58]

Alfred Barnaby Thomas, who received his Ph.D. two years after Nasatir, started his career as a Spanish Borderlands historian, with a focus on regions north and east of New Mexico. He spent a decade at the University of Oklahoma, where he published on Spanish exploration and Indian policy in North America, and offered classes on Latin American history. He later moved to the University of Alabama to develop a program in Latin American history, and there he began to publish not only on the Spanish in the U.S. South—helping create a useable past for his new home, much as Bolton had in Texas and California—but also broadly on Latin America. He wrote histories of Brazil and Argentina, and authored a general Latin American history textbook. Then, in the late 1950s, a new topic beckoned from a North American landscape that was already familiar to Thomas. The Indian Claims Commission needed historical data for Jicarilla Apache, Mescalero and Chiricahua Apache, Lipan Apache, and Yavapai land claims. After shifting to the eastern Spanish Borderlands, and then south into Latin America, Thomas crossed yet another border into Native American history—a field that had existed as a mere shadow on Bolton's Eurocentric map of greater America.[59]

These were only three of a number of ambidextrous, border-crossing historians that Bolton produced in his lifetime. As their pedagogical and scholarly trajectories suggest, Bolton's continental and hemispheric stories might have fallen to the margins of U.S. and Latin American paradigms, but his wider horizons endured. Trained to cross borders, Bolton's students adapted quite readily to the bounded academic terrains of their generation: Flashing passports from the national "territories" of U.S. and Latin American history (and the U.S.-centered Spanish Borderlands), many migrated at will across the larger, hemispheric past. Fortunately, their scholarly world allowed limited forms of dual citizenship. Such border-crossing scholars may have been in the minority, but they were a tolerated phenomenon of a world that had not completely hardened along sectional lines. This is not to say that borders did not matter—Bolton had faced the academic border patrol as early as 1902 when he had to smuggle his way into the United States through Texas—but that the rules of scholarly citizenship were anything but settled.

This earlier scholarly community emerged from a world where U.S. historians had just begun to think transnationally about the American past. It was the larger crucible of international relations tied to the rise of the United States as a world power that created space for a greater American perspective. A similar context would, after World War II, forge new distinctions between the story of the United States and that of Latin America. With new federal funding for area studies, history departments were, in turn, more formally divided into separate—and, many insisted, self-sufficient—communities for studying the Americas. Scholars now took the international American past for granted, but they also took for granted the ways of dividing up this past. In short, that which seemed new and exciting for Herbert Eugene Bolton became assimilated and codified under the separate signs of U.S. and Latin American history. Since these bifurcated American tales now seem so natural to us, we show surprise at new continental and hemispheric stories that transcend and challenge these bordered terrains. "It's about time!" some have exclaimed. "Why didn't we think of this before?" others ask.

This is possibly a good thing. Maybe our desire to imagine ourselves at the edge of a brave new world will inspire new bursts of creativity and lead to perspectives that our forebears could have only imagined. Yet we can also learn from those who came before. Wandering through the fog and ruins of Bolton's graveyard, one may find it hauntingly familiar. Bolton's mission to rescue America from the clutches of national history resonates not only for prophets of a new global world, but also for a growing guild of borderlands and transnational historians. Borders and their crossings are, by conventional standards, peripheral to histories that really matter—as candidates for jobs or tenure in U.S. and Latin American history can be reminded. Yet those who thrive in these scholarly spaces in-between are learning again what Bolton told us in 1932. "In a larger framework," he insisted, "many things which have seemed obscure and secondary become outstanding and primary."[60]

Building on Bolton today, historians might consider the range of histori-cal scales he proposed for future study: the hemispheric frame of his "Epic of Greater America," the continental setting of Bolton and Marshall's *The Colonization of North America*, the local transnational (but also subnational) stage of borderlands history, and the transoceanic and imperial contexts of European American and "Pacific Ocean" history. Those following Bolton today might add to the list: pan–Native American histories, epics of greater African America and Asian America, the Americas within world systems, and so on. Even environmental historians find an important place in such open-ended frameworks. Who, Bolton proposed, "has written the history of the introduc-tion of European plants and animals in the Western Hemisphere as a whole, or the spread of cattle and horse raising from Patagonia to Labrador?" And how, environmental historians might today add, could the history of nature and its transformation take us on the even larger stages of the "wider world"?[61]

Such open-ended inquiries should warn us—just as Edmundo O'Gorman warned others in his critique of Bolton—of the pitfalls of simply replacing one historical container with another. We might instead try, from a range of per-spectives, to contextualize, decenter, and denaturalize national and transna-tional narratives alike. Conversely, we might also learn from Bolton about the enduring power of conventional historical containers. U.S. readers embraced Bolton's borderland pioneers as the heroic forefathers of their own cultural legacies—transformed by the racial and cultural alchemy of the epic form into precursors of a white "American" history. Although Bolton laced these "pre-national" epics with references to wider horizons, teleological forces at work in these narratives were never completely tamed. Even today, borderlands schol-ars fuel this nation-centered telos when they focus on lands now within the United States, and end their stories in 1821, with Mexican Independence, or in 1848, with the division of Mexico's far north into U.S. and Mexican halves.

Bolton tried to escape this conundrum with his greater American narra-tive, which had many endings in many places, and so claimed significance for more than the select national few. Yet in the long run, it was precisely the unepic-like nature of this narrative—the fact that it seemed to speak to nobody in particular—that helped seal its fate. In the end, Bolton's students were des-tined to carry his hemispheric horizons into a greater American landscape that was more concerned than ever with mapping proper boundaries between nations and cultures.

Yet to say that Bolton's legacy was about the rise and fall of a paradigm is to miss its broader significance. One must also consider not only the enduring linkages between the "greater America" and Latin American history, but also how Bolton's wider horizons took on new form in the work of his students, who regularly crossed the continental divides of American history. His enduring legacy should remind us that all paradigms, no matter how grand, are sustained by small, local practices—practices as basic as taking Spanish lessons, crossing a border, or losing one's place in the archives of a foreign land. If we want to understand how his wider horizons have endured, and how they might be of use to future generations, we might begin our greater American journeys—much as Bolton did in the summer of 1902—at the nearest international checkpoint, armed with a passport, a respect for new languages, and an open mind.

NOTES

1. Anthony DePalma, *Here: A Biography of the New American Continent* (New York: Public Affairs, 2001), xiii, 7–13; Richard Kiy and John D. Wirth, eds., *Environmental Management on North America's Borders* (College Station: Texas A & M Press, 1998), 3. DePalma described Wirth as a "fellow North American *voyageur*." As head of the North American Institute, a trinational public affairs group, Wirth not only studied post-NAFTA issues until his untimely death in 2002, but like DePalma, he wrote history to shape a new continental consciousness. See preface to John D. Wirth, *Smelter Smoke in North America: The Politics of Transborder Pollution* (Lawrence: University Press of Kansas, 2000); and John Wirth and Robert L. Earle, eds., *Identities in North America: The Search for Community* (Stanford: Stanford University Press, 1995). For Moyers's quote, see fly jacket of DePalma, *New American Continent*.

2. Arthur Whitaker, *Latin American History Since 1825* (Washington, D.C.: Service Center for Teachers of History, 1961), 4; John Higham, *History: Professional Scholarship in America* (New York: Prentice-Hall, 1965), 41; and Lewis Hanke, ed., *Do the Americas Have a Common History? A Critique of the Bolton Theory* (New York: Alfred A. Knopf, 1964). This latter collection contained pre-1960s critiques of Bolton, but placed them in a polemical framework that particularly resonated in the 1960s.

3. Herbert Eugene Bolton, *The Spanish Borderlands: A Chronicle of Old Florida and the Southwest* (1921; reprint, with a foreword by Albert L. Hurtado, Albuquerque: University of New Mexico Press, 1996); Herbert Eugene Bolton, "Defensive Spanish Expansion and the Significance of the Borderlands," in Bolton, *Wider Horizons of American History* (Notre Dame: University of Notre Dame Press, 1939), 98; and John Francis Bannon, ed., *Bolton and the Spanish Borderlands* (Norman: University of Oklahoma Press, 1964), 3, 301. See discussions of Bolton's Borderlands history in Albert L. Hurtado, "Parkmanizing the Spanish Borderlands: Bolton, Turner, and the Historians' World," *Western Historical Quarterly* 26, 2 (summer 1995): 149–67; David J. Weber, "The Idea of the Spanish Borderlands," in *Columbian Consequences*, vol. 3, *The Spanish Borderlands in Pan-American Perspective*, ed. David Hurst Thomas (Washington, D.C.: Smithsonian Institution Press, 1991), 3–20; and David J. Weber, "John Francis Bannon and the Historiography of the Spanish Borderlands: Retrospect

and Prospect," in *Myth and the History of the Hispanic Southwest: Essays by David J. Weber* (Albuquerque: University of New Mexico Press, 1988), 55–88.

4. The romantic image of the Spanish Southwest had already begun to emerge in the nineteenth century with such writers as Charles F. Lummis and Hubert Howe Bancroft. For discussions of the Black Legend in the United States, see Philip Wayne Powell, *Tree of Hate: Propaganda and Prejudices Affecting United States Relations with the Hispanic World* (Vallecito, Calif.: Ross House Books, 1985); and David J. Weber, "'Scarce more than apes': Historical Roots of Anglo-American Stereotypes of Mexicans," in *New Spain's Far Northern Frontier: Essays on Spain in the American West, 1540–1821*, ed. David J. Weber (Albuquerque: University of New Mexico Press, 1979), 293–307. For counter-vailing romantic images of the U.S. Southwest, see David J. Weber, *The Spanish Frontier in North America* (New Haven: Yale University Press, 1992), 341–53.

5. Mikhail Bakhtin, "Epic and Novel: Toward a Methodology for the Study of the Novel," in *The Dialogical Imagination: Four Essays by M. M. Bakhtin*, ed. Michael Holquist (Austin: University of Texas Press, 1981), 13–14. In the borderlands, Spanish history laid the space for—and played foil to—national history in both Black and White Legend variants. I do *not* propose Bakhtin's model as a strict recipe for understanding how Americans made sense of their past, but *would* suggest that the general assumptions that went into a nation's literary epics also shaped the ways citizens made sense of their own national and cultural histories vis-à-vis "others."

6. This is what allowed the poet Virgil, for instance, to incorporate heroes of Asia (Troy) into the foundational national story of Rome, through his epic, *The Aeneid*. See, for Aneas and the phenomena of incorporating the "other" as "ancestor," Robert Pogue Harrison, *The Dominion of the Dead* (Chicago: University of Chicago Press, 2003), 90–105. Quoted passage is from Bakhtin, "Epic and Novel," 15–16.

7. John Francis Bannon, *Herbert Eugene Bolton: The Historian and the Man, 1870–1953* (Tucson: University of Arizona Press, 1978), 7–22, 32. For Turner's thesis, see Frederick J. Turner, "The Significance of the Frontier in American History," *Annual Report of the American Historical Association for the Year 1893* (Washington, D.C.: GPO, 1894), 199–227; William Cronon, "Revisiting the Vanishing Frontier: The Legacy of Frederick Jackson Turner," *Western Historical Quarterly* 18 (April 1987): 157–76; and John Mack Faragher, ed., *Rereading Frederick Jackson Turner: "The Significance of the Frontier in American History" and Other Essays* (New York: Henry Holt and Co., 1994).

8. Bannon, *Herbert Eugene Bolton*, 31–33; and Herbert Eugene Bolton to Frederick E. Bolton, 17 June 1902, Herbert E. Bolton Papers, Bancroft Library, University of California at Berkeley.

9. Bannon, *Herbert Eugene Bolton*, 35–38; and John Francis Bannon, "Herbert Eugene Bolton, His *Guide* in the Making," *Southwestern Historical Quarterly* 73, 1 (July 1969): 37.

10. For a general discussion of how Texans saw their history at this time, see Stephen Stagner, "Epics, Science, and the Lost Frontier: Texas Historical Writing, 1836–1936," *Western Historical Quarterly* 12 (April 1981): 164–81. By "romance," I mean an open-ended story, often marked by incessant wandering, and devoid of the *telos* that marks the epic form. For epic and romance, see David Quint, *Epic and Empire: Politics and*

Generic Form from Virgil to Milton (Princeton: Princeton University Press, 1993). For the ways that Texans wove Spanish ruins into their own history, see Holly Beachley Brear, *Inherit the Alamo: Myth and Ritual at an American Shrine* (Austin: University of Texas Press, 1995); and Lewis T. Fisher, *Saving San Antonio: The Precarious Preservation of a Heritage* (Lubbock: Texas Tech University Press, 1996), 37–87.

11. Herbert Eugene Bolton, "Some Materials for Southwestern History in the Archivo General de Mexico," *Texas Historical Association Quarterly* 6 (October 1902): 103–12; and "Some Materials for Southwestern History in the Archivo General de Mexico, II," *Texas Historical Association Quarterly* 7 (January 1904): 196–213.

12. Bannon, "*Guide* in the Making," 42–52; and José de Onís, "The Americas of Herbert E. Bolton," *The Americas* 12, 2 (October 1955): 159.

13. J. Franklin Jameson to Herbert Eugene Bolton, 6 June 1907, in Incoming Correspondence, Bolton Papers; Herbert Eugene Bolton, *Guide to Materials for the History of the United States in the Principal Archives of Mexico* (Washington, D.C.: The Carnegie Institution of Washington, 1913), vii–viii, 2; and Bannon, "*Guide* in the Making," 43.

14. It is hard to know how Carnegie officials imagined this "mutual understanding" working, but it is important to note that the Carnegie Foundation in general played a large role in the study of U.S. international relations. By 1934, the Carnegie and Rockefeller foundations had over half of the known capital funds of foundations funding the study of international relations. The Historical Section of the Carnegie Institution of Washington was for years home to the *American Historical Review*. This all reflected the investment that national and private interests could have in American history. See discussion in Edith W. Ware, *The Study of International Relations in the United States: Survey for 1934* (New York: Columbia University Press, 1934), 24–27.

15. Bolton, *Guide to Materials*, vii–viii. I use the word "mined" in explicit reference to a letter that Bolton wrote his brother in 1902, in which he expressed his excitement to get into the "mine of sources that lie in Mexico." Herbert Eugene Bolton to Frederick E. Bolton, 8 July 1902, Bolton Papers.

16. Bannon, *Herbert Eugene Bolton*, 58–88; Robert A. McCaughey, *International Studies and Academic Enterprise: A Chapter in the Enclosure of American Learning* (New York: Columbia University Press, 1984), 80; John F. Davis, *California: Romantic and Resourceful: A Plea for the Collection, Preservation, and Diffusion of Information Relating to Pacific Coast History* (San Francisco: A. M. Robertson, 1914); and Jorge Basadre, "Introduction," in *Courses on Latin America in Institutions of Higher Education in the United States, 1948–1949*, comp. Estellita Hart (Washington, D.C.: Division of Education, Department of Cultural Affairs, Pan American Union, 1949). Bancroft had the world's largest collection of Spanish *Americana*; for his legacy, see John W. Caughey, *Hubert Howe Bancroft: Historian of the West* (Berkeley: University of California Press, 1946); and Charles S. Peterson, "Hubert Howe Bancroft: First Western Regionalist," in *Writing Western History: Essays on Major Western Historians*, ed. Richard W. Etulain (Albuquerque: University of New Mexico Press, 1991), 43–70. More research needs to be done on the Native Sons of the Golden West; Albert Hurtado says they were hardly ready to trade in Anglo-California heroes for Spanish pioneer heroes, but bases this on sentiments in the 1920s. Earlier pro-Spanish sentiments were likely shaped by Charles

Lummis and other pro-Spanish writers of his era. Albert L. Hurtado, "Herbert E. Bolton, Racism, and American History," *Pacific Historical Review* 42, 2 (May 1993): 129.

17. Herbert Eugene Bolton, "Need for the Publication of a Comprehensive Body of Documents Relating to the History of Spanish Activities within the Present Limits of the United States," in *Bolton and the Spanish Borderlands*, ed. John Francis Bannon (Norman: University of Oklahoma Press, 1964), 25–27, 30.

18. H. Morse Stephens and Herbert E. Bolton, *The Pacific Ocean in History* (New York: The Macmillan Company, 1917), 7. Notably, Turner's frontier thesis and the essays in *The Pacific Ocean in History* were both presented as academic adjuncts to worlds' fairs; the first was in the U.S. heartland and celebrated the nation's development, and the second was in the far West, and celebrated a new era of U.S. expansion abroad.

19. Herbert Eugene Bolton, *Anza's California Expeditions*, vol. 1, *An Outpost of Empire* (Berkeley: University of California Press, 1930), vi.

20. John F. Davis, "The History of California," in Stephens and Bolton, *Pacific Ocean in History*, 86. Anza quote is from Bolton, *Outpost of Empire*, vi.

21. Herbert Eugene Bolton to Frederick E. Bolton, 2 June 1912, Bolton Papers; and Herbert Eugene Bolton and Thomas Maitland Marshall, *The Colonization of North America, 1492–1783* (New York: The Macmillan Company, 1920), v–vi. Macmillan negotiated with Bolton for a multivolume history of the United States through the twentieth century, and said they would consider a collaborative work. Bolton convinced Marshall to join him. *The Colonization of North America* was the only volume that was published; chapters of a second volume can still be found in the Bolton Papers. Bannon, *Herbert Eugene Bolton*, 98.

22. O. G. Libby, "Review of *The Colonization of North America, 1492–1783*," in *The Mississippi Valley Historical Review* 7, 4 (March 1921): 398–99, and Lewis R. Harley, "A New Treatment of American History," *Education* 15, 1 (September 1919): 22.

23. Libby, "Review of *Colonization of North America*," 397–98. The ideas behind the Good Neighbor Policy can be traced back to this same context. What I propose is a corrective to the idea that Bolton's greater America was an academic derivation of 1930s political ideas. Instead, the ideas of Bolton and Roosevelt's advisors developed along parallel tracks leading back to the 1920s, and in Bolton's case even farther. For post–World War I roots of Latin American history, see Basadre in Hart, comp., *Courses on Latin America 1948–49*, xvi–xix.

24. Herbert Eugene Bolton, *History of the Americas: A Syllabus with Maps* (Boston: Ginn and Company, 1928), iii; Bannon, *Herbert Eugene Bolton*, 141–44; Ware, *Study of International Relations*, 282; Herbert Eugene Bolton, "The Confessions of a Wayward Professor," *The Americas* 6, 3 (January 1950): 361–62; and Herbert Eugene Bolton to Edith E. Ware, 4 April 1933, Bolton Papers.

25. Herbert Eugene Bolton, *History of the Americas: A Syllabus with Maps* (Boston: Ginn and Company, 1928), iv. Letters of recommendation are scattered throughout the Bolton Papers. A synopsis of Bolton's 1923 speech can be found in the *American Historical Review* 28, 3 (April 1923): 419; followed by Herbert Eugene Bolton, "An Introductory Course in American History," *The Historical Outlook* 15, 1 (January 1924): 17–20.

26. "Report on the Teaching of Latin American History," *Bulletin of the Pan American Union* 61, 6 (June 1927): 547–49; and Ware, *Study of International Relations*, 282–83. Bolton

noted in 1933 that "History of the Americas" had been set up "in a large number of colleges and universities throughout the country." Herbert Eugene Bolton to Robert Gordon Sproul, 4 August 1933, Bolton Papers. To keep up with a growing demand, Ginn and Company came out with a second edition of Bolton's printed syllabus in 1935.

27. Bolton, *History of the Americas*, 310.

28. I borrow the term "foundational fiction" from Doris Sommer, *Foundational Fictions: The National Romances of Latin America* (Berkeley: University of California Press, 1991).

29. John W. Caughey, "Herbert Eugene Bolton," in *Turner, Bolton, and Webb: Three Historians of the American Frontier* (Seattle: University of Washington Press, 1965), 53–54; Bolton, *History of the Americas*, iii–iv; Bolton and Marshall, *Colonization of North America*, vi–vii; and Bolton, *History of the Americas*, iii. Bolton and Marshall gave special instructions for rearranging chapters, for those wishing to "treat the development of the colonies of a single nation as a continuous movement." Bolton and Marshall, *Colonization of North America*, vii.

30. Herbert E. Bolton, "The Epic of Greater America," *American Historical Review* 38 (April 1933): 448 (compare to Bolton, *History of the Americas*, iii), and 472. Emphasis is mine.

31. Bolton, "Epic of Greater America," 474, 448, 473.

32. Whitaker, *Latin American History*, 41.

33. Bannon, *Herbert Eugene Bolton*, 255–56; and Bolton, "Epic of Greater America," 473–74.

34. Herbert Eugene Bolton to Walter N. Sage, 31 January 1933, in Bolton Papers; and Herbert Eugene Bolton to Eugene Barker, cited in Bannon, *Herbert Eugene Bolton*, 185; Herbert Eugene Bolton, *Wider Horizons of American History* (New York: Appleton-Century, 1939); Arthur P. Whitaker, "Review of Herbert E. Bolton, *Wider Horizons of American History*," *The Mississippi Valley Historical Review* 26, 3 (December 1939): 459; and Edmundo O'Gorman, "Do the Americas Have a Common History?" in *Do the Americas Have a Common History? A Critique of the Bolton Theory*, ed. Lewis Hanke (New York: Knopf, 1964), 104–6, which originally appeared in the review *Universidad de la Habana* (January 1939) as "Hegel y el moderno panamericanismo."

35. Bolton, "Epic of Greater America," 470.

36. O'Gorman, "Common History?" 109.

37. Bolton, "Epic of Greater America," 469–70, and O'Gorman, "Common History?" 109, 105.

38. Bannon, *Herbert Eugene Bolton*, 187; and Herbert E. Bolton, "Some Cultural Assets of Latin America," in *Hispanic American Historical Review* 20, 1 (February 1940): 5, 3. Bolton gave this paper at the Conference on Inter-American Relations in the Field of Education, Washington, D.C., on 9 November 1939.

39. Bannon, *Herbert Eugene Bolton*, 208–11; and Bolton, "Some Cultural Assets," 7, 3. Emphasis is mine.

40. Herbert Eugene Bolton, *Rim of Christendom: A Biography of Eusebio Francisco Kino, Pacific Coast Pioneer* (New York: The Macmillan Company, 1936), 21–22, 56; and Herbert Eugene Bolton, *The Padre on Horseback: A Sketch of Eusebio Francisco Kino, S.J.,*

Apostle to the Pimas (San Francisco: The Sonora Press, 1932), 5, viii.

41. See discussion of the larger cultural and political context of the Coronado Cuarto Centennial in Charles Montgomery, *The Spanish Redemption: Heritage, Power, and Loss on New Mexico's Upper Rio Grande* (Berkeley: University of California Press, 2002), 217–29.

42. Herbert Eugene Bolton, *Coronado, Knight of Pueblos and Plains* (New York: Whittlesey House, 1949), 395–96.

43. Bolton, *Rim of Christendom*, vii; and Bolton, *Knight of Pueblos and Plains*, vii, x. Also see the discussion in Bannon, *Herbert Eugene Bolton*, 220–21. Bolton was part of a delegation set up by the National Park Service to bring the proposal for a transnational Coronado monument to Mexico City. The plan eventually failed.

44. For Bolton's festschrift and Hanke's review, see Adele Ogden and Engel Sluiter, eds., *Greater America: Essays in Honor of Herbert Eugene Bolton* (Berkeley: University of California Press, 1945); Lewis Hanke, "Review of *Greater America*," in *American Historical Review* 52, 1 (October 1946): 205. Information on Bolton's students and the waning popularity of "History of the Americas" based on data compiled from Hart, ed., *Courses on Latin America, 1948–1949*. Ten of Bolton's 43 students who taught Latin American history taught "History of the Americas" in 1949. This was still a large percentage, considering that the percentage of Americas courses versus those on Latin American history in general for 1949 was just under 10 percent (98 out of 1186).

45. Caughey, "Herbert Eugene Bolton," 64. For the new boom in Latin American studies (and history) in the 1930s and 1940s, see Lewis Hanke, "The Early Development of Latin American Studies in the United States, 1930–1949," in *Studying Latin America: Essays in Honor of Preston E. James*, ed. David J. Robinson (Ann Arbor, Mich.: Published for Department of Geography, Syracuse University, by University Microfilms International, 1980); and Basadre in Hart, comp., *Courses on Latin America, 1948–49*. In the 1930s, the history of the western United States emerged as a newly inscribed *regional* (rather than frontier) paradigm. See Richard W. Etulain, "Prologue: A New Historiographical Frontier: The Twentieth-Century West," in *The Twentieth Century West: Historical Interpretations*, ed. Gerald D. Nash and Richard W. Etulain (Albuquerque: University of New Mexico Press, 1991). For the larger North American construction of Latin America as an alter-ego to the United States, see Román de la Campa, *Latin Americanism* (Minneapolis: University of Minnesota Press, 1999).

46. For early parallel historiographies of Bolton's greater America and Latin American history, see Ware, *Study of International Relations*, 223, 263; and Basadre in Hart, comp., *Courses on Latin America, 1948–49*, x–xii. My claims for the 1930s and 1940s come from data from *Latin American Studies in American Institutions of Higher Learning: Academic Year 1935–1936* (Washington, D.C.: Division of Intellectual Cooperation, Pan American Union, 1936); *Latin American Studies, 1938–39*; and Hart, ed., *Courses on Latin America, 1948–49*.

47. One might see the 1948–1949 figures as a sign of decline, but this is only relative to Latin America history, and it was not a dramatic decline.

48. Ware, *Study of International Relations*, 282–83; and data from *Latin American Studies, 1935–36*; *Latin American Studies, 1938–39*; and Hart, ed., *Courses on Latin*

America, 1948–49. The reasons why the course did so well in Catholic college settings calls for further research. From the perspective of *research* institutions, the History of the Americas was doing poorly. In terms of classes taught nationwide, it was increasing marginally, from 13 in 1935–1936, to 19 in 1939–1940, to 20 in 1948–1949, even though it was certainly not in *decline*. It is worth noting that more of the smaller schools *in general* appeared in later reports, but it is hard to tell if this is because early surveys missed these schools, or if it took time for Latin American courses to "trickle down."

49. In 1935–1936, 17 of 32 professors (53 percent) told Pan American Union surveyors they used *History of the Americas*, compared to 22 of 48 (48 percent) in 1938–1939, and 14 of 98 (14 percent) in 1948–1949.

50. *Latin American Studies, 1938–39,* 29; and Hart, ed., *Latin American Studies, 1948–49,* 7, 170–72.

51. This is particularly evident in the classes described in Hart, ed., *Courses on Latin America, 1948–49.*

52. James F. King and Samuel Everett, "Latin American History Textbooks," in *Latin America in School and College Teaching Materials: Report of the Committee on the Study of Teaching Materials on Inter-American Subjects* (Washington, D.C.: American Council on Education, 1944).

53. Ibid., 130.

54. Here, again, I follow a line of thought articulated for more recent decades in Román de la Campa's *Latin Americanism.* For discussion of national and transnational "scales" of historical inquiry, and their subjects, see Richard White, "The Nationalization of Nature," *Journal of American History* 86, 3 (December 1999): 976–86.

55. Bannon, *Bolton and the Spanish Borderlands,* 3, 301; and Hanke, *Do the Americas Have a Common History?* 27.

56. I base these figures (and the ones that follow) on a database of Bolton students with data from a variety of sources. My main source is Ogden and Sluiter, eds., *Greater America,* where Bolton student Gregory Campton compiled a bibliography of Bolton students before June 1944. I combined this with publications in the on-line directory of University of California libraries (MELVYL) and a variety of other sources.

57. Agapito Rey, "A Dedication to the Memory of Herbert Ingram Priestley, 1875–1944," *Arizona and the West* 6, 3 (autumn 1964): 188–89; and *Latin American Studies, 1935–36,* 6–7.

58. Eugene K. Chamberlin, "Abraham Phineas Nasatir (1904–1991)," *Hispanic American Historical Review* 71, 4 (1991): 859; *Latin American Studies, 1938–39,* 60; Hart, ed., *Courses on Latin America, 1948–49,* 169; and Janet R. Fireman, "Abraham Nasatir, Dean of Documents," *Pacific Historical Review* 41, 4 (1987): 514–15.

59. John Francis Bannon, "Alfred Barnaby Thomas," in Eugene R. Huck and Edward H. Moseley, *Militarists, Merchants and Missionaries: United States Expansion in Middle America; Essays Written in Honor of Alfred Barnaby Thomas* (Alabama: University of Alabama Press, 1970), ix–xi; and *Latin American Studies, 1935–36,* 43.

60. Bolton, "Epic of Greater America," 473.

61. Ibid. 474.

Chapter Nine

Afterword—Echoes of Colonialism
Peninsulares, Wholesome Hispanics, Steamy Latins

John Nieto-Phillips

ne fall morning in 1971, an unlikely group of elected officials and political activists convened at a motel in a suburb of Washington. Their objective was to forge a coalition among 9 million Cubans, Puerto Ricans, and Mexican Americans in the United States, based on their common concerns: police brutality, education, job discrimination, and housing. Participants wore badges in red print on an orange background that proclaimed them "UNIDOS." But far from uniting the three major constituencies behind a shared agenda, the meeting underscored the groups' divergent interests and historical experiences in the United States. The *New York Times* reported that "militants" had succeeded in pushing through a platform advocating Puerto Rican independence and the establishment of a Spanish-speaking political party in Washington. So-called moderates took flight, literally, and caught early planes home. Thus, what began as a well-intended effort aimed at unity ended, for some, in disillusionment. One of the conference's organizers, Nuyorican stalwart Hermán Badillo, lamented that the "coalition will have to wait—maybe for another generation."[1]

More than a generation has passed since that meeting took place, and Latinos are hardly closer to political unity than they were in 1971. Despite the growing visibility of such organizations as the National Council of La Raza and the Congressional Hispanic Caucus, despite the founding of Latina/o Studies programs on university campuses nationwide, and notwithstanding recent U.S. census figures that proclaim Latinos "the nation's largest minority group" (as if this were an honorific title), Latinos have yet to coalesce into a political force equal to their numbers. But this should come as no surprise to anyone who has studied the vast and varied landscape of Latin American history. The fragmented nature of Latino politics is rooted deep in particular colonial legacies and national memories. And those memories are, as we have seen in the foregoing essays, tenuous and subject to change, contestation, strategic deployment, and manipulation.

Spain's imprint on national imaginations has been resilient, to say the least. National histories of the emerging republics were, as Jeremy Adelman aptly noted, "inevitably bound up with their shadow, the colonial past." From the ruins of the past were born new peoples and new cultures, as well as new historical memories. The most enduring cultural marker of Spanish colonialism, the Spanish language, was likened by the Colombian scholar José Antonio León Rey to a "majestic river, ever open to smaller streams and brooks that enrich it."[2] Its tributaries, León Rey said, flow from the indigenous, African, and European peoples who comprise the Western Hemisphere. Not by happenstance, these linguistic streams and brooks have converged in recent years into a veritable torrent of *hispanidad*, in the land that stole Spain's imperial glory more than a century ago: the United States. At least, this is the impression rendered by global media outlets.

Perhaps no country is more cognizant of the *latinoamericanización* of the United States than Spain, whose journalists regularly report, with obvious delight, on the proliferation of Spanish (and Spanglish) in California, New York, Texas, or Florida. One recent article in the Madrid-based *El Mundo* noted that of the 35 million Latinos in the United States fully 28 million consider Spanish their native language. "'El sueño americano,'" the paper proclaimed, "se escribe con 'eñe.'"[3] Similar stories have appeared in Paris and Berlin and London. The impression abroad is that Latinos are flocking to the United States in such numbers that their demographic presence and, by extension, Spain's cultural and linguistic legacy, is now impossible to ignore. The basic tenor of foreign press reports is that Uncle Sam's imperial chickens have come home to roost; and those chickens speak Spanish, a point not lost on the Real Academia Española (RAE).

José del Valle's article reminds us that any pretense on the part of RAE to assert Spain's linguistic authority over its former colonies historically has been viewed by Latin American intellectuals with suspicion, if not outright resistance. The RAE's vision of "pan-Hispanic" unity rooted in a common language betrays Spain's lingering nostalgia for its former splendor. Several of the articles in this collection have shown that nostalgia has been a vital force in shaping Spain's official remembrances of its past. Whether conceived as a "White Legend" or a *paradigma española*, Spain's colonial record has been glorified by *hispanófilos*, but contested by rivals and by chroniclers of national independence.

As we have seen, both the Black Legend (of decadence) and the White Legend (of beneficence) have historically gained some form of state sanction; for they were born in particular contexts, ideologies, and political aims. Pan-Hispanic identity, if it ever can be said to exist, will be arguably more a by-product of U.S. imperialism than Spanish colonialism. Yet the Spanish language remains at the core of Latino identity in the United States, according to some. As the world bears witness to the Latinization of this mostly English-speaking country, it cannot help but view the phenomenon as an extension of earlier European exploits and rivalries.

In October of 2003, the town of Biarritz hosted a conference focusing on the "Reconquête silencieuse," an expression (originally: *la reconquista silenciosa*) coined by Carlos Fuentes to explain Latinos' "demographic explosion" in the United States. According to *Le Figaro*, the conferees addressed two fundamental questions: How will Latinos manage to integrate themselves (into American society)? and, Will the country one day become the United States "of Latinos"? The Latino explosion is clearly *un objet de curiosité* in France.[4]

Much of the foreign press's newfound fascination for Latinos can be attributed to Hollywood, which has disseminated considerable footage of steamy Latins (speaking English with muted accents) making their debut in America. For many audiences, it is the Mexican actor of Lebanese and Spanish ancestry, Salma Hayek, and the Spaniard, Antonio Banderas, who have come to embody Latin glamour onscreen. Their Mediterranean features no doubt resonate with European audiences. But they also belie the varied racial phenotypes that comprise Latino peoples. Like latter-day *criollos* and *peninsulares* who, in Baroque *casta* paintings, broadcast to Europe the promise of a grand life in the Americas, today's fair-skinned Latin actors give the world a sense that the United States, or at least Hollywood, is the land of milk and honey. Of course, there are notable exceptions to the fair-skin rule, such as Jennifer López, whose racial ambiguity, sexuality, and commercial appeal have been the subject of popular and academic intrigue. Both onscreen and off, she has epitomized the rags-to-riches trope that audiences yearn for.[5] Hollywood has done little to complicate Latino images and, instead, has exploited stereotypes and "success stories" to meet popular tastes and expectations.

Other media have followed suit. North American television and print media are today saturated with advertisements geared toward "the Hispanic market." Envisaged as a kind of rainbow of national cultures unified by the Spanish language and supposedly shared cultural values, this market has been defined by advertising agencies in idealized terms: as middle-class, Spanish-speaking, brand-loyal, immigrant families that possess considerable purchasing power. And while some of these attributes may apply to particular segments of the Latino population, they hardly reflect reality of the greater part. Nor do they mirror the complexity and wide-ranging circumstances of Latino as defined by class, language, race, region, national origin, and residency or immigrant status. As Arlene Dávila correctly points out in her monograph on the subject, the U.S. media routinely convey a romanticized knowledge about Latinos that does not correspond to everyday life.[6] Yet, the impulse to reduce "Hispanics" to a set of essential cultural traits persists, as it has done for decades.

The ideological thrust behind "the Hispanic market" has the faint ring of Hispanist rhetoric that emanated from politicians and academics in the first half of the twentieth century. "The Spanish world," Francisco Franco proclaimed in 1941 in welcoming Chile's new ambassador to Madrid, "must be something one and indivisible, of full and universal understanding, in which they will have equal parts of Spain each of 'the free, independent and sovereign nations of America.'" Framed partly as a strategic reply to Roosevelt's Pan-American designs, Franco's Hispanism professed a transnational "spiritual brotherhood" among Spanish-speaking peoples, founded in essential beliefs, values, and a common language.[7] Hispanismo encompassed a wide range of moral values, traditions, and emphasis on family and community that set the Spanish-speaking world apart from, and in binary opposition to, U.S. hegemonic culture. This opposition, a source of pride for Hispanists, has also been a source of anti-immigrant sentiment and English-only initiatives dating to the 1910s.

When Congress passed bills to restrict the flow of migrants to the United States in 1917, 1921, and 1924, it did so with southern and eastern Europeans in mind. However, the impact of these laws quickly spread from Ellis Island to El Paso, where Mexican migrant workers were forced to undergo a literacy test, medical examination, and, sometimes, a delousing shower. Just as European immigration subsided, the "greaser invasion" began in earnest. "Those who enter," the *New York Times* opined in 1929, "are largely Indian in blood, with only a veneer of Spanish culture."[8] Calls for a crackdown on the flow of "wetbacks" were followed by increased vigilante violence on the border, segregation in the schools, and efforts to "repatriate" Mexicans. One need not recite the litany of state initiatives passed in recent years to conclude that anti-immigrant feeling is alive and well, and is still strongly infused with racism. While the media have, on the one hand, celebrated things "Hispanic" in popular culture, they have also exacerbated deep-seated and widespread fears that "illegals" are invading the public schools, the workplace, and the body politic.

In slogans reminiscent of the 1930s, politicians and commentators today denounce undocumented immigrants as civic pariahs or economic parasites that threaten to drain public coffers dry. Headlines periodically announce tales of illicit border crossings that end in death by suffocation in a sealed tractor-trailer or by dehydration and exposure in the Sonora Desert. The moral tone of such reports generally confirms the need for greater "control over our borders." Whereas the glamour media adore their royal family of "Hispanic" luminaries, popular news outlets are, as ever, feverishly stoking anti-immigrant sentiment and Latinophobia. In September 2003, for example, the Cable News Network's (CNN) television economist Lou Dobbs initiated an "investigative reporting" series entitled "Broken Borders," which took aim at the "millions of illegal aliens" who are crossing into the United States, stealing jobs, depressing wages, and threatening the nation's security and well-being. Week after week, in shrill terms Dobbs denounced the influx of mostly Spanish-speaking border breakers, proclaiming in one broadcast that "[s]even hundred thousand illegal aliens enter this country each year, some carrying deadly diseases" (20 Nov. 2003).[9] Often blurring the distinction between "legals" and "illegals," Dobbs blamed "aliens" for clogging the nation's courts and prisons, for invading the public schools, and for straining medical services.

Employing more academic, though equally naïve terms, Harvard University's Samuel P. Huntington has reduced the matters of immigration down to what he calls "the Hispanic challenge": that is, the failure of Spanish-speaking (most notably, according to Huntington, Mexican) immigrants to "assimilate" into the English-speaking Anglo society. What the challenge really amounts to is a brewing "cultural division between Hispanics and Anglos [that] could replace the racial division between blacks and whites as the most serious cleavage in U.S. society." Mexicans' "contempt of [American] culture," of borders, and of the English language, Huntington warns, will inexorably deepen that cleavage. "Blood," he argues, "is thicker than borders."[10]

Thus, the popular imagination is fed two seemingly contradictory stereotypes: the wholesome, light-skinned Hispanic who believes in tradition, family, and the American Dream; and the lawbreaking, desperate, dark-skinned day laborer who will stop at nothing to enter the United States, even at great peril. Like the White and Black Legends, these stereotypes can be found on opposite sides of the same ideological coin. One is inspired by Hispanophilia, which can be conceived as a kind of love of the exotic white other, while the other is molded from Latinophobia, or a fear of the dark, treacherous, nonwhite interloper.

In an age when capital, technology, information, and goods traverse the globe with ease, it seems ironic that governments are increasingly preoccupied with the regulation of human movement. The horrific events of 9/11 have heightened popular anxiety about the permeability of national borders: Any immigrant seems now a potential threat to national security. Yet perhaps this is a propitious moment to reflect upon the nature of borders, boundaries, and frontiers in defining our histories, much as Herbert Eugene Bolton sought to do. Such a reflection might compel us to study the interconnectedness of our colonial and national narratives. It might induce us to understand the structures that have, for centuries, impelled people to distant lands. And it might also hold lessons for understanding the "Latina/o condition" in the United States.

One of the most widely publicized facts from the 2000 U.S. census is that the Latinos have eclipsed African Americans as the largest minority population. Not surprisingly, persons of Mexican descent continue to lead the numbers (comprising 58.5 percent of Latinos). But there is a growing debate over ways Latinos identify themselves by race and national origin. There are also important changes in the way the U.S. Census Bureau conceives of ethnic and racial categories.

Responding to protests that the "Hispanic" ethnic category not only conveyed "white" racial connotations or "Spanish" cultural undertones, and that it glossed over both the racial and ethnic diversity of the population it sought to measure, the Census Bureau authorized the use of the terms "Hispanic" and "Latino" interchangeably. Additionally, it allowed respondents to identify themselves using any combination of six racial categories: American Indian or Alaska Native; Asian; Black or African American; Native Hawaiian or Other Pacific Islander; White; and Some Other Race. What resulted were 63 possible racial combinations, and a considerably more complex picture of the country's racial composition.

The result among "Hispanic or Latino" respondents is open to interpretation. In 1990, 3 out of 4 "Hispanics" (75.6 percent) classified themselves at "white." In 2000, fewer than half (47.9 percent) classified themselves as "white," while fully 42.2 percent could not classify themselves by any of the five usual racial categories or combinations. Instead, they checked the box "Some other race." This latter figure compares with just 1.9 percent for the "non-Hispanic or Latino" population. What does this suggest? It may well indicate that, by checking the "Hispanic or Latino" ethnic box, respondents are in fact choosing a "racialized ethnicity," something akin to *la raza*. Or it may hint that the Census Bureau's racial categories are indeterminate, inadequate, or irrelevant to many Latinos. What is certain is that Latinos' concept of self often defies U.S. government racial formulations and conventions, as it has since colonial times.[11]

Paralleling the shift away from the "white" racial self-definition, national categories appear to be losing some of their currency among Latinos. The vast majority of Latinos (82.7 percent) identified themselves with a national origin (e.g., Mexico, Puerto Rico, Cuba, etc.); however, at least 1 in 6 Latinos (17.3 percent) did not do so, but instead specified their identity under the rubric "All Other Hispanic or Latino." This figure represents a significant increase over the 1990 census, when fewer than 1 in 25 Hispanics (3.9 percent) did not identify themselves by national origin.[12]

The implication of both trends is that Latinos are in a period of rather intensive self-redefinition, which I submit is both aided and complicated by media representations, trends in popular culture, and the shifting terrain of ethnic/racial politics in the United States. Are the media, in fact, succeeding in forging a "Hispanic nation" within a nation? Or is there a more fundamental shift in ethnic consciousness taking place, grounded in face-to-face relations, continued discrimination, a common sense of marginality in society and the economy, and an unfulfilled desire for full entry into the body politic? For certain, Latinos' perceptions of themselves are shaped both by their immediate circumstances, as well as their historical relation to the white, English-speaking body politic. But I would hazard to say that popular memories of Spain's colonial past—among Latinos and Americans, generally—will continue to fade, as the progeny of conquest become authors of their own history and identity.

NOTES

1. Jack Rosenthal, "The Goal among the Spanish-Speaking: 'Unidos,'" *New York Times*, 31 October 1971.

2. "Unity is Sought on Spanish Words; Experts from 19 Countries Hold Parley in San Juan," *New York Times*, 7 December 1969.

3. Carlos Fresneda and María Ramírez, "Pujanza del idioma español. Es la segunda lengua oficial, impulsada por esos 35 millones de hispanos que son ya la primera 'minoría.'" *El Mundo*, 13 October 2003.

4. *Le Figaro*, 4 October 2003.

5. Frances Negrón-Muntaner, "Jennifer's Butt," *Aztlán* 22, 2 (fall 1997): 182–85. A significant and growing body of scholarship examines media represeatations of Latinas. A few works include: Angharad N. Valdivia, *A Latina in the Land of Hollywood and Other Essays on Media Culture* (Tucson: University of Arizona Press, 2000); Clara E. Rodríguez, *Heroes, Lovers, and Others: The Story of Latinos in Hollywood* (Washington, D.C.: Smithsonian Books, 2004); and Rodríguez, *Latin Looks: Images of Latinas and Latinos in the U.S. Media* (Boulder, Colo.: Westview Press, 1997).

6. Arlene Dávila, *Latinos, Inc.: The Marketing and Making of a People* (Berkeley: University of California Press, 2001).

7. "Franco Denies Aim to Regain Americas: Welcoming New Chilean Envoy, General Explains Spanish Hopes," *New York Times*, 21 February 1941.

8. *New York Times*, 13 October 1929.

9. Peter Hart, "Dobbs' Choice: CNN Host Picks Immigration as His Ax to Grind," *Extra! The Magazine of FAIR—The Media Watchgroup* 17, 1 (Feb. 2004): 13–14.

10. Samuel P. Huntington, "The Hispanic Challenge," *Foreign Policy* 141 (Mar./Apr. 2004): 30–45.

11. Betsy Guzmán, "The Hispanic Population." U.S. Census Brief, Bureau of the Census, May 2001. For an insightful examination of evolution of racial terminology in the U.S. census, see Clara Rodriguez, *Changing Race: Latinos, the Census, and the History of Ethnicity in the United States* (New York: New York University Press, 2000).

12. Ibid. For a critical inquiry into the creation and accuracy of U.S. Census Bureau designations for Latinos (particularly the "All other Hispanic or Latino" category), see Eileen Diaz McConnell and Edward Delgado-Romero, "Latino Panethnicity: Reality or Methodological Construction?" *Sociological Focus*, special issue: *The Latino Experience in the United States* 37 (4): 297–312.

Suggestions for Further Reading

For those interested in pursuing some of the debates discussed across these essays, we have compiled a brief bibliography, organized thematically.

The origins, nature, and significance of the Black and White Legends have been a matter of fierce debate over the years. Though referring to bodies of knowledge and representations stretching back to the late Middle Ages, the term "Black Legend" was coined only in the twentieth century. In 1914, Julián Juderías earned laudits from some of his Spanish countrymen with his classic work *La leyenda negra y la verdad histórica*. Three years later, he prefaced a new and revised edition of the book with a letter in which he explained to King Alfonso XIII that he wrote the book simply "to vindicate Spain's good name" against the country's foreign critics. Juderías's work, which was reissued in 1997, stands as one of the vociferous reactions to the Black Legend and its authors. A more finely nuanced Spanish discussion of the Black Legend is to be found in Ricardo García Cárcel, *La leyenda negra: Historia y opinión* (Madrid: Alianza Editorial, 1992).

On this side of the Atlantic, scholars have long regarded Spain's past with considerable ambivalence. Following Francisco Franco's rise to power and his regime's embrace of Spain's colonial legacy, U.S. scholars proved far less enamored of the romantic "White Legend." In North American historiography, a good starting point is the exchange between Benjamin Keen and Lewis Hanke that took place in the *Hispanic American Historical Review* between 1969 and 1971. Other important contributions include the collection of essays on the central figure in the elaboration of both legends, Bartolomé de las Casas: Juan Friede and Benjamin Keen, eds., *Bartolomé de las Casas in History: Toward an Understanding of the Man and His Work* (DeKalb: Northern Illinois University Press, 1971). See also the documentary collection edited by Charles Gibson, *The Black Legend: Anti-Spanish Attitudes in the Old World and the New* (New York: Knopf, 1971). Recent discussions of the Black Legend and the White can be found in Richard Kagan, "Prescott's Paradigm: American Historical Scholarship and the Decline of Spain," *American Historical Review* 101 (1996): 423–46; and Kagan, ed., *Spain in America: The Origins of Hispanism in the United States* (Urbana: University of Illinois Press, 2002).

Intimately related to the Black and White Legends is the scholarship on the impact of Spanish conquest and colonization, not just on the former colonies but on the former metropolis as well. J. H. Elliot has written incisively on the latter, for instance concerning the *arbistristas*, essayists who pondered the nature of the Spanish monarchy and the consequences of its global empire. See the essays collected in *Spain and Its World, 1500–1700* (New Haven: Yale University Press, 1989). On how the conquest shaped Spanish and European political and scientific paradigms, see Elliott, *The Old World and the New, 1492–1650* (Cambridge: Cambridge University Press, 1970); Edmundo O'Gorman, *The Invention of America* (Bloomington: Indiana University Press, 1961); Anthony Pagden, *Lords of All the World: Ideologies of Empire in Spain, Britain and France c. 1500–c. 1800* (New Haven: Yale University Press, 1995); and Jorge Cañizares-Esguerra, *How to Write the History of the New World: Histories, Epistemologies, and Identities in the Eighteenth-Century Atlantic World* (Stanford: Stanford University Press, 2001). On the modern period, a good introduction to a growing literature is Josep M. Fradera, *Gobernar colonias* (Barcelona: Ediciones Península, 1999).

The literature on the colonies is vast. Charles Gibson, *Spain in America* (New York: Harper Torchbooks, 1966) and Stanley Stein and Barbara Stein, *The Colonial Heritage of Latin America* (New York: Oxford University Press, 1970) are fundamental works on the social and economic consequences of Spanish conquest and colonization. A seminal history of the origins of Spanish American independence is John Lynch, *The Spanish American Revolutions, 1808–1826* (New York: Norton, 1973). Among works that have reconsidered these earlier approaches, see Jaime Rodríguez O., *The Independence of Spanish America* (Cambridge: Cambridge University Press, 1998); and Jeremy Adelman, ed., *Colonial Legacies: The Problem of Persistence in Latin American History* (London: Routledge, 1999). On the Philippines, see John Leddy Phelan, *The Hispanization of the Philippines: Spanish Aims and Filipino Responses, 1565–1700* (Madison: University of Wisconsin Press, 1959). Recent perspectives on conquest, colonization, and nationalism are to be found in Vicente Rafael, *Contracting Colonialism: Translation and Christian Conversion in Tagalog Society under Early Spanish Rule* (Ithaca: Cornell University Press, 1988); and Benedict Anderson, "Nitroglycerine in the Pomegranate: José Rizal: Paris, Havana, Barcelona, Berlin—1," *New Left Review* 27 (2004): 99–118, part of a series of articles on the Filipino patriot José Rizal.

For a broad overview of Spanish colonialism in North America, see David J. Weber, *The Spanish Frontier in North America* (New Haven: Yale University Press, 1994). For a highly readable introduction to Latina and Latino experiences in the context of colonialism and postcolonialism, see Juan González,

Harvest of Empire: A History of Latinos in America (New York: Viking, 2000). On the colonial roots of Latina and Latino identities, see Ramón A. Gutiérrez, "Unraveling America's Hispanic Past: Internal Stratification and Class Boundaries," *Aztlán* 17 (1986): 79–101; and Suzanne Oboler, *Ethnic Labels, Latino Lives: Identity and the Politics of (Re)Presentation in the United States* (Minneapolis: University of Minnesota Press, 1995).

Several works have recently questioned whether the Spanish empire and the independent nation-states that emerged from decolonization fit into broader patterns of European imperialism and national liberation, with differing conclusions. For example, see Frederick Cooper et al., *Confronting Historical Paradigms: Peasants, Labor and the Capitalist World System in Africa and Latin America* (Madison: University of Wisconsin Press, 1993); the special issue of the journal *boundary2* 20 (1993), entitled "The Postmodernism Debate in Latin America"; and Mark Thurner and Andrés Guerrero, eds., *After Spanish Rule: Postcolonial Predicaments of the Americas* (Durham, N.C.: Duke University Press, 2003). Colonial and postcolonial studies are burgeoning fields and several recent collections offer useful insights for studying the Iberian empires and postcolonial societies. These include Gyan Prakash, ed., *After Colonialism: Imperial Histories and Postcolonial Displacements* (Princeton: Princeton University Press, 1995), in which Jorge Klor de Alva goes to some length to defend Iberian peculiarity; and Frederick Cooper and Ann Laura Stoler, eds., *Tensions of Empire: Colonial Cultures in a Bourgeois Age* (Berkeley: University of California Press, 1997). See also Antoinette Burton, ed., *After the Imperial Turn: Thinking with and through the Nation* (Durham: Duke University Press, 2003); and Craig Calhoun, Frederick Cooper, and Kevin Moore, eds., *Lessons of Empire* (New york: The New Press, 2005).

CONTRIBUTORS

Jeremy Adelman is the Walter S. Carpenter III Professor of Spanish Civilization and Culture and chair of the History Department at Princeton University. His most recent books include the prize-winning *Republic of Capital: Buenos Aires and the Legal Transformation of the Atlantic World* (Stanford University Press, 1999), and *Worlds Together, Worlds Apart: A History of the Modern World from the Mongol Empire to the Present*, coauthored with Robert L. Tignor et al. (W. W. Norton, 2002). He is currently finishing a major work on the end of the Spanish and Portuguese empires and the origins of the nation-state in Latin America.

Astrid Cubano-Iguina is Professor of History at the University of Puerto Rico in Río Piedras. She received her Ph.D. from Princeton University in 1988 and has written on the nineteenth-century social and political history of Puerto Rico, the comparative history of Cuba and Puerto Rico, and the history of violence, gender notions, and the law. Her article "Legal Constructions of Gender and Violence against Women" appears in *Law and History Review* 22, 3 (fall 2004). Cubano-Iguina is completing a book about the role of violence, gender, and the law in late-nineteenth-century identity formation process in Puerto Rico.

José del Valle is Associate Professor of Hispanic Linguistics at the Graduate Center of the City University of New York. He is the author of *El trueque s/x en español antiguo: aproximaciones teóricas* (Max Niemeyer, 1996) and coeditor, with Luis Gabriel-Stheeman, of *The Battle over Spanish between 1800 and 2000: Language Ideologies and Hispanic Intellectuals* (Routledge, 2002). A Spanish edition of the latter, *La batalla del idioma*, was published in 2004 (Vervuert/Iberoamericana). His research focuses on language ideologies in Spain's and Latin America's recent linguistic history.

Antonio Feros teaches history at the University of Pennsylvania. He writes about politics, culture, and ethnic relations in the early modern Spanish empire, and early modern European intellectual history. Feros is the author of *Kingship and Favoritism in the Spain of Philip III, 1598–1621* (Cambridge University Press, 2000), which has been translated into Spanish (Marcial Pons,

2002), and is currently working on two new projects: "Constructing Self and Other: National and Ethnic Identities in the Early Modern Spanish World," and "The Constitution of Empire," which involves an examination of the political, administrative, and social foundations of the early modern Spanish empire (1500–1820).

Javier Morillo-Alicea has taught history and anthropology at Carleton College and Macalester College. He is also the author of "'Aquel laberinto de oficinas': Ways of Knowing Empire in Late-Nineteenth-Century Spain," in *After Spanish Rule: Postcolonial Predicaments of the Americas*, ed. Mark Thurner and Andrés Guerrero (Duke University Press, 2003).

John Nieto-Phillips is Associate Professor of History and Latino Studies at Indiana University, Bloomington. The author of *The Language of Blood: The Making of Spanish-American Identity in New Mexico, 1880s–1930s* (University of New Mexico Press, 2004), his interests include race, language, education, and civic identities among Latinas and Latinos. He is currently engaged in a comparative study of "Americanization" programs in the schools of Puerto Rico and New Mexico, 1890s–1940s. Prior to coming to Indiana, he was a researcher-in-residence at the Centro de Estudios Puertorriqueños at Hunter College, a visiting professor at the University of Paris, and taught at New Mexico State University, Las Cruces.

Christopher Schmidt-Nowara is Associate Professor of History and the Director of the Latin American and Latino Studies Institute at Fordham University. He is the author of *Empire and Antislavery: Spain, Cuba, and Puerto Rico, 1833–1874* (University of Pittsburgh Press, 1999) and is currently completing a manuscript entitled *The Conquest of History: Spanish Colonialism and National Histories in the Nineteenth Century*, also to be published by Pittsburgh. With Mónica Burguera he has edited a special issue of *Social History* (fall 2004) dedicated to contemporary Spanish historiography.

Dale Tomich is Professor of Sociology and History at Binghamton University of the State University of New York. He is author of *Slavery in the Circuit of Sugar: Martinique and the World Economy, 1830–1848* (Johns Hopkins University Press, 1990) and *Through the Prism of Slavery: Labor, Capital, and World Economy* (Rowan and Littlefield, 2004), as well as various articles on Atlantic slavery. His current research interests include landscape, environment, and plantation architecture and slavery in Brazil, Cuba, and the United States during the nineteenth century.

Samuel Truett is Assistant Professor of History at the University of New Mexico. He is the author of *Transnational Dreams: Transforming the U.S.-Mexico Borderlands* (Yale University Press, forthcoming), and coeditor with Elliott Young of *Continental Crossroads: Remapping U.S.-Mexico Borderlands History* (Duke University Press, 2004).

Index